APPARITIONS

APPARITIONS

CELIA GREEN

AND

CHARLES McCREERY

HAMISH HAMILTON

LONDON

First published in Great Britain, 1975
by Hamish Hamilton Ltd
90 Great Russell Street London WC1

Copyright © 1975 by Institute of Psychophysical Research,
Oxford

SBN 241 89182 5

Proceedings of the Institute of Psychophysical
Research, Volume 5

Printed in Great Britain by
Western Printing Services Ltd, Bristol

Contents

An Open Letter to Millionaires

'Maecenas atavis edite regibus'

NEW and original ideas in science do not spring unbidden from the ground. They come only at the call of some rare genius, and they need to be backed and protected against the bitter opposition and blind prejudice of the established system of belief. Human psychology has not changed since the sixteenth century, and the man who questions the orthodoxies of modern science can expect to be imprisoned as effectively as was Galileo—and if the chains are less visible, they are the more binding.

The Institute of Psychophysical Research in Oxford exists to carry out research in hitherto unexplored areas. Its activities have, so far, been severely restricted due to inadequate financial resources.

What is needed is for some far-sighted individual to recognise the revolutionary potential of the Institute's work, and to endow its research on a scale commensurate with its importance.

The Institute now represents a unique collection of talent, especially equipped to open up this field of knowledge; but converting theory into practical results is an expensive process, and as long as the Institute is starved of the finance needed, this talent will remain imprisoned, and no significant advance will be possible.

Yet once the prison door is opened the effects of the flood of discovery that will burst on the world will be out of all proportion to the effort expended in turning the key.

It awaits only the time when some princely Maecenas shall step forward and turn that key.

'Wird dieser Fürst sich finden'—RICHARD WAGNER?

Introduction and Acknowledgements

IN 1968 and 1974 the Institute of Psychophysical Research made appeals, by means of the Press and Sound Radio, for first-hand accounts of experiences of perceiving apparitions, this term being intended to cover experiences involving any of the senses and not just visual ones. Approximately 300 people responded to the first appeal and 1,500 to the second, and in each case more than half of those who replied claimed to have had more than one experience. About a third of the respondents to the second appeal were from overseas countries, English-speaking or otherwise. Questionnaires were sent to all those who responded to these two appeals, except for those who wrote in some language other than English, and a total of 850 completed questionnaires were received.

The material on which this book is based consists of the written narratives by our subjects of their experiences and their replies to the questionnaire, together with previously published first-hand case material.

Any generalisations about the characteristics of apparitional experiences made in the text are to be understood as referring to the population of such cases collected by the Institute and as reported to it.

Where percentages are given they are based on the total population of cases, or of subjects, for which it was possible to ascertain the factor in question. Indeterminate cases have been omitted.

The age of the cases reported to the Institute was very variable. Some were very recent, including a few in each of the two main appeal populations which were sent in as having happened after the date of the appeal.

It would be possible, with a sufficiently large number of cases, to conduct a statistical analysis designed to demonstrate whether certain factors were, or were not, reported more frequently in connection with old cases than with recent ones—i.e. whether there are any directions in which the experiences tend to become modified with the lapse of time. In general, it is of course known that older memories tend to be less reliable than recent ones. On the other hand it should be borne in mind that apparitional experiences (at least those that are reported) are usually regarded as vivid and memorable, and the subjects probably stabilise their memories of them soon after the event by repeated narration or mental examination.

It was not possible to establish, in a way that would have been statistically significant, whether any factors did, or did not, tend to be reported more frequently in either older or more recent cases. No trend of this kind was perceptible. The cases were, therefore, for the purposes of this analysis accepted as forming part of the same population.

Seventy-two per cent of the responding subjects were women and 28 per cent men. This finding cannot, of course, be taken as shedding light on the relative frequency of the occurrence of apparitional experiences in the male and female populations, but only on the frequency with which women and men respectively report apparitional experiences in response to appeals of this nature.

With a few exceptions, proper names (christian names, surnames and place names) referred to in our subjects' statements have been replaced by pseudonyms or initial capital letters, which do not correspond to the true initial of the name, in cases where the real name might lead to recognition of the subject's identity.

Any case which is quoted in this book without a reference is drawn from material in the possession of the Institute.

The main sources of published material drawn on are the following:

E. Gurney, F. W. H. Myers and F. Podmore, *Phantasms of the Living*, 1886—referred to throughout as 'Gurney I' and 'Gurney II', according to whether Volume I or Volume II is being referred to.

Mrs. E. M. Sidgwick, Miss Alice Johnson, and others, *Report on the Census of Hallucinations*, 1894—referred to throughout as *Census*.

Various volumes of the *Journal* and *Proceedings* of the Society for Psychical Research, London—referred to throughout as

Journal of the S.P.R., and *Proceedings of the S.P.R.* respectively.

Sir Ernest Bennett, *Apparitions and Haunted Houses*, 1939—referred to throughout as 'Bennett'.

Full particulars of these and other works referred to in the text will be found in the Bibliography.

We are grateful to the Society for Psychical Research, London, for permission to quote from copyright material. Detailed references will be found following each quotation.

On behalf of the Institute, we should like to thank the following for their advice and assistance in this project: Professor W. Ross Ashby, Professor D. E. Broadbent, Professor Colin Cherry, Professor H. J. Eysenck, Professor O. R. Frisch, Professeur Henri Gastaut, Mr. G. W. Lambert, Professor Gardner Murphy, Dr. Ian Oswald, Professor Sir Rudolph Peters, Professor H. H. Price, Mr. J. B. Priestley, Professor W. H. Thorpe, Dr. R. H. Thouless, Dr. W. Grey Walter, and Professor Graham Weddell.

We should like to express our gratitude to our colleagues at the Institute, in particular to William Leslie and Christine Fulcher, for their unremitting labours and unfailing patience at all stages in the production of this book.

We should like also to thank the Press at home and abroad, and the BBC for their cooperation in enabling the two appeals to reach the public; and we should like to extend very particularly our thanks to the subjects themselves, who showed such patience in providing answers to our questions, and who made such efforts to make sure that we understood exactly what they meant.

CHAPTER 1

Apparitions and Waking Dreams

WHAT is an apparition? Here is an example:

> When living in Oxford . . . I had an odd experience when walking from New College to Broad St.
>
> There is a curve in the road with the back gates of Queen's College on the left and before reaching Hertford bridge. As I came down the road I saw two undergraduates in short gowns, one was sitting on a chestnut coloured horse with white socks, the other was holding the bridle rein with one hand and had the other hand on the horse's neck. I was surprised to see a horse there and took a good look at it. Just as I came near the group another undergraduate on a cycle, with a tennis racket, came round the curve very quickly. I shrank back as I thought there would be a nasty accident, but to my surprise the cyclist came through the hindquarters of the horse. Very startled I realised the horse and the young men were no longer there.
>
> It is the only time I have ever seen anything unusual and the group looked quite ordinary. The undergraduates were, however, wearing riding breeches. They both had short hair, and short black gowns. They were talking to each other quite naturally.
>
> It was not until later, when I made some enquiries, that I learnt that these large doors had led to the Queen's College stables in the past.
>
> I was going to a meeting of the Oxford Writer's Circle at the time and I was sufficiently pale when I arrived to make the members ask if I was all right. They were very intrigued when I told them the story—although I think very few believed me!

We think of an apparition, typically, as a figure of a person who 'isn't really there' superimposed on the normal environment. The surroundings of the person who perceives the apparition do not change. The figures seen in New College Lane in the case just quoted seem to be hallucinatory, but the street in which they appeared seemed to be as usual, and the subject seemed to be perceiving them in the normal way.

There is another type of experience in which the subject, who is awake at the time, temporarily loses his awareness of his normal environment, and seems to be perceiving a different one. That is to say, his field of perception is temporarily replaced by a hallucinatory one. We shall call this type of experience a 'waking dream' by analogy with dreams which occur in sleep, in which the subject is completely unaware of his physical surroundings, such as the bedroom in which he is asleep, and his attention is instead engaged by the substitute field of perception provided by his dream.

We shall call experiences in which the subject's field of perception is completely replaced by a hallucinatory one 'metachoric', so we see that both waking dreams and ordinary dreams are examples of metachoric experiences.

In a waking dream a subject may perceive a figure which he might call an 'apparition'. For example, in the following case, the subject sees his wife moving about.

> One afternoon in or about the year 1930 I was seated at my desk in Millbank, London, when I went into what I can only describe as a day dream. Suddenly I was at home at No. —, St. Mary's Grove, Chiswick. My wife was just leaving the kitchen to go into our common bedroom, which was also on the ground floor, in order to tidy it up. I knew this because her thoughts were my thoughts just as though we were jointly one individual. She (or rather we) entered the room to find that Bert (me) had flung his best suit, worn the night before, untidily, and characteristically, down in a corner. Jennie thought 'That's just like him, and he will want it tonight for the party. I haven't time to press it. I know, I'll put the trousers between brown paper and under the mattress of his bed.' We had twin beds at that time.
>
> In accordance with her plan she did put the trousers under the bed and just afterwards I 'woke up' back at my desk. The experience was so vivid that I looked at my watch to mark the time. It was 3.10 p.m. I could hardly wait to get home, but when I did I went straight to my bed and lifted the mattress. The trousers were there, in brown paper, just as I had seen them put there at 3.10 p.m. Jennie my wife confirmed that her thoughts and actions were exactly as I described them, but of course she could not confirm the exact time.

(The subject's wife confirms that on getting home from the office that evening he 'described exactly' her actions and thoughts of earlier in the day, and went straight to the bedroom and found his trousers under the mattress before telling her of his experience and before they had held any conversation.)

Figures of people which occur in waking dreams are, of course, provided with a complex hallucinatory surrounding, whereas the more typical apparition seems to have no accompanying surrounding, but stands, or possibly moves around, in the normal surroundings of the percipient.

We have to ask ourselves how close is the relationship between these two types of phenomena—the 'waking dream' type of apparition and the 'normal' type. Let us begin by considering some intermediate types of apparition, in which the main figure was provided with some hallucinatory environment of its own, but in which this hallucinatory environment seemed to replace only a part of the subject's normal surroundings.

In one case in our collection the subject reports seeing, not merely a single hallucinatory figure as in the preceding case, but a quite complex street-scene on a wall, rather as if it were thrown there by a film projector. The percipient's account is as follows:

> Four years ago next april we were home on leave from Germany, and I took my son, then 9, to stay for a couple of days, with my sister. As she had only one spare room, Timothy (my son) had a camp bed in the corner of my room, rather a low bed, his was. On our 2nd night there, at about 11.30 p.m. I switched off the light and lay in bed facing the wall against which my son's camp bed was set. The room was quite dark, except for a thread of light showing beneath the door, and I could hear my sister and her husband coming upstairs to bed. Suddenly a patch of light appeared on the wall in the form of a square, like a T.V. screen, but the light was natural looking, a golden sunlight, and in this square was a busy street scene, in fact, it was crowded with people, all on the move, in the foreground a young man wearing a dark suit, coat undone and one hand in his trouser-pocket, hatless, and as he walked briskly along, he looked slightly backwards and downwards where my son lay sleeping, and he kept looking until he walked out of sight, and as he did so, the picture gradually faded, and the room was dark again. By then of course I was sitting up and staring nearly pop-eyed I'm sure.
>
> I've never seen anything like this before or since and still find it inexplicable. I had not been watching television earlier.

The following example will illustrate how part of the percipient's normal environment may seem to disappear and be replaced by a new piece. In this case the subject reports that a building, which formed part of the scene she was looking at before the start of the experience, vanished and in its place she saw some rhododendron bushes:

I was in the sick-room at Boarding School with a small bone broken in the foot. My parents hardly ever came to see me. But I do remember my Father paid me a visit, which was lovely for me and unusual.

I can't remember if it was before or after his visit, that I was looking out of the sick room window, where one saw brick buildings as music and piano practice rooms. Suddenly the brick building vanished and I saw a large Rhododendron bush or bushes instead. I saw the colour and shape distinctly. Out of this bounded the biggest black dog I'd really ever seen, very fierce with a small piece of either chain or leather attached to his neck. He bounded out and ran a small way before it all went and I was again looking at the red brick building.

(The subject adds that years later she learnt by chance from her father that he had had what was apparently the same experience on looking out of her sick-room window on the day of his visit. Not having known of his daughter's experience he had not thought to tell her of his own before.)

So far we appear to have three distinct classes of apparition: waking dreams, typical apparitions and a type intermediate between them. In the waking dream the subject's normal environment is completely replaced by a different environment in which he sees the figure of a person; in the typical apparitional case the subject seems to remain in his normal environment, and the apparitional figure appears superimposed on it; and in the intermediate type there is a partial replacement of the subject's normal environment by a different environment within which the apparition is seen. However, the distinctions between these three types may be less absolute than they appear at first sight.

Consider, for example, the following case in which the subject seems to see an apparitional figure in her normal environment, that is to say, in her own living-room. Although the subject seems to be in her normal environment we gather from her account that an external observer would have seen her lying in bed throughout, and from the fact that she comments on the displacement of the settee we gather that what she was perceiving was a hallucinatory imitation of her living-room, and not the room itself. That is to say, this was a metachoric experience.

I thought just recently, that I would try to see my eldest son living in Rhodesia. For five nights just before I fell asleep, I willed very strongly that I would be allowed to 'see Charles in Rhodesia'. On the sixth night, I almost forgot to put my mind to the matter, and being almost asleep I just thought 'I wish I could see Charles', not mentioning Rhodesia. I was just beginning to wake up about 7.45 a.m. when suddenly I found myself in the living room, seated on the settee, which had by some means been pushed back against the wall, so that I had a clear view of the door. I had a great feeling of elation and knew that some Being was clearing the way as it were; the whole atmosphere seemed to be in motion. Presently I heard hurrying footsteps, and knowing it was morning, I thought my eldest daughter must have come back home, instead of going on to College. The footsteps drew nearer still hurrying, but I now realized that it was a man's footsteps I could hear. Suddenly the door opened, and a man's head and shoulders appeared; I thought at first it was that of one of my brothers whom I had not seen for some years, then to my delight I realized that it was Charles, five years older than when I last saw him and very lean and brown; his skin much darker than I would have expected. He looked around the room impatiently, and with a very surprized look on his face; he must have wondered what on earth he was doing there, as he has never seen this flat and he did not turn round far enough to see me, though I willed it with all my heart. I knew that this was a gift, and the moment would soon be gone; so I eagerly took in every aspect of his features and clothing. In another moment I was back in bed.

This case can actually be classified as an out-of-the-body experience, and it is interesting to note that it is true to type in so far as the experience is 'experimental', that is, brought about as a result of some exercise of deliberate intention on the part of the subject, and contains an element of unrealism in the departure from the true position of the settee. This case, however, reminds us of the facility which out-of-the-body experiences have for providing the subject with a precisely imitated but hallucinatory replica of his normal surroundings. In cases which are not experimental, but occur entirely spontaneously, the correspondence between the hallucinatory imitation environment and the normal environment appears usually to be virtually complete, so that the subject is not able to observe any point of discrepancy. This obviously raises the possibility that in at least some apparitional cases in which the subject seems to see an apparition superimposed on his normal environment, he may actually be having a metachoric experience and be seeing a completely hallucinatory substitute environment. If and when this happens, the experience is obviously much the same as what we have called a waking dream, except that the substitute environment is an imitation of that in which the subject actually finds himself at the time, and no discontinuity is perceptible at the beginning and end of the experience.

Again, it might at first sight appear that the type of case in which a part of the subject's normal environment seems to be replaced by a hallucinatory scene is what it seems to be. That is to say, we might think that the subject was still perceiving some of his normal environment in the normal way, and was hallucinated about only a part of it. However, it is also possible, in the light of the observations we have just made, that the whole environment is actually hallucinatory throughout the experience, and it is just that a part of the hallucinatory environment provides an accurate imitation of the subject's normal surroundings. Various cases, among which is the following, shed interesting light on this hypothesis.

> I was put to sleep in that same room, along with another maid-servant. We went to bed and turned down the gas till only a little button of gas was alight. Then it seemed to me that the gas turned red and there came more light in the room than the gas would make. The wall opposite my side of the bed, a few feet away, seemed to disappear, and I saw a round table with a red cover and an old lady reading at it, and girls sitting round it. They seemed to be about 12 years old, in high dresses, but I could not see more than their heads and shoulders. They made no noise. Then they disappeared, and then came men with daggers and hilts and girdles, and a sort of capes and plumes in their hats, and sandals on their feet, who seemed to fight. These made a loud noise. When one of them was struck he seemed to fall down. The fight seemed to take place in daylight. All this seemed to last about half an hour, then all vanished. I was so terrified that I could not move or speak while it went on. I perspired so much with fear that the mattress was soaked on the side where I lay.
>
> This happened night after night about 20 times, the same figures appearing, except that sometimes there would be a man with spectacles reading at the table instead of the old lady. And one night a white figure seemed to leave the group of men who were fighting and to pass round by the end of the bed and disappear into the wall.
>
> I told my fellow servant something of what I saw, and asked her to notice that the gas turned red as soon as it was turned low. But she could not see this, and laughed at me, and said that it was all nonsense, and always went to sleep before the figures came. (*Journal of the S.P.R.*, Vol. VI, 1893–4, p.13)

The fact that the gas seemed to the percipient to turn red, which her companion could not see, suggests in itself that she was hallucinated about this in addition to the scenes which she saw instead of the opposite wall. However, she also mentions that 'there came more light in the room than the gas would make'. This change in the lighting presumably affected practically all parts of her field of vision, and strongly suggests that from this point on everything that she seemed to see around her was actually hallucinatory, although part of it was a close imitation of her actual surroundings at the time.

Cases such as this suggest that, in experiences which appear to be partly hallucinatory, the subject's environment may actually be entirely hallucinatory, even when the subject reports no obvious reason for suggesting this to be so. That is to say, the type of apparitional experience in which a part of the subject's environment seems to be replaced may also be metachoric, as is the 'waking dream' type.

CHAPTER 2

The Illumination of the Environment

CONSIDERING for the moment only those apparitional cases which are not of the waking dream type, but in which the subject's normal environment appears to be unchanged throughout the experience, we find that in the majority of these the illumination of the environment seems to be unchanged throughout. There is, however, an interesting minority in which the illumination of the environment is modified in various ways while the apparitional experience is taking place. It is interesting to examine what light the question of illumination sheds on the problem of the hallucinatory nature or otherwise of the subject's environment during apparitional experiences. There seems to be a strong case for regarding the entire environment as hallucinatory in cases where the illumination differs from the normal, whereas in cases in which the illumination does not change this interpretation seems less inevitable.

*

There is a small class of cases in which the subject reports that the apparition appeared to reduce the overall illumination of his visual field. For example, the subject may report seeing an apparition leaning in at a window and seeming thereby to cut off some of the day-light entering from outside, so that the whole room in which the subject is situated is temporarily darkened somewhat, just as if a real person were partly blocking the window. Alternatively, an apparition may seem to pass near to a candle in such a way that it intercepts some of its light, and casts a shadow over the whole room.

The following two cases will illustrate these possibilities.

One day in the '40s, when I was living in the Rectory at Marlborough, my father's house, my mother and sister had gone out, and

I was lying on a sofa in the drawing-room; at about 3 p.m. I was reading a book, when the light seemed to be slightly darkened, and looking up I saw, leaning in at the window farthest from me, about three feet from the ground, and beckoning, a gentleman whom I had only seen once, about a fortnight or three weeks previously. Supposing that my father wanted me to sign my name (as a witness to a lease, or something of that kind), I got up, went out of the window (which led down into the garden), and passed along in front of the house, and up six steps into my father's study, which was empty. I then went into the yard and garden, but found nobody; so I returned to my sofa and my books. When father came in, two hours afterwards, I said, 'Why did you send Mr. H. to call me, and then go away?' My father replied, 'What are you talking about? H. is down in Wales.' Nothing more was said. I did not like to dwell on the subject to either of my parents, and I did not mention the occurrence to any one for several years. About a fortnight afterwards, I was told by my mother that Mr. H. had written, proposing for my hand (some property of his adjoined some property of my father's in Wales). I cannot fix *exactly* how close the coincidence was; but my strong impression is that the letter was received within 24 hours of my experience. (Gurney II, p. 527)

. . . It was still just about 9.30 . . . and I just pulling myself into a half-sitting posture against the pillows, thinking of nothing but the arrangements for the following day, when to my great astonishment I saw a gentleman standing at the foot of the bed, dressed as a naval officer, and with a cap on his head having a projecting peak. The light being in the position which I have indicated, the face was in shadow *to me*, and the more so that the visitor was leaning upon his arms which rested on the foot-rail of the bedstead. I was too astonished to be afraid, but simply wondered who it could be; and, instantly touching my husband's shoulder (whose face was turned from me), I said, 'Willie, who is this?' My husband turned, and for a second or two lay looking in intense astonishment at the intruder; then lifting himself a little, he shouted 'What on earth are you doing here, sir?' Meanwhile the form, slowly drawing himself into an upright position, now said in a commanding, yet reproachful voice, 'Willie! Willie!'

I looked at my husband and saw that his face was white and agitated. As I turned towards him he sprang out of bed as though to attack the man, but stood by the bedside as if afraid, or in great perplexity, while the figure calmly and slowly moved *towards the wall* at right angles with the lamp . . . As it passed the lamp, a deep shadow fell upon the room as of a material person shutting out the light from us by his intervening body, and he disappeared, as it were, into the wall. My husband now, in a very agitated manner, caught up the lamp, and turning to me said, 'I mean to look all over the house, and see where he is gone.'

I was by this time exceedingly agitated too, but remembering that the door was locked, and that the mysterious visitor had not gone towards it at all, remarked, 'He has not gone out by the door!' But without pausing, my husband *unlocked the door*, hastened out of the room, and was soon searching the whole house. Sitting there in the dark, I thought to myself, 'We have surely seen an apparition! Whatever can it indicate—perhaps my brother Arthur (he was in the navy, and at that time on a voyage to India) is in trouble: such things have been told of as occurring.' In some such way I pondered with an anxious heart, holding the child, who just then awakened, in my arms, until my husband came back looking very white and miserable.

Sitting upon the bedside, he put his arm about me and said, 'Do you know what we have seen?' And I said, 'Yes, it was a spirit. I am afraid it was Arthur, but could not see his face'—and he exclaimed, 'Oh! no, it was my father!' (*Proceedings of the S.P.R.*, Vol. VI, 1889–90, pp. 27–8)

Now when the overall level of illumination is reduced, this must affect virtually all parts of the visual field. Let us consider what explanations of this phenomenon may be possible in cases such as the two we have just quoted.

One can of course suppose that the apparition in each of these cases was some kind of temporary physical entity, which really did intercept the light, and that the subject was perceiving everything in his environment, including the apparition, in the normal way. This theory, however, would raise considerable difficulties. It would be difficult to suggest that all apparitions were temporary physical entities of this kind, as such a view would fit very badly with what we observe of the behaviour of apparitions in general.

One difficulty, for example, is that apparitions are sometimes seen by some, but not all, of those present at the time. This difficulty, and others like it, can always be got round by supposing that there are at least two quite different kinds of apparition. It would be necessary for someone adopting this point of view to suppose that some apparitions were physical, including those few instances in which the figure is seen to occlude a light source, and that in cases of other kinds the apparitional figure is not physical, but hallucinatory.

Another possible explanation of the two cases just quoted is that the lighting in the room happened to alter at the time the apparition was seen due to some physical cause, and that the subconscious mind of the subject timed the actions of the apparitional figure so that it appeared to be the cause of the reduced illumination. For example, in the first of the two cases it might be supposed that the day was predominantly sunny, but that a cloud passed over the sun just before the percipient looked up and saw the figure at the window. The hallucinatory figure would then seem to be the cause of the reduced level of illumination in the room. The percipient's subconscious might have anticipated the approach of the cloud to the sun by extrasensory perception, or simply noticed the onset of shadow and immediately initiated the hallucination of the figure at the window.

A third possible explanation is that experiences in which there is a reduced overall level of illumination are entirely hallucinatory, or metachoric. For example, in each of the two cases we have quoted, the percipients may have been hallucinating the entire room at a level of illumination lower than that which was actually prevailing in that room in reality.

*

In addition to the class of cases which we have just been discussing, in which the overall environment is darker than would be expected, there are also reports of cases in which the overall level of illumination is abnormally bright.

For example, we shall shortly proceed to quote two cases which will illustrate how the subject's whole environment may appear illuminated, without there being any evident source for the illumination.

The only alternative to the view that both the figure and the environment are hallucinatory in such cases would be to suppose that the figure of the apparition is hallucinatory, while the light illuminating the environment is generated by some kind of psycho-kinetic process.

This would mean that the apparition would not be visible to any independent observer who happened to look into the room, unless he also happened to be hallucinated, but that the heightened illumination of the room would be visible to anyone who happened to look at it. Furthermore, if a photograph was taken of the room while the subject was seeing the apparition, the resulting print would show the temporarily heightened illumination of the room but not the figure of the apparition.

But if no additional physical light is introduced into the

situation by psychokinesis, the conclusion seems unavoidable that the whole of the subject's environment is hallucinatory throughout the experience, or at least so long as the increased illumination is present.

The two following cases illustrate this kind of increase in the overall illumination of the surroundings which may accompany an apparition.

> On New Year's Eve, 1852, I awoke about 12.40 a.m. and found my room so brilliantly illuminated that I imagined I had forgotten to put out my candle, and that something must have caught fire. I got up and, on looking round, saw at the foot of the bed a coffin resting on chairs, on each of which was a silver candlestick with a large wax taper alight; in the coffin was a figure of my father. I put out my hand and touched him, when it became quite dark. I felt for my matchbox and lighted a candle, looked at my watch and wrote down the time. The next morning I told my friend, with whom I was staying in Paris at the time, and on the morning of the 2nd of January we received a letter from Marseilles, saying that my father had died suddenly at 12.40 on New Year's Eve, and that he had expressed such a strong wish to see his youngest child (i.e., myself) again just before his death. (Gurney, I, pp. 436–7)

> One night in the year 1882 or 1883, I awoke completely and sat up in bed. There was light enough in the room to see all the objects in it distinctly. My bed faced the door. Coming from the door, which was shut, I saw distinctly, and noticed the dress she had on, a lady friend staying in the house. She was advancing on her hands and knees. My first thought was that she had suddenly lost her reason. I asked her what she wanted. She did not answer but disappeared under the bed. I leaned over the side of the bed to see if I could see her, believing her really to be there; almost immediately the room became quite dark. I had no feeling of fear, and I am sure that I was wide awake. I was teaching at the time, and had been overworking. I was in the habit of seeing the lady almost daily, and had done so for some years. She was presumably asleep in bed at the time on the other side of the passage. I was alone. (Census, pp. 79–80)

Another way in which the apparition may be more visible to the subject than the normal lighting conditions would appear to warrant is that the apparition may seem to have an intrinsic luminosity of its own. The following case is an example of this type.

> This experience occurred in Hovelhof, a village in Westphalia, Germany.
> I lived alone in a self-contained flat, over a bank. By day, meals

were served there to a number of British soldiers and civilians, who were waited on by staff of German domestics, but by 10 p.m. the last of the domestic staff left and any of the soldiers or civilians who remained were usually out by 11 p.m. . . . .

I was awakened from sleep by my left shoulder being shaken, it seemed to me quite roughly. I sat up in bed. The room was dark but I could just see that somebody was standing at the foot of the bed. At first I assumed that it was a member of the domestic staff and I was puzzled at being woken in that manner and while it was still dark. I waited for the visitor to speak, and while I did so the figure became increasingly visible; it was a woman, hatless and with dark hair, and not anyone I recognized. Up to that time I still thought it was an ordinary person, but then the figure seemed to become gradually illuminated by an internal glow. It was not a glow as bright as when a hand is held round an electric bulb, and the illumination was yellow, rather like a luminous clock-dial.

The features became quite clearly visible, the face seemed to be smiling and I could see the outline of the arms. From the start I had assumed that the visitor was a domestic which probably accounts for the fact that, in recalling the incident, I had the impression that she was wearing an apron, but I did not really notice the clothes. She slowly moved forward, her hand extended at arm's-length as though with the intention of shaking my left shoulder again. To move forward, she came round the bed as a tangible person would have done.

Suddenly, I became very frightened and tried to switch on the main light which was operated by a cord hanging down the wall behind my head, while at the same time moving away to my right to avoid the approaching figure. There was nothing menacing about the woman's demeanour, in fact I had the impression all the time she was smiling. I groped about desperately with my left hand behind my head but could not find the cord. So I moved round sideways in bed, put my right hand out, so that I could lean on the floor, and managed to switch on the table lamp with my left hand. This lamp was to my right when I was in bed, but in the cross position to which I had now got, half out of bed, it was on my left. As soon as the light came on, the figure disappeared. The bedroom door was, as usual, shut. (*Proceedings of the S.P.R.*, Vol. 53, 1960, pp. 150–1)

When an apparition seems to glow from within, the surroundings may remain dark, or the surroundings themselves may also seem to be illuminated, either by radiance emanating from the apparition or by light seeming to come from some other source.

Now if the subject's surroundings appear illuminated, as well as the figure of the apparition itself, we seem driven to the conclusion that the experience is metachoric, and the whole environment the subject is seeing is hallucinatory.

If the figure has an intrinsic illumination, but this does not appear to have any effect on the environment by increasing its level of illumination at all, it seems to be more optional whether or not we regard the experience as metachoric. One may either suppose that the subject is perceiving his surroundings in the normal way, with the exception of the hallucinatory glowing figure which he sees superimposed on them, or we may suppose that the whole environment, including the glowing figure, is hallucinatory although much of it is an accurate reproduction of what the subject would be perceiving normally.

In the following case, although the apparition is itself luminous, the rest of the subject's surroundings appear to be darker, and not lighter, while it is present. This clearly suggests that the environment is completely hallucinatory.

> At about 3 a.m. (i.e., to be precise, on the morning of September 22nd), I woke up, naturally, so far as I know; I was lying on my right side—that is, with my face towards the west wall. I was perfectly conscious and wide awake, and though not aware of anything abnormal occurring in the room, I had a feeling of constraint to turn round to look towards the east wall. Turning my head over my shoulder I saw there a hazy column of light, extending from about a foot, or a little more than a foot, above the ground, and some five feet in height. The room was pitch dark, and I could see absolutely nothing but the light, which was, I noticed, about where I remembered the wardrobe was. (The wardrobe has plain, painted doors, not glazed, and is not capable of reflecting light.) I then turned round again, shut my eyes, and settled myself with the idea of getting to sleep, but soon again turned to look at the object. I had not any feeling of actual fear, only a slight nervousness and chilliness, except for a moment when I fancied it was coming towards me. Upon looking intently at the light, I observed it to be of a misty, almost phosphorescent nature, having the distinctive character of appearing to be illuminated from within. It then appeared gradually to assume a definite form, and in the course of, say, 5 or 10 seconds—though it seemed to me longer at the time—I concluded it was of the form of a woman in a night-dress, whether an old woman or young I could not say; in a few seconds more, however, I made out that it had the appearance of a young woman bending slightly forward, with the near right arm slightly extended, and the hand a little raised; the face—of which I remember seeing only about half or three-quarters—also somewhat forward, the attitude altogether giving the idea that she was looking for something on the floor. The head was covered by a white hood, with a white band passing underneath the chin, like a nun's headdress. The contour of the face was rather oval, but I could not distinguish any features. The light was brighter and less misty just below what I took

to be the nightdress, giving me the idea that I saw feet, though without definite form; the face also was, I think, somewhat brighter than the rest of the body, and it appeared as though the dress veiled the light and thus rendered it misty. I now remembered Mrs. Robinson's[1] explanation of the appearance as being caused possibly by a light from outside the window being thrown into the room. I therefore turned my head quite round to the right—I was reclining with my body a little raised on my left elbow, I think, and my head turned a little to my left—in order to see if any rays of light were crossing the room. There was no light whatever across the room, of this I am perfectly certain; but I was struck with the fact that I saw no sign of the window: the apparition was the only thing in the room that was visible.

. . . then it vanished and I saw the window and the whole of the room normally.

During the whole of the vision the room seemed to me unnaturally dark, and I am not conscious of having been able to see any object in the room (except perhaps the bar at the foot of the bed), while the apparition was at C,[2] but of this I have only a confused recollection. Directly the column of light vanished, however, I could see the window and other things with some distinctness. (*Journal of the S.P.R.*, Vol. IV, 1889–90, pp. 43–4)

In the case just quoted, it will be observed that while the apparition was present the subject could see no sign of the window, but once it had vanished she was able to see 'the window and the whole of the room normally'. This could easily be explained if the experience was metachoric, and the subject was perceiving a completely hallucinatory environment while the apparition was present.

In another case a luminous apparition is seen against some white blinds in a dark room. The percipient says that while the apparition was visible in front of the blinds they appeared quite dark, but resumed their normal whiteness when the apparition disappeared. This again suggests that, while seeing the apparition, the percipient was also hallucinating at least part of her visual field, viz. the area occupied by the blinds. The following is part of the percipient's narrative:

On Friday evening, November 15th, 1912, I retired to bed as usual about 9 o'clock. . . . Being rather tired, I soon fell asleep, but awoke, as near as I can judge, in the middle of the night or the very early hours of the morning. I had no clock in the room, so am not

---

[1] A caretaker in the house.
[2] A reference to a plan of the room drawn by the percipient.

positive of the time. I turned my head towards the window, when my eyes were attracted to a white figure hovering near the dressing-table. The figure was in the form of a baby, and was clothed from head to foot in a white robe which fitted rather closely. The robe appeared to be in one piece, part of which fitted closely round the head and formed a hood. No arms were visible, so the robe went straight down. I saw no feet, but I had a feeling at the time that the robe just covered them. As near as I can tell, the figure was about eighteen inches high. It seemed to me that some invisible hand was holding it at the back, which caused it to bend slightly forward. Although appearing so suddenly, I felt too fascinated to be frightened, and gazed at it until it disappeared. I tried to sleep, but that was impossible. Whether through curiosity or not (I cannot tell), but I felt compelled to look up, and there was the figure in exactly the same spot as before. I must confess I felt a little uncomfortable, but far from frightened. It was at this second appearance I noticed it turn to the window and bow. It disappeared, but came again the third time. After the third disappearance I did not see it again. I lay awake for a long time and then fell asleep. . . . It is interesting to note that when the figure was present the robe was so white and seemed to shine so much in the darkness that the white blinds appeared quite dark, though they resumed their ordinary whiteness when the figure disappeared. (*Journal of the S.P.R.*, Vol. XVI, 1913–14, pp. 114–16)

The optical effects associated with the presence of the luminous apparition, in both the last two cases, are similar to those which might have been expected if the apparition had been a real bright object. In the first case, everything else in the environment which was not itself brightly illuminated became invisible until the bright apparition disappeared, at which point other objects again became perceptible. This is what might have been expected to happen if the apparition had been a real bright object; in the presence of the bright object the percipient's vision would have adapted to this level of brightness, and would not have been able to pick out the other objects in the room, but when the bright object had disappeared his night vision would have returned and he would have been able to see them.

If the apparition had been a real object, this might correspond to a shift from rod to cone vision, and back to rod vision again when the bright object was removed.

In the second case, the variation in the brightness of the blinds behind the apparition resembles a typical brightness contrast effect, such as would have arisen if the apparition had been a real bright object. A real object that was much whiter than the blinds would have made them seem dark in just the same way if it was placed in front of them, and similarly its removal would have made the blinds appear white again.

In the light of present knowledge of the physiology of visual perception, both these optical effects seem to arise at a much more peripheral level of the visual system (such as the retina of the eye) than the parts of the nervous system which might be expected to be involved in perceiving hallucinations. If such is the case, then these optical effects could only be caused either by the apparition being a real physical object, or else by their being themselves a part of the hallucination. That is to say, either apparitions of this kind are producing real light photons which impinge on the subject's retina, or else the whole scene is produced at a higher level of the brain, in mimicry of normal optical effects. Seeing a bright hallucinatory object should not cause optical effects of this kind in the perception of the environment, supposing the rest of the environment to be perceived in the normal way.

CHAPTER 3

The Substitution of the Environment

As we have seen, apparitions which occur in association with certain kinds of modified illumination seem to require us to suppose that the subject's entire visual field is hallucinatory, and not just the figure of the apparition. There is another class of apparition cases which also seems to involve us in supposing this. These are the cases in which the percipient sees the apparition in an 'impossible' way, such as through the back of his head or round a corner.

The following is a case in which the subject apparently sees an apparition through the back of his head. The percipient was sitting reading a book, waiting for two friends to return from a concert, and the apparition was of one of these friends (called 'A.H.' in the percipient's account):

> I had read some twenty minutes or so, was thoroughly absorbed in the book, my mind was perfectly quiet, and for the time being my friends were quite forgotten, when suddenly without a moment's warning my whole being seemed roused to the highest state of tension or aliveness, and I was aware, with an intenseness not easily imagined by those who have never experienced it, that another being or presence was not only in the room but close to me. I put my book down, and although my excitement was great, I felt quite collected and not conscious of any sense of fear. Without changing my position, and looking straight at the fire, I knew somehow that my friend A.H. was standing at my left elbow, but so far behind me as to be hidden by the arm-chair in which I was leaning back. Moving my eyes round slightly without otherwise changing my position, the lower portion of one leg became visible, and I instantly recognised the grey-blue material of trousers he often wore, but the stuff appeared semi-transparent, reminding me of tobacco smoke in consistency. I could have touched it with my hand without moving more than my left arm. With that curious instinctive wish not to see more of such a 'figure', I did no more than glance once or twice at the apparition and then

directed my gaze steadily at the fire in front of me. An appreciable space of time passed—probably seconds in all, but seeming in reality much longer,—when the most curious thing happened. Standing upright between me and the window on my left, and at a distance of about four feet from me and almost immediately behind my chair, I saw perfectly distinctly the figure of my friend,—the face very pale, the head slightly thrown back, the eyes shut, and on one side of the throat, just under the jaw, a wound with blood on it. The figure remained motionless with the arms close to the sides, and for some time, how long I can't say, I looked steadily at it; then all at once roused myself, turned deliberately round, the figure vanished, and I realised instantly that I had seen the figure behind me without moving from my first position,—an impossible feat physically. I am perfectly certain I never moved my position from the first appearance of the figure as seen physically, until it disappeared on my turning round. (*Journal of the S.P.R.*, Vol. VII, 1895-6, pp. 26-7)

The percipient later discovered that at about the time of his experience his friend A.H. had fainted in the street, and in falling on the edge of the kerb had cut his face under the jaw.

It is possible that in this case the subject experienced a kinaesthetic hallucination, so that he continued to experience the physical sensations appropriate to looking at the fire in front of him although in reality he was turning round in his seat and should have been experiencing the physical sensations appropriate to such a movement. However, if this was not the case, then it appears that the subject's eyes were not involved in the experience of seeing the figure behind his chair, and that his whole visual field while apparently looking at it was thus hallucinatory. As we do not have the report of any witness in this case, it is not possible to determine whether the subject was really sitting in the position that he thought he was, i.e. facing the fire.

*

Cases in which the subject sees his normal environment as temporarily illuminated while he sees an apparition, or in which he sees the apparition in some physically impossible way, form only a small minority of the cases reported to us.

However, if the subject's entire visual field in such cases is hallucinatory, then the question arises whether the percipient's entire visual field may not be hallucinatory in all cases in which he sees an apparition. If not, we should have to suppose that there were two distinct kinds of experience of seeing an apparition: one in which the percipient's entire visual field was hallucinatory, and one in which only a part of it was, namely the figure of the apparition.

It may be helpful at this point to remind the reader that there are other types of metachoric experience in which the whole environment seen by the subject is hallucinatory, although it appears to represent his normal surroundings.

The first of these types of experience is the 'out-of-the-body' or ecsomatic experience. The following is an example which was reported as occurring in Oxford:

> I was working as a waitress in a local restaurant and had just finished a 12-hour stint. I was terribly fatigued and was chagrined to find I had lost the last bus. . . . However I started walking as in those days I lived in Jericho, a fifteen minute walk at most. I remember feeling so fatigued that I wondered if I'd make it and resolved to myself that I'd 'got to keep going'. The next I registered, was of hearing the sound of my heels very hollowly and I looked down and watched myself walk round the bend of Beaumont Street into Walton Street. I—the bit of me that counts—was up on a level with Worcester College chapel. I saw myself very clearly—it was a summer evening and I was wearing a sleeveless shantung dress. I remember thinking 'so that's how I look to other people'.

When one says that the percipient's field of perception in a case such as this is hallucinatory one does not mean to imply that it is not an accurate representation of her environment. As far as one can tell, this subject sees just what she would if she were really hovering at the point near Worcester College chapel at which she seems to be. However, what she sees is obviously not the same picture of Beaumont Street as that provided by the information, if any, coming from her retina. It is a different perspective of the street altogether. It is for this reason that one may for convenience call it 'hallucinatory'—because the subject's eyes do not appear to be involved in it, at least not in the way in which one's eyes normally appear to be involved in seeing.

The following is an example of the second type of metachoric experience, the Type 2 false awakening. A false awakening is an experience in which a subject believes that he wakes up from sleep, but does not really do so. A Type 2 false awakening is one in which he appears to wake up in his own bed and normal surroundings, in a very realistic way. The percipient is 'Subject E', whose lucid dreams and out-of-the-body experiences are discussed in Charles McCreery's book, *Psychical Phenomena and the Physical World*:

> I awoke to the realisation that the bedside radio was still on. Someone passed the door on the way downstairs. I turned the music low: strange, I thought, the radio being on this time of night—what *was* the time? I reached out of bed to look at the clock (about six feet away) but as I did so an eerie feeling came over me, and I hesitated; yet everything looked perfectly natural so I went ahead, against a mounting tension of the atmosphere, and picked up the clock—whereupon it suddenly changed in my hands! Hastily I put it down; its black dial had turned white and the hands moved to the 9 and 10. I recognised this was the false awakening. Pausing a moment to ponder the significance of the position of the hands (for I knew this could not represent the actual time) I dived back under the blankets. Monsters were pressing in on me, I called for help but could not wake up—not until I had seized hold of the monsters and fought them, and flung them on the floor.

We would say that the subject's entire field of perception was hallucinatory in an experience such as this for the following reason. At the end of the experience the subject wakes up in bed, even if he had seemed to be out of bed just before waking. We may therefore suppose that he was in bed all the time. Also, when the subject does wake up he opens his eyes in the normal way, so we may presume that he had them closed throughout the preceding experience.

*

Whether or not it is true that the subject is provided with a complete substitute field of perception in all apparitional cases, this is probably true at least of those apparitions which occur in states which resemble a Type 2 false awakening. We have some reports of apparitions which certainly did occur in states recognised by the subjects as being false awakenings, but it seems quite likely that not all false awakenings of this kind are recognised as such. As they provide such a good imitation of a normal awakening, some subjects have reported having had false awakenings several times before realising what they were. It is therefore quite possible that some of the apparitions which are reported as associated with waking in the night may have occurred in a Type 2 false awakening, which the subject never identified as such because of lack of experience of this state.

The following two cases are examples of apparitions which occurred in the false awakening, in both cases to subjects with some previous experience of these states.

I knew that X was reading a book and would probably be staying up late, when I went to bed myself about 1 a.m.

I was woken in the night by sounds of someone in the house going to the lavatory, and thought that this must be X who had finished reading his book and was going to bed. I looked at my watch, which was luminous, and the time seemed to be about ten past four. Some time later it seemed to me that I was being woken again by somewhat similar noises in the house. There was a period of gradual awakening, as it seemed, and I then found myself awake and realising that the sounds had resolved themselves into the sounds of someone coming up the last flight of stairs towards my bedroom. I wondered if this might be Y, but when someone seemed to enter the room, and said, rather softly as if trying to find out if I was awake, 'Hello,' I realised it was X.

The room was very dimly lit and he didn't come in far from the door, but the shape of the figure appeared characteristic, and the verbal exchanges were very realistic, at least on the purely auditory level. I said, 'I'm awake', and raised my head a bit. I added, 'I heard the first time you went to the lavatory,' referring to the time when I had really been awake previously. X said, 'The first time? It was about the fourth,' and I took this to be some joking reference to the length of time he had been sitting up reading while I was asleep.

When I thought about this incident the next day, it still seemed very real and convincing, but I could not understand why I had not continued the conversation and could not remember X leaving the room. I concluded that I must have fallen asleep again and he must have gone away. But I found it hard to understand how I had fallen asleep so quickly and completely.

X later told me that he had not been near my room all night, and had only been to the lavatory once. I then realised the whole experience had been hallucinatory.

I awoke in the middle of the night, in most tranquil mood, and lay on my back in quiet reverie, eyes open. After some while Mother suddenly came into the room (as I remember the door was already wide open). I felt a little surprised, not having heard her about, also slightly anxious thinking she must have gone downstairs some time ago. I watched casually as she approached her bed and prepared in the usual way to get in. Her hair hung loose. I then returned to my quiet reverie. Presently, however, an increasingly eerie feeling began to steal over me—it began to dawn on me that there had been something indefinably 'odd' about the occurrence. Mother was normally quiet in her movements, but that scene had been quite noiseless— then full realisation broke as I recalled her putting her hair in rollers the night before, while in the vision (as I now concluded it must have been) her hair was loose and straight! I felt disconcerted, belatedly raising myself to look across at her in bed. I tried to think there might possibly be some normal explanation, but in the morning Mother confirmed she hadn't been up in the night, and her hair was still in rollers.

*

Once we have accepted that the idea of total substitution of the environment is virtually forced upon us in certain types of apparitional cases, and more or less strongly suggested in others, we have to bear this possibility in mind even in connection with apparitional experiences which are not of any of these types, and in which there is no particular feature of the case to suggest this interpretation.

There are a certain number of relatively unusual or anomalous types of apparitional experience which are easier to interpret if we suppose they are metachoric.

For example, let us consider the following case in which the subject reports that a visual apparition of a human figure seemed to pick up and then let fall a physical object in the environment, some snuffers. (The apparition represented the percipient's brother, who was in reality in another part of the country.)

> I dreamt one night that I saw my brother on horseback, who said to me that he was on a journey; he would therefore give me several commissions to my parents. I observed that his expression of countenance appeared very strange, and asked him why he looked so blue-black in his face? On which he made answer that it was occasioned by the new cloak he had put on, which was dyed with indigo. On this he reached me his hand, but whilst giving him mine, his horse began to plunge, which terrified me, and I awoke. Not long after awaking, the door of my room opened, someone came to my bedside, and drew aside the curtains, when I perceived the natural figure of my brother in his nightgown. After standing there a few minutes, he went to the table, took up the snuffers, and let them fall, and then shut the room door again. Fear, apprehension, and terror overpowered me to such a degree that I could not stay in bed any longer. I begged my elder sister, who also witnessed this scene, to accompany me to my parents. On entering the chamber of the latter, my father was astonished, and asked me the reason for my nocturnal coming. I besought him to spare me the answer till the morrow, and only permit me to pass the night in his room, to which he assented.
>
> As soon as I awoke in the morning, I was called upon by my parents to relate what had happened, which my eldest sister confirmed. The circumstance seemed so remarkable to my father that he

noted down the night and the hour. About three weeks afterwards my father received the melancholy intelligence of my brother's decease; when it appeared that he had died the same night, and the same hour, of an epidemic disorder, in which he had been suffocated, and his face had become quite black. In the last days of his illness he had spoken continually of his family, and had wished for nothing more ardently than to be able to speak once more with me. (Quoted in Gurney II, pp. 612–13)

There are a number of ways in which one might interpret this case, assuming of course that the percipient has accurately described his experience.

First, one might take the account at face value and suppose that the snuffers really did leave the surface of the table and fall back onto it. On this view we should have to suppose that two distinct but co-ordinated phenomena were taking place: the subject was hallucinating the figure of his brother going through the motions of picking up the snuffers; and simultaneously the snuffers were being raised by psychokinesis. Unfortunately, the subject does not comment on whether the snuffers were in the same position at the end of the experience as they had been before it started, or whether he thought he was able to detect an appreciable difference in the position in which the snuffers were lying after the experience had ended.

Another view might be that the subject hallucinated the figure of the apparition and also hallucinated a pair of snuffers rising into the air in the apparition's hand. If we suppose that the subject was perceiving the rest of the room in the normal way, then we should also have to postulate that he experienced a negative hallucination with respect to the real pair of snuffers, which lay on the table throughout. Otherwise the percipient would presumably have seen two snuffers simultaneously, one real one lying on the table, and another hallucinatory one rising into the air.

We may simplify this situation somewhat if we suppose that the percipient's whole field of view was hallucinatory when he saw the apparition pick up the snuffers. On this interpretation he was seeing a hallucinatory representation of his physical surroundings that was identical with what he would have seen if he had been perceiving it normally, except in two respects: first, the hallucinatory scene contained a human figure which was not there in reality, and second, it represented the snuffers as rising into the air and falling back again when in fact they remained motionless throughout.

There is another small class of unusual apparitional cases which may be explained by supposing them to be metachoric. Usually apparitions seem to avoid being touched, and speak only to a limited and somewhat imperfect extent, as though whatever subconscious mechanism may be responsible for projecting them found it difficult or undesirable to construct a convincing hallucination of too many senses at once. We shall be discussing this issue at greater length later (see Chapter 11). There are, however, a few cases on record which are distinctly atypical in this respect, and in which the apparition seems to function as freely as a real person, conversing in a perfectly realistic manner. One case of this type is quoted on pages 45-6 of Charles McCreery's book *Psychical Phenomena and the Physical World*. In this case the percipient reports shaking hands and talking with an apparition for some time in a busy street. If the passers-by really all saw the same apparition as the percipient, this apparition would have been collective to a very remarkable extent; in fact it would be difficult to find any other reported case in which so many people saw the apparition. On the other hand, if they did not, and saw the percipient shaking hands and chatting with thin air, they would presumably have shown some signs of surprise. But the difficulty vanishes if we accept the possibility that the subject may have been walking along as usual, or perhaps standing for a short time looking thoughtful. The fact that he thought he moved—e.g. shook hands—during the experience, does not present any particular difficulty; in Type 2 false awakenings the subject may appear to sit up and move about in his bed, but is presumably in reality lying down all the while.

CHAPTER 4

Apparitions and Out-of-the-Body Experiences

WE have observed that apparitions certainly do on occasion occur in Type 2 false awakenings and in fact may do so more often than is realised. Type 2 false awakenings are closely related to out-of-the-body experiences, and in this chapter we shall consider the possible relationship between experiences of seeing apparitions and out-of-the-body experiences.

*

Ecsomatic experiences sometimes occur in close conjunction with experiences of seeing apparitions. The subject may have the experience of seeing an apparition just before having an out-of-the-body experience, or he may have an out-of-the-body experience first and see an apparition directly after it. There may also be some degree of overlap between the two kinds of experience, and the subject may 'leave his body' at some point in the process of seeing an apparition.

The following are two instances in which the subject reports first seeing an apparition and then having an ecsomatic experience.

> I was in the W.A.A.F. during the war and at one point I was stationed in a hotel in W— called the A— Hotel . . . we were given beds in the basement leading off the kitchen and were reasonably settled for quite a few months. There were two of us and two maid-servants also there. Anyway one night when all had gone to sleep I was lying awake thinking about whether we should go into B— the following night to see a film, when the kitchen door opened and a figure walked in dressed in what I thought was a nightdress, though it didn't seem quite real. I looked at it for a moment and thought it was one of the owners, and then as it advanced towards me a feeling of terror swept through me and the next thing I knew I was on the ceiling looking down at myself in bed. The figure seemed to be doing

something to the bedclothes around my face, tucking me in as it were, I'm not quite sure, and then it vanished.

In the above case we note that the subject reports first seeing the apparition enter the room from her real position in bed, and then seeing it from a point near the ceiling as it appeared to do something to the bedclothes by her own physical body in the bed.

The second case is rather similar. The subject was lying awake in bed, but on perceiving the apparition he 'got up' to greet it, only to find subsequently that he had really been lying on his bunk all along. It will be seen that this subject also seems to have first seen the apparition from the real position of his physical body, and then to have seen it from a position other than that of his physical body.

> At the time of the occurrence I was living in Australia, in the 'bush' at a place about 60–70 miles from Perth, W.A. A certain young lady and myself were head over heels in love with one another. At the time, she was staying at a place about 200–250 miles away. I had finished my work for the day, it was quite dark, and I had lit the hurricane lamp which was in the hut where I slept. I had washed and was lying on my bunk waiting for a call to the evening meal, when I saw the certain young lady approach the open doorway out of the darkness. As she approached into the light, I got off my bunk and went towards her. We greeted one another, and as we did so, I realised I was *still lying on my bunk*. With the realization, the whole thing vanished, and I was indeed still lying perfectly still on my bunk. I was back in my body, on the *inside* looking *out*, instead of being on the outside and looking back at one's own body which appeared to be quite dead.

In both these last two cases it seems clear that at least the latter part of the experience was metachoric, since the subject was seeing the scene in a form which did not correspond to the form in which it was being presented to him by the information, if any, coming from his retina. Throughout the first experience, for example, the subject's retina was presumably presenting her with information about the room as seen from the bed, if her eyes were open at all; whereas towards the end of the experience she was seeing the room as it would have been seen by someone placed near the ceiling.

It seems to be more optional whether or not we regard the subject's environment as completely hallucinatory at the beginning of the experience. One might suppose that, until seeming to leave her body, the percipient was perceiving her environment normally, and only hallucinating the figure of the apparition which was superimposed on it.

However, it seems rather arbitrary to suppose that at the moment when the subject seemed to leave her body the experience suddenly changed from being partially hallucinatory to being wholly hallucinatory, and this clearly suggests the possibility that the experience was metachoric from the outset.

*

It appears that an out-of-the-body experience or a Type 2 false awakening can present the subject with such a detailed and realistic picture of his normal environment that he may not realise at first that what he is experiencing is hallucinatory and not normal perception. The following is an example of an ecsomatic experience in which the percipient did not realise that she was no longer in a normal state:

> I was seated at the tea-table with my family . . . about 5 p.m. on an autumn afternoon. My mother or father suddenly reminded me . . . that I should be at my music lesson, so I hurriedly collected my music case and rushed out of the front door and out of the gate on to the wet pavement which was strewn with leaves.
> *What I thought:* I must hurry. I must be careful. It would be awful if I slipped on one of those leaves and fell. Vivid picture of my prostrate body on the pavement outside the house, while 'I' sped along the road, almost reaching the corner of the block.
> *What actually happened as told me later:* The parents watched me leave the house . . . They saw me fall, then my mother said 'She's not getting up.' My father got out to me and I heard him say to another person who had crossed the road to help me 'I'll take her. I'm her father.'

It appears that an experience similar to an out-of-the-body experience could happen without the subject ever becoming aware of the fact, provided there was no noticeable discontinuity in his perceptual experience at either the beginning or the end of it. The question arises whether apparitions are ever perceived while the subject is in such a state.

We have suggested that the subject's whole visual field may be hallucinatory while he is perceiving an apparition of, say, a human being, and not just the figure of the apparition itself. If this is the case, the question arises whether the hallucinatory visual field of the subject's surroundings (apart from the apparition) always corresponds to what the subject would be seeing if he was perceiving his environment normally, or whether he may sometimes see it from a position other than that of his physical body, as in an out-of-the-body experience. That is to say, do the movements which the subject thinks he makes while seeing an apparition always correspond to those which he is really making? In cases in which they do not correspond, we may say that the subject has been seeing the apparition while having an out-of-the-body experience.

For example, a subject might wake up during the night and perceive an apparition in his bedroom. He might then proceed to get out of bed in order to investigate the apparition at closer quarters, only to find, when the apparition vanished, that he was still in bed and had never really got out of bed at all.

Of course, for the subject to be completely deceived about his true position it might be necessary for his subconscious mind to present to him hallucinatory tactile and kinaesthetic sensations appropriate to getting out of bed, standing on the floor, etc., as well as a hallucinatory visual field appropriate to someone standing outside the bed rather than lying in it.

The question is whether any cases of the type we have described are actually reported to occur. That is to say, are cases reported in which the subject's physical position at the end of the experience is found not to tally with what it should have been if his impression of his movements throughout the experience had been correct?

The answer to this seems to be that some cases of this type are reported, but they are relatively rare and the transition from one position to the other is usually reported only rather obliquely or allusively by the subject, so that it is difficult to estimate exactly how many cases fall into this class.

For example, in the following case the percipient, Lord Brougham, describes seeing an apparition while lying in his bath, and then, after the apparition had ended, finding himself on the floor outside the bath without knowing how he had got there. (The percipient was travelling in Sweden at the time of his experience. The apparition represented a school-friend, G., with whom Lord Brougham had made a compact to the effect that whichever died sooner would try to appear to the other. Since leaving school Lord Brougham had more or less lost contact with this friend.)

> We set out for Gothenburg, [apparently on December 18th] determined to make for Norway. About 1 in the morning, arriving at a decent inn, we decided to stop for the night. Tired with the cold of yesterday, I was glad to take advantage of a hot bath before I turned in, and here a most remarkable thing happened to me. . . .
> I had taken, as I have said, a warm bath, and while lying in it and enjoying the comfort of the heat, after the late freezing I had undergone, I turned my head round, looking towards the chair on which I had deposited my clothes, as I was about to get out of the bath. On the chair sat G., looking calmly at me. How I got out of the bath I know not, but on recovering my senses I found myself sprawling on the floor. The apparition, or whatever it was, that had taken the likeness of G., had disappeared. (Quoted in Gurney I, pp. 394–5)

(Lord Brougham adds that shortly after his return to Edinburgh from Sweden he learnt that G. had died in India on the 19th of December.)

There are two possible interpretations of the discontinuity reported by Lord Brougham at the end of his experience.

It is possible that the whole experience of perceiving the apparition occurred while he was still in the bath, and that he suffered a period of amnesia from the moment when the apparition ended until he found himself on the floor. During this period he got out of the bath but was not subsequently able to remember having done so.

Alternatively, it may be that, while seeming to look at the apparition from a position in the bath, he was in fact climbing out all the while, so that when the apparition came to an end and the figure disappeared he also became aware of his true physical position, which was outside the bath and on the floor.

The following is also an interesting case in the present connection. The subject was a pupil at a convent school in Belgium.

> One Saturday morning I was in the church helping Mère Columba to dust. I was up a ladder dusting a statue when I was rather surprised to see a girl, who had left some time, dressed as a nun, come towards me, and beckon me to follow her; it gave me rather a shock to see myself on the ladder when I was in the act of following the nun. Passing through a door I reached the chapel by a way I had never been before. When I was kneeling in one of the pews, I was very surprised to see Uncle Oldham come up to me, as mother had not told me he was coming to Belgium. I thought something was wrong

as he had such a pained expression; he took my hand and said he had done something very wrong and that it would help him a great deal to have me to pray for him; then he told me he had been refused by the woman he loved and that he had shot himself in his despair; after that he visited me every morning. When I found myself again on the ladder I must have looked rather pale, so Mère Columba made me lie down for some time; but she only said it was my imagination. I made her promise not to tell any one, as I knew no one would believe it and thought I should be laughed at; a few days after I heard from mother that Uncle Oldham had died suddenly. It gave me a shock, as I did not know who to believe and could not write, as all letters are read before leaving the convent. I only heard the truth from mother when I came home. (*Journal of the S.P.R.*, Vol. XIII, 1907–8, p. 232)

(It appears that 'Uncle Oldham', the percipient's godfather, had in fact shot himself on the Wednesday before her experience.)

This case may be classified as an apparitional experience with a discontinuity of location at the end, and possibly also at the beginning. The account does not make it clear whether the subject remembered seeming to climb down the ladder at the beginning of the experience in response to the summons from the nun. She only recalls that while in the act of following the nun she was surprised to see herself still on the ladder. At the end of the experience the subject says that she 'found herself again on the ladder', and does not describe any return journey on foot from the chapel in which she saw her uncle. Since this case includes the experience of seeing the subject's own body from outside, we could classify this as an out-of-the-body experience.

*

It is not, however, typical for apparitional cases to end with a reported discontinuity in the percipient's experience, even with one that is reported rather vaguely. When a subject appears to himself to be moving about during an apparitional experience, he usually finds himself at the end of the experience in the position he expects to be in, so clearly he has not actually been lying or standing still throughout the experience. For example, in the case which we have already quoted on p. 12, the percipient describes finding his bedroom illuminated one night and getting out of bed to investigate a coffin which he saw at the foot of his bed. When the whole scene faded, leaving the percipient in darkness, it seems he really was out of bed, investigating the apparition, as he believed himself to be. At any rate, he does not mention noticing any discontinuity in his position as the apparition faded, such as suddenly finding himself back in bed.

This correspondence between the subject's expected and actual position at the end of an apparitional experience does not constitute an absolute proof that he has not been having an out-of-the-body experience while seeing the apparition. His movements may have been, to a greater or lesser extent, different from what he believes them to have been, provided only that he finds himself in the correct position at the end of the experience. In an ecsomatic experience also the subject's position at the end of the experience may tally with his observations of the movements of his physical body. The subject may, for example, seem to float along above his physical body as it is walking. When the experience ends he may find himself walking along at the correct point of the road, as indicated by his observations of his progress from the ecsomatic position.

CHAPTER 5

The Substitution of Physical Sensation

WE have observed in the last chapter that the subject's physical movements in the course of an apparitional experience may not tally exactly with those which he believes himself to make. In this chapter we shall consider what indications may be provided by reports of apparitional experiences that in at least some of them the subject is provided with hallucinatory impressions of his own physical movements.

The following apparitional experience is interesting in this context. Gurney describes the percipient as a 'distinguished Indian officer'.

> I had been taking luncheon with some friends, and after it was over, my host proposed that I and my fellow guest should accompany him to see some alterations he was making in his grounds. After we had been out some little time, looking at these changes, a native servant approached me with a message from my hostess, asking me to go into the house to speak to her. I at once left my friends, and accompanied the man back to the house, following him through the verandah into the room where the luncheon had been laid. There he left me, and I waited for my hostess to come, but no one appeared; so after a few minutes I called her by name, thinking that she might not be aware that I had come in. Receiving no answer, after once again repeating her name, I walked back into the verandah, where, on entering, I had observed a durzee (or tailor) at work, and asked him where the man was who came in with me. The durzee replied, 'Your excellency, no one came with you.' 'But,' I said, 'the man lifted the chik' (the outside verandah blind) 'for me.' 'No, your Excellency, you lifted it yourself,' the durzee answered. Much puzzled, I returned to my friends in the grounds, exclaiming, 'Here's a good joke'; and then, telling them what had happened, and what the durzee had said, I asked them if they had not seen the servant who called for me shortly before. They both said they had seen no one. 'Why you don't mean to say I have not been in the house?' I said. 'Oh, yes, you were

in the midst of saying something about the alterations, when you suddenly stopped, and walked back to the house; we could not tell why,' they both said. I was in perfect health at the time of the occurrence, and continued to be so after it. (Gurney I, p. 499 *n.*)

Although the percipient does not report any discontinuity at the beginning or end of his experience, his movements in the course of the experience evidently did not tally exactly with those which he himself thought he had made. The subject seems to have been under the impression that a hallucinatory figure, which at the time he thought was real, had lifted a verandah-blind to enable him to enter a house. However, an eye-witness failed to see the hallucinatory figure at all and reported that the subject had lifted the blind for himself. It seems that the percipient must have hallucinated the position of his arm and the physical sensations appropriate to walking straight into the house, instead of those appropriate to lifting the blind.

When the subject of an out-of-the-body experience sees an environment which resembles his actual surroundings but differs from it in some particular, such as in the presence of a piece of furniture which is not there in reality, we take this as an indication that his visual field may be hallucinatory. In the same way, since in the apparitional case which we have just quoted the subject's impression of his physical movements differed, at least at a certain point, from those which he was really making, we should consider the possibility that he may have had, throughout this experience, a substitute field of perception as regards his physical sensations, even though for much of the time this tallied with his real movements.

In the case quoted in the last chapter of the subject who walked to the chapel with the apparitional nun, her impression of her movements does not appear to have corresponded to any movement which she was seen to make by her companion, so in this case we have to conclude that the subject was provided with substitute impressions of her own physical movements throughout. As we have already pointed out in connection with visual phenomena, substitute hallucinatory impressions may show a close correspondence with the real perceptions which the subject might be expected to be having.

In the following case the subject saw an apparition while walking round a cathedral:

I lived in Trondheim for four years and left the city in 1... have often visited the city since that time. I was much interest the construction work done at the Cathedral and often went in to s how the work was progressing . . .

One sunny morning I went into the cathedral. I walked along the north passage, walking towards the altar, which is, as is usual in the churches, situated in the east. The large pillars in gothic style are alike on both sides of the main body of the church. Looking across towards the south wall, I noticed a *Nun* sitting quietly in one of the many niches along the wall. I walked up to the front of the altar and turned left, down the south side passage. The *Nun* was looking straight at me and I wondered what she was doing here at this time of the day. I walked along the passage, all the time looking at the Nun and she at me. I thought I would talk to her as I came closer, but when I was just 6–7 feet away from her, she faded away and I saw her no more! I must say I was puzzled, but walking into the West end of the Cathedral I stopped and talked to one of the women cleaning the church and said to her: 'I thought I saw a Catholic Nun over in the West End, sitting in a niche, but when I came near she disappeared—how could that be?' 'Oh' answered the woman 'we often see her.' And this I have verified by others.

We note that in this case the percipient actually was walking round the cathedral at the time. We do not have a report from any external observer in this case, but it appears probable that a bystander would have reported seeing him making the movements which he himself thought he did. However, we are unable to ascertain whether the correspondence between his real and supposed movements was very close indeed, or only approximate. Even if the movements he thought he was making were a precise replica of those which he actually made, it is still a possibility that his physical sensations were a hallucinatory replica of what he would normally have had.

*

The question might be raised, when a subject speaks to an apparition, or addresses some real person in his environment while perceiving an apparition, is he really speaking out loud, or only hallucinating doing so?

If this part of his experience were hallucinatory, then it is possible that a kinaesthetic as well as an auditory hallucination might be involved. Not only would he hear a hallucination of his own voice, but he might hallucinate the sensations of muscular contraction and sound vibration in the throat, mouth, etc., which we normally experience when speaking. We may not usually be very conscious of these sensations when we speak, but it is possible that the apparition subject would notice their absence, unless his subconscious presented him with some hallucinatory equivalent.

An interesting case in the present context is the following, in which the subject reports seeing a girl in his room after experimenting with out-of-the-body experiences. He says that he was 'cataleptic' and that his teeth were tightly clenched, but he nevertheless heard himself speaking to the girl and saying, 'Hallo, what are you doing in my room?'

> One night after practising astral projection I woke up completely cataleptic. A golden light seemed to suffuse the room from some unseen source to within a foot or two of the ceiling. On my left stood a young woman dressed in leg-of-mutton sleeves, with a high collar and artifically constricted waist and buttons down the centre of the bodice. She had golden hair arranged over the top of her head. Although I was cataleptic, my teeth tightly clenched, I heard myself saying, 'Hallo, what are you doing in my room?' She replied 'I shan't be long now, I was just looking at the gas behind the plate.' A clear silvery girl's voice then said 'I shan't be long either.' The second speaker I did not see.
>
> I went to sleep and woke up quite normal in the morning. I thought, I must have been dreaming, the expression 'the gas behind the plate' does not make sense. Then I realised that I had switched on a small electric radiator, it was a very cold night. The radiator was circular and dish shaped, rarely seen now. A thick lead was attached to it. The dress suggested a time when gas may have been used for heating but not electricity. Cannot the spirits keep up-to-date in house gadgets, if not in clothes?

If this subject's teeth really were tightly clenched, as he thought, then it was presumably impossible for him to speak normally. We should therefore have to suppose that the sentence he heard himself speaking was an auditory hallucination. It would not have been heard by an independent observer, had one happened to be in his room, or recorded by a tape-recorder, had one happened to be picking up sounds in his vicinity at that moment.

Alternatively, it may be that the subject's jaws and vocal chords were working normally, that he did indeed speak the sentence he heard himself saying, and that his sensation of having his teeth tightly clenched was hallucinatory. On this view an independent observer might have seen and heard him speaking normally, even though the percipient himself was under the impression that his teeth were together and he was unable to do so.

This particular experience occurred after the subject had been making a deliberate attempt to induce an out-of-the-body experience, and was experiencing paralysis, so it is not a very typical experience of seeing an apparition.

We have no other cases in which the subject's impression that he was talking seems to have been hallucinatory. In all other cases it seems that the subject really did speak out loud to an apparition when he thought he did. For example, in one of our cases, the subject reports that while redecorating in her late mother's bedroom, she heard her mother say that she had never cared for a certain wallpaper. The subject replied out loud: 'I did not know that, why did you not say ?' It seems that her husband, who was downstairs, heard her speak and called to her to come down (see pp. 65–6).

The following is an auditory case in which a bystander heard the percipient talking down a speaking-tube but did not hear anyone at the other end with whom the percipient might be having his conversation. The percipient was a doctor.

> It was in the early morning of a Christmas Day, about 12.30 a.m., when I heard a ring at my night bell, and speaking down my speaking tube (which is close to my bed)—my wife heard me conversing—I was told by a gentleman, whose voice I well knew and recognised, that I was to go at once to see his wife, who was in labour and urgently needed my assistance. I got up, dressed, and went to the house, knocked with my stick several times on the back door, but failing to get an answer returned home to bed. I went to church the next morning, Christmas Day, at 7 a.m., and shortly after 9 the same gentleman called again and said I was to go at once to his wife. I asked him whether he came in the night and he said, 'No, but I *nearly* did at 12.30 this morning.' I said nothing, but went and attended the lady, and then asked for particulars, *without putting any leading questions*. They told me she had been much worse at 12.30 a.m., and had wanted me to be sent for, but that the nurse didn't think it necessary. They also said they heard my knocks on the back door, but being Christmas morning they thought it was 'the waits', and so did not answer. . . .
>
> April 23rd, 1890   E. West Symes, M.D.

Mrs. Symes corroborates as follows:

> I perfectly well remember the events of the night in question, which

are exactly as my husband states. I was awakened by hearing him speaking down the tube, and said, 'Who are you talking to, the night bell has not rung?' He said, 'Yes, it has; I have to go to Mrs. S.' As I *always* hear the bell, I thought this curious, and I listened carefully while he spoke down the tube. He answered several questions (apparently) though I could hear no voice but his own; which surprised me, as I can always hear the voice but not the words unless they are very loudly spoken. I said to my husband, 'I think you are mistaken, there is no one there,' but he said, 'Nonsense, it is S. himself, and I must go immediately,' which he did, returning in a short time, and saying that S.'s house was all in darkness, and he could make no one hear.

May 16th, 1890   M. Evelyn Symes
(*Journal of the S.P.R.*, Vol. IV, 1889–90, pp. 326–7)

It might be argued that the subject's companion in a case such as this may have hallucinated the sound of the subject's voice. However, when the companion is apparently not sharing in the rest of the subject's experience, there seems no particular reason for supposing him to be undergoing any sort of hallucination.

Of course, when two or more people both perceive what they take to be the same apparition simultaneously, and speak to each other while perceiving it, the situation is rather different. If both of them are experiencing visual hallucinations, it is more reasonable to suppose that they might both be experiencing a hallucinatory conversation between each other as well.

*

It is also interesting to ask whether someone's eyes are moving when he believes he is following the movement of an apparition across his field of vision.

The following case is relevant in this respect. An onlooker apparently saw the eyes of the percipient moving as she watched a hallucinatory figure cross a room.

That same evening, it must have been in the summer, because it was daylight, Miss St. Leger and I were having supper in her room with the door open. I was sitting with the door on my right, with a good view of the door opposite, which was shut, when I saw a small inconspicuous old lady, without hat or coat, in an old-fashioned dress; she was thin, rather shrunk and head bent; I only saw her back. She seemed quite at home and knew where to go, and seemed to fade away into the door of this room opposite me. I looked so tremendously astonished that Miss St. Leger asked me what was the matter, and I looking at her face knew she knew what I had seen without my telling her.

I ought to have said that I watched her moving along the passage to the door. Miss St. Leger said she could see my eyes moving. Of course the whole thing only lasted a second and I was too staggered to say anything, while I watched.

We lived there for another eight months, but didn't see anything more of the old lady. (Bennett, p. 304)

It does not follow from the fact that someone's eyes are moving that there is any particular kind of activity going on in his retina. If someone is seeing a hallucinatory figure, he may be so conditioned by his experience of perceiving real objects that he unconsciously moves his eyes in the appropriate way to follow its movements, although his eyes are not actually involved in perceiving it.

A phenomenon which demonstrates how eye-movements may be associated with the movement of objects in a hallucinatory field of perception is the eye-movements which occur during dreaming, in which the subject is obviously not making use of his eyes to perceive things in the normal way, but in which the movements of his eye-ball are sometimes found to correspond to what one would expect if he were following the movement of objects in his dream, as he subsequently describes it to the experimenter.

There are some reports which suggest that the apparition subject's eyes certainly do not always move in the appropriate way to follow the hallucinatory figure. The most obvious of these are those in which the subject claims to have seen a figure in an 'impossible' position, such as standing directly behind him. The following is a case of this kind:

I was lying awake in the dark in bed one night when the room became full of a strange vibrance, and at the head of the bed (a divan) I saw quite clearly although I was not looking that way with my physical eyes, a figure clothed in black, with grey (or white—the room was dark) hair, and with some peculiarity around the nose and mouth. He seemed to land on the floor as if he had leaped from somewhere. He lifted up the skirt of his black robe, and I saw that his feet and ankles were clothed in grey socks or stockings (no shoes).

Then he turned towards another figure whom I then perceived standing in front of the fireplace, wearing a sort of clerical dress—a white surplice over a black gown. For some unknown reason I took this to be a bishop.

The first figure lifted his left hand up to his right shoulder and then extended his right hand to that of the 'bishop' in a handclasp.

There ensued quite a prolonged conversation between them, which I did not hear (and did not try to hear). Then the first figure was at my bedside and I heard him utter just the two words, 'this girl' (I was about 41 at the time I think).

The person just vanished after saying 'this girl' at my bedside (speaking presumably to the other 'apparition') . . .

At first I must have perceived him through the top of my head. He was facing the bed and near my head.

CHAPTER 6

Collective Hallucinations

APPARITIONS are sometimes seen by more than one person at a time, and in this case are called collective. There are reports of groups numbering from two up to about eight people seeing the same apparition at the same time, but there are no well authenticated cases of groups much larger than this doing so. For example, audiences in theatres or other public places do not seem to witness collective apparitions.

The accounts given by the different witnesses of a collective apparition often appear to tally with one another, and this has led some writers to comment with amazement on the precise co-ordination required to enable a number of people to see an identical figure, as if viewed from the appropriate angle in each case. But as a matter of fact we do not know how precise the correspondence is between the images perceived by the various subjects. There are cases on record where, although the reports of the different subjects show some resemblance to one another, there are distinct indications of discrepancies. Even in cases where the reports reveal no discrepancies, we cannot be sure that there were not some which did not emerge from the verbal statement.

If you were shown two films in succession of the same actress walking across the same room, you would find it very difficult to decide for certain whether what you had seen was the same piece of film run twice over or two separate pieces of film. Only very detailed observations of the precise spots on which the actress placed her feet when walking, for example, would enable you to convince yourself that the two pieces of film were different. If the two films managed to be closely similar in all the particulars which you might notice in trying to distinguish between them, it would be virtually impossible for you to reach a firm conclusion whether they were the same or different.

Now suppose that two different people are shown two different films, of similar actresses dressed in a similar way, walking across a similar room, and that these people have to try to determine by comparing their verbal reports whether they have seen the same film or two different ones. It is clear that in this case a much wider degree of discrepancy could go undetected than in the case of two films which are seen by the same person.

The subjects, and even investigators, writing about collective apparitions in which there is some discrepancy between the reports of the various witnesses, sometimes seem to be implying that one of the witnesses must have been correct, and the others mistaken, instead of simply accepting that the various witnesses may actually have seen different things. This tendency probably arises from people's habitual attitude toward their perceptions of the physical world, in which it is assumed that there is always one correct version of the events perceived, and if anyone reports some discrepancy they are mistaken.

As a matter of fact, quite wide discrepancies could exist between the perceptions of one person and those of another without attracting any attention. For example, if two people walk down a street together, their conversation will refer only to very few features of the environment. So long as their pictures of the scene tally in these respects, and are sufficiently consistent with each person's memory of the locality, they could actually differ quite widely. Suppose, for example, they both see a piece of paper blown across the street. They might see it performing quite a different series of movements without either of them suspecting that their experiences differed.

It may be pertinent to point out that even the existence of such a peculiarity as colour-blindness was not suspected until the work of Dalton in 1794. Presumably the colour-blind person's experience of the world is somewhat different from the experience of a normally sighted person. They may both look at the same object in their environment, but may perceive it in different ways. Nevertheless, they may never realise there is a difference between their several perceptions of the same object. To quote Sir Francis Galton: 'That one person out of twenty-nine or thereabouts should be unable to distinguish a red from a green, without knowing that he had any deficiency of colour sense, and without betraying his deficiency to his friends, seems perfectly incredible to the other twenty-eight; yet as a matter of fact he rarely does either the one or the other.' (Galton, *Inquiries into Human Faculty*, p. 31.)

As it is so difficult to detect minor differences in different people's perceptions of the physical world, it seems likely that hallucinations of a fairly trivial kind may well be more common than is supposed. Even if people notice a minor discrepancy in their reports of their observations, they will be likely to dismiss it as a 'mistake' on the part of one of the observers.

It is when what is perceived is at variance, not only with the reports of other observers, but with our beliefs about the continuity of nature, that it is subsequently regarded as an apparition or hallucination.

People sometimes report, for example, seeing an electric light on in a room where it is actually switched off at the time, or seeing the dial of a wireless light up when they turn it on although it is not plugged in. When the true situation is discovered, they decide that they were hallucinated. An illustration of this type of experience is the following:

> I was walking into a room from outside. It was bright sunshine outside, but because the only window in this room is north facing, it is poorly lit and the lights are frequently switched on even in the daytime. As one opens the door, one of the light-bulbs (unshaded) is directly in one's line of view. As I opened the door on this occasion, I saw that this light-bulb was on, and I immediately thought of turning it off at the switch by the door. As I opened the door wider and stepped into the room, I realised that I had been wrong and that the light had been off.
>
> The duration of the hallucination had been very short; merely the split-second between the door being slightly open and the door being wide open.
>
> · I am not sure whether the room was lit up as it would have been with the light on, or whether it was dark. What I *saw* was the light-bulb glowing; I have no distinct impression of what the rest of the room was like before I realised that the light was not really on.

We shall now discuss some actual examples of collective cases in which we have independent reports from each of the persons concerned.

In the following case three people were returning from visiting a sick man, and all three report that on their way home together they more or less simultaneously saw an apparition of this man crossing a lake at about the time he died.

Here is the account of the first percipient in this case, a Miss Godley:

> One afternoon in February 1926 I went to visit a former old farm labourer of mine, Robert Bowes, who lived about a mile away, but inside the place: it was about 2.30. He had been ill for some time but was not any worse. I had lately broken my leg and was in a donkey trap, the steward was leading the donkey and my masseuse walking behind. I talked to Robert through the open window and he sat up and talked quite well, and asked me to send for the doctor as he had not seen him for some time. I then came straight back. The road runs along the shores of a big lake and, while the steward stopped to open a gate there, he asked me, 'if I saw the man on the lake'. I looked and saw an old man with a long white beard which floated in the wind, crossing to the other side of the lake. He appeared to be moving his arms, as though working a punt, he was standing up and gliding across but I saw no boat. I said, 'Where is the boat?' The steward replied 'There is no boat.' I said, 'What nonsense! there must be a boat, and he is standing up in it,' but there was no boat and he was just gliding along on the dark water; the masseuse also saw him. The steward asked me who I thought he was like, I said, 'he is exactly like Robert Bowes, the old man.' The figure crossed the lake and disappeared in among the reeds and trees at the far side, and we came home. I at once went to take off my hat and coat and to write a note for the doctor, but, before I left my room, the bell rang and the doctor came in. I said I was glad to see him as I wanted him to go and see Robert Bowes; he said, 'I have just been there' (he went in a car by a different road to the one I had been on) 'and the old chap is dead.'
>
> That is all; but no living man crossed the lake, and there was no boat on it. (Bennett, p. 37)

The account of the second percipient, the steward referred to by Miss Godley in the above account, is as follows:

> Miss Anna Godley, Miss Goldsmith and I were visiting a sick man on the estate. We had no idea that he was so near passing out of this earthly life, but on parting from him on his sick bed, and on our way home we were amazed when passing Killegar lake, at the close of the same day, to see him walking on the surface of the water. His whiskers were floating in the breeze and when near the shore, in the shadow of the wood, he completely disappeared. We all three beheld the same sight. (Ibid., p. 38)

It will be seen that neither of the first two percipients refer to a boat in which the apparitional figure was standing; they seem to have seen it as merely walking or gliding over the surface of the water. However, the third percipient in the case, Miss Goldsmith, the masseuse, seems to have hallucinated a boat as well as the figure of the old man. Her account is as follows:

> We had just left the cottage where the old man was lying in a terribly weak condition, and on walking back, we were impelled to glance towards the lake, and saw a shadowy, bent form step from the rushes, and into a boat, and after an interval just disappear. We learnt later on that the old man had passed away at that moment. Though not in the least given to seeing visions, but being of an extremely practical nature, I certainly saw the spectre as I describe it. (Ibid., p. 39)

It seems clear from these various accounts that the three percipients' experiences differed in at least one particular; namely, the masseuse saw a boat which one might say rationalised the figure's passage across the water, whereas the other two percipients, Miss Godley and her steward, did not. Nevertheless, we find Miss Godley making the following remarks about this discrepancy:

> There was no boat on the lake when we saw Robert Bowes crossing. My masseuse thought he was standing up in one, but he wasn't; there was nothing except what looked like a pole being used by him to help himself across. . . . (Ibid., p. 39)

It will be seen that Miss Godley apparently assumes without question that her masseuse must be 'wrong' when she asserts that the apparition was standing up in a boat, as if there was some objective criterion of what was a correct and what was an incorrect way of seeing the figure. Such an attitude may or may not be justified if a number of people are discussing the several ways in which they perceived what they believed to be a real object in their environment, such as a real man crossing a lake. But it is scarcely necessary to point out that the attitude is quite unjustified if the object perceived by the various observers is hallucinatory.

The following is another case in which there seems to have been a discrepancy between the experiences of the percipients, in this case a married couple, Mr. and Mrs. Barber. They each report seeing a figure of a lady approaching the front door of their house as they returned to it. But the wife believes she saw the figure raise its hand as though to ring their door-bell, a feature which the husband does not mention, and both percipients seem to be aware that the appearance of the figure, its dress, etc., may have looked different to the two of them.

The husband's account is as follows:

> In April of last year, while the light was still good, I was returning home from a walk with my wife, and when within a few yards of the gate, which opens into a straight path leading to the house, both my wife and I saw a woman pass through the open gate and walk straight to the house, when, on reaching the door, she disappeared. I ran to the door, opened it with my latchkey, and expected in my astonishment to find her inside, for she seemed to have walked through the door. It all seemed so real that I at once searched the house, but in vain. We were the only two people in the street, and did not see the figure until she entered the gate, when we simultaneously exclaimed, 'Who is that?' She seemed to come out of space and go into space again in a most marvellous manner. She wore a plaid shawl, and her bonnet was a grey-black with a bit of colour in it. We could not remember hearing any sound as she walked, but otherwise we have never seen anything more apparently substantial. It is impossible for us to conceive how she could have disappeared if she had been of flesh and blood. . . .
>
> When I heard Mrs. Barber telling friends of our experience, I have noticed that the figure presented to her mind does not seem to have been exactly the same as that which was evident to my mind. . . . Again, Mrs. Barber is sure she spoke first (though I thought we spoke at once) . . . (*Proceedings of the S.P.R.*, Vol. XXXIII, 1922, p. 372)

The relevant part of Mrs. Barber's account is as follows:

> My husband now began to cross the road, bidding me follow, and take care not to fall on the loose stones. I did so, naturally looking down at my feet, until a little more than half way across the road, or about 6 yards from the gate, when on raising my eyes I saw a grey figure walking up the path to the door. She was then about a yard inside the gate, and although she had appeared so mysteriously, I felt no surprise, she looked so thoroughly commonplace and substantial. My husband saw her enter the gate, so there can be no question as to which of us saw her first, but I was certainly the first to exclaim: 'Who is that?' although my husband's exclamation followed so quickly that they might almost be considered simultaneous, as indeed I believe Mr. Barber described them in his letter to you. I next said: 'Stop a moment and let us see who it is,' but he answered, 'No, it is no good letting her ring,' and hurried forward with his latchkey. The distance from the gate to the door is 7½ yards, and when I first saw the figure I should be about 6 yards from the gate.
>
> My husband would be at least a couple of yards in front of me, and as he saw the figure actually turn in at the gate he had a better view

of her shawl and bonnet. I only saw that she was in grey, and that it was no one we knew. She walked quietly up the path and then up the two steps to the door, and I always fancy I saw her raise her hand as though to ring the bell, but of that I cannot be sure, and then against the dark door she vanished completely, certainly not more than 4 yards from where my husband was standing. We were expecting no visitor, and our thoughts were far away from the supernatural, for just before crossing the road we had been saying how hungry we were, and how we should enjoy our supper.

I took special note of the date and hour, fully expecting we should hear of some occurrence which nearly concerned us, but nothing has, so far, transpired. (Ibid.)

In a case such as this even the percipients seem to be in some doubt as to how much their several experiences differed from each other. But at least it is clear that there was scope for a considerable degree of discrepancy between what they each saw, and we certainly cannot conclude that their experiences were identical as we tend to do when two people perceive a real object.

Another example of a discrepancy between two percipients' descriptions of what they took to be the same apparition is to be found in a case which we shall quote in a later chapter (pp. 208–9). It seems that the husband merely saw the figure of an apparition gesture towards a night-light, whereupon it went out, whereas his wife saw the apparition actually put its hand over the night-light and seemingly extinguish it by doing so.

*

When two people are looking at some real object in their environment such as a third person close by them, we assume that their perceptions of this person are closely co-ordinated, rather like two photographs of a single object taken from different angles. We imagine that this close co-ordination results from both observers continually receiving large amounts of information from their environment in the form of light-waves reflected from the figure they are looking at and acting in a characteristic way on their retina.

When two or more people are simultaneously hallucinating the figure of a third person at the same point in their communal environment there is no such normal source of information that could explain the co-ordination of their several perceptions of the third, hallucinatory person. If the percipients are not communicating by any normal means, verbal or otherwise, about what they are each seeing, we seem driven to suppose that telepathy is taking place between them at a subconscious level to enable their visual experiences to harmonise with one another.

If one supposes that their perceptions are very exactly co-ordinated, in the way that we imagine two people's simultaneous perception of a real object are co-ordinated, then we have to postulate a remarkable amount of telepathic information being exchanged at a subconscious level.

However, if we consider each collective case at face value, and do not assume that the various percipients' perceptual experiences were any more closely correlated than is strictly implied by their various first-hand accounts, then one usually finds that the amount of information that would need to have been exchanged at a subconscious level by the various percipients is actually relatively small, and can be expressed in a sentence or two.

For example, consider the case in which three people report seeing a man passing across a lake. The various common elements in their several perceptual experiences might be summarised as follows: 'Robert Bowes, crossing the lake, from near side to far side, now.'

We do not know whether each percipient saw the figure of Robert Bowes follow exactly the same line across the lake; nor whether they each saw him advance at exactly the same speed; nor whether they each saw him appear and disappear at exactly the same moments in time and at exactly the same places. They may have done, but we have no information on which we can decide one way or the other.

CHAPTER 7

Emotions and Insight

WE have pointed out that some, or possibly all, cases of apparitions may be metachoric experiences, as are out-of-the-body experiences. We might wonder how closely related these two types of experience may be. However, when we consider the emotions which subjects report having experienced at the various stages of the two kinds of experience, we find that distinctly different emotional states seem to preponderate in the two cases.

Let us consider the emotional state the subject is in before the experience starts. In our study of out-of-the-body experiences there was an appreciable proportion of cases in which the subjects were under some kind of stress at the time, for example in crisis or accident situations, or alternatively feeling particularly happy or elated, although there was also a substantial proportion of cases in which subjects could find no particular way of characterising their state of mind, except that they were feeling quite ordinary. In the case of apparitional subjects there is seldom any sign of subjects having felt unusually elated, or having had any reason to feel shocked or stressed before the experience started. The great majority can find little of a distinctive kind to say about their state before the experience began.

*

We asked our subjects at what point in their experience they had realised they were perceiving an apparition. The results were as follows:

%

(a) Realised immediately they started to perceive
the apparition   46

(b) Not immediately, but before they stopped
      perceiving it   18
(c) As it ended   5
(d) Not until after it had ended   31

Many subjects seem to achieve insight as a result of the apparition disappearing. However, most of these chose (d) and not (c)
to describe the timing of the process. This may be because their
realisation that something is an apparition, even when it disappears, is somewhat delayed. We may relate this to the fact that
subjects sometimes seem to accept without surprise rather a high
degree of abnormal behaviour on the part of the apparition. For
example, the following is a case in which the percipient seems not
to have thought that what she was looking at might be an
apparition, although its movements were extremely difficult to
account for on normal terms, and its manner of dress was very
unusual. The subject, at one point in her narrative, remarks that
'no sensation of fear, no suspicion of the supernatural, entered
our minds'.

> We were walking home from Richmond, my husband and I, one
> bright July day about half-past five, having ordered the boat to meet
> us and take us up to our own steps.
> Between Richmond and Twickenham, on the Surrey side, is a
> splendid avenue of large trees; between the avenue and the river is a
> long and wide stretch of beach, and at the Twickenham end the
> ground is very open, and one sees the curve of the river and glimpses
> of some houses at Twickenham and Teddington; there is no bank or
> tree to intercept the view, and any one walking along the towing path
> can be seen for a long distance.
> When a little way down the avenue, at the third tree, perhaps, a
> man passed stealthily behind me, to my left side, and went outside
> the trees—I was walking the furthest from the river. Two or three
> times he passed me thus, always in the same stealthy manner, as if
> not wishing to be seen.
> I did not draw my husband's attention to him, because, although
> the last man to commence a quarrel, he never submitted to an
> impertinence, and this stranger's movements appeared so spy-like.
> I did not know my husband had seen him till he passed the third
> time; then R. said:—
> 'What is that fellow dodging about for? the avenue is open to all,
> why does he not keep in or out of it? he appears anxious to know
> what we are talking about; as it does not concern him, we will go
> out into the open.'
> We were then about the seventh or eighth tree down. As he spoke

he stepped onto the open beach, and gave me his hand to help over some obstruction in the path, a fallen branch, if I remember rightly. Both these movements were made in less time than it would take me to speak of them.

As I put my hand in his, I looked round, and saw the stranger standing between the trees. It was the first full look we had, and I said, 'He looks as if he had stepped out of an old picture!'

We could see only his boots, his cloak, and hat. The boots were peculiar, high, and falling over at the knee, his cloak large and round, and thrown over his left shoulder, in the Spanish fashion, and his hat, apparently a soft felt, had a very wide drooping border, and was worn so much on one side we saw no face.

We both distinctly remember that in all the times we saw him that day, no face was visible. His whole costume was of one tone, and that of a dusty cobweb is the only thing I can liken it to.

We stood looking at him, I wondering if he would resent my husband's speech, but he made no movement, and I put my hand in R.'s to step into the open. As my husband's fingers closed on mine, he started, and as I looked up to see the cause I saw his eyes fixed steadily on the open space at the remote end of the avenue.

There, clearly defined by the bright background of the towing path and the river, stood the figure that, less than an instant before, was by our side, and which we certainly thought to be that of a fellow creature (of rather ill-bred manners, utterly inconsistent with the decided dignity of his appearance).

Had he been shot out of a gun, he could not have gone faster.

The distance I have since measured: it is [about 150 yards]; the time occupied in traversing it I could not have counted a dozen in, however rapidly.

Now comes the most peculiar part of our experience, that which has made me very chary of telling it, for fear of ridicule.

When we saw the figure standing out there on the open ground, we were simply perplexed; no sensation of fear, or suspicion of the supernatural, entered our minds. We walked towards him with our eyes fixed on him.

There stood the figure, clearly defined, till we got within a certain distance; then it changed. It is so difficult to describe what did take place; the only way I can suggest it even is thus: You have seen a thick volume of smoke come out of a railway engine and gradually become thinner and thinner as it hovers over the ground, till you see through it the objects behind.

That is what took place. The figure stood there still, but, though it did not lose its shape, it gradually became transparent, till we saw the river and the bank and the distant trees through it. Still it was there. Then it got fainter and fainter, till there was not the least suggestion of it left; nothing but the large, bright, open space, without a single object behind which any one could have hidden.

(*Journal of the S.P.R.*, Vol. I, 1884–5, pp. 247–8)

Related to the fact that subjects sometimes do not seem to notice unrealistic behaviour on the part of the apparition is their tendency not to remember immediately facts which might arouse an awareness that they were seeing an apparition. This is shown most strikingly by a number of cases in which the subjects, when perceiving an apparition of a deceased person, do not immediately call to mind their knowledge of his death. The two following cases illustrate this. In both cases, the schoolgirl percipients were extremely frightened as soon as they did remember that the person they had seen was dead.

> One November afternoon I arrived home from school and passing through the diningroom I noticed my grandfather in his sitting room talking to my grandmother (who had been ill). She was sitting on the couch brushing and combing her hair. She was in her nightgown and robe. I entered the room and said hello to them, and told my grandmother it was nice to see her feeling up to being out of bed. After a minute or two of polite conversation, I said I had better go do my homework. My grandmother then said 'Barbara, it would be best if you don't tell anyone I was up and that you spoke with me.'
>
> I went on upstairs and as I entered my own room it suddenly came over me that my grandmother was dead! She had died a month earlier. My school books dropped out of my hands, my heart raced, I had goose pimples all over. I remained in my room until I had heard my parents come home and the sounds of supper being prepared. . . . After my grandmother (the apparition) deceased my grandfather was often known to sit in his room alone talking.
>
> After seeing the apparition I did not talk to anyone about it for several months. Eventually, I did relate the story to my mother, who told me I must have been dreaming. I never accepted this theory as I was not sleeping. I have always regretted that as an adult I never had the opportunity to discuss this with my grandfather. He was in the room. He was sitting in a separate chair from the apparition and was not near enough to touch her but he was talking to her. He is now deceased.

> My experience was by sight sound and touch. I was then 11 years old. We lived in my grandmother's house in Slough, along with many other relatives, due to the housing shortage. I shared a large double bed with my sister Janet, who was then 6 years old. She had been to sleep for some time, but I was awake because there were visitors downstairs and the noise was considerable. It was a bright, frosty moonlit evening and very light still in our room. Suddenly I realized I felt squashed and turned over to push Janet back to her side of the bed. My grandfather was lying in between us, on his back but with his head turned, looking at Janet. I asked him what was the matter,

thinking it most strange that he should be in our bed at all. He turned his face towards me, when I spoke, and I put my hand out and started stroking his beard. (He always allowed me to brush it for him as a special treat.) He answered quietly, saying not to jump around too much in case I woke Janet, and that he was only making sure we were alright. It was only then that I remembered that he had died the previous June, and the fear and horror I felt then can be imagined and I started screaming for my mother. The grown-ups passed it off as a bad dream, but I was able to tell them a lot of their conversation of the evening, that had drifted up to me, as I lay awake.

I'd like to stress that in no way was I conscious that he was a 'ghost'. He felt solid, warm and looked and spoke quite naturally.

If the apparition represents someone with whom the percipient is familiar, it is quite common for the percipient to believe for a time that he must be seeing the person in the flesh, so to speak, even if on rational grounds such a conclusion is rather unlikely. The following case illustrates this point. The percipient, Dr. Howard, was in Fort Smith, Arkansas, U.S.A. in 1867, a time in the nineteenth century when communications were relatively difficult, and his wife was in Michigan. Nevertheless, on seeing an apparition of her, he at first assumed she was really there and had made the long journey to be with him.

I went to my room, as I have said, for the purpose of rest. I turned the key in the lock, and lay down on the bed with my back towards the door. I had not been there 10 minutes when I heard someone coming upstairs with a light step, and I wondered who it could be. I had expected several of my friends would call as soon as they knew I had returned, and I was too tired to see anyone. I took this course to get rested. While this idea was in my mind that I needed rest, I heard the door open, or seem to open, and I heard footsteps coming towards the bed. I turned over so as to look in that direction, and there stood my wife. I was a little excited, as it was so unexpected. I immediately got up and reached for a chair that stood near, and whilst doing so I said, 'Why, Libbie, when did you come? You look so tired; you must be—you have had 300 miles of staging.' She spoke, and said, 'Yes, I am a little weary.' I stepped forward with the chair, and was about to ask her to be seated when, to my surprise, she was not there. I stepped to the door and found it was locked. Not being accustomed to such apparitions, I felt sure that she had passed from the mortal form. As soon as I could compose myself, I sat down and wrote her what I saw, describing the dress she had on, also the collar on her neck, together with a ring she had on her finger, all of which I had never seen before. On receiving an answer, which was as soon as possible, my wife said, 'On the day you speak of I dressed myself with the dress and collar you saw in your vision, also the ring, which you have described as perfectly as you could have done if it were in your hand. I felt tired, and went to my room about 11 o'clock, and immediately fell asleep, and slept soundly for three hours.' (*Journal of the S.P.R.*, Vol. IV, 1889–90, pp. 305–6)

Mrs. Howard confirmed her husband's account and claimed that he had never seen the dress, collar or ring she was wearing, although he accurately described them in his letter to her.

*

In the case of out-of-the-body experiences fear or anxiety of any kind are usually only experienced after the subject has seen his own body from the outside, and so realised what a paradoxical state he is in. Similarly, in apparitional experiences, 33 per cent of our subjects report 'apprehension', 'alarm', 'terror' or 'panic', but this is virtually always as a result of realising that what they are seeing is an apparition as a result of something unnatural about it.

For example, in the following case the subject reports that she at first merely experienced mild annoyance at being kept awake by sounds from a room next to her bedroom but that she felt 'absolute terror' on realising that no one had been in the neighbouring room at the time she heard the sounds. The percipient was aged 21 at the time and living with her grandparents. Also in the house was an elderly woman, Mrs. MacAlpine, and an aunt.

> One evening I went to bed early and so had my grandmother. The maids were also in bed. I could not get to sleep because of the extraordinary amount of noise going on in Mrs. MacAlpine's bedroom. She seemed to be walking backwards and forwards, opening and shutting her chest of drawers very violently. I was not in the least alarmed, only astounded that such a usually quiet old lady should be making such a commotion. Then I heard my Aunt and Mrs. MacAlpine coming up the stairs, pause just by my grandmother's bedroom door and say goodnight to each other. Then I felt a sensation of absolute terror, for I realised that Mrs. MacAlpine was not in her bedroom at all, and when she went in she did not speak to anyone, nor did anyone come out. Nothing more happened and I went to sleep. The next morning when I mentioned the matter at breakfast, my aunt immediately shut me up and said I had dreamed the whole thing, and I was so upset I did not mention it again to anyone—I mean upset at being laughed at. But years later I found that my sister-in-law and my brother had had strange experiences in that room, as had my grandparents, my mother and her three sisters, in other parts of the house.

The realisation of being in an abnormal state does not seem to occur spontaneously to the out-of-the-body subject. It is only as a result of seeing his own body from the outside that this realisation is aroused, together with the possible accompaniment of shock or fear. In a somewhat similar way, apparition subjects do not usually seem to realise by a direct intuition that what they are seeing is an apparition, but it requires a definite departure from realistic behaviour on the part of the apparition to arouse this awareness, and the fear or surprise which may go with it. Incidentally, one difference between out-of-the-body experiences and apparitional experiences is that the former are usually terminated very rapidly once the subject's emotional equanimity is disturbed, while apparitional experiences may continue for a considerable time after the subject has become alarmed.

As we have observed, emotions of fear or surprise are only aroused once the apparition has shown itself to be such, but of course there are many apparitions which are unnatural in some way from their first appearance. The following percipient, for example, reports that she was 'thoroughly startled' by the sight of the apparition which appeared 'shimmering' and not entirely solid. The percipient in this case is Mrs. Barbara Barr, and the apparition was of her late stepfather, D. H. Lawrence.

> After Lawrence's death I stayed on with my mother (I was 25 years old then) but had a serious illness in the same villa in which Lawrence had died. One morning at the end of October 1930, my mother brought up the early letters of Lawrence to herself which had just been retrieved from German relatives of hers. I read halfway through one letter, but feeling ill and weary, laid it down again. At that moment I saw what appeared to be the apparition of Lawrence leaning over me—the effect was of a shimmering mass—not entirely solid. His expression seemed benign. I was thoroughly startled and blinked, or shut my eyes—when I looked again, this apparition, or image, had gone. I have never experienced any other kind of psychic phenomenon.

It is noticeable that apparitions are much less frequently than out-of-the-body experiences associated with a positive emotional state, and when they are, it does not seem to be so extreme. Three per cent of our apparition subjects mentioned 'wonder' in connection with their experience, and 6 per cent 'happiness', 'elation' or 'delight'. Nearly twice as many out-of-the-body subjects described their emotions during the experience in this kind of positive way, and tended to use more extreme terms such as 'excitement', 'exhilaration' and 'exaltation', which were practically never used by apparition subjects.

A type of reaction which is quite commonly reported by both out-of-the-body and apparition subjects is that of 'interest', 'curiosity' or 'fascination'. Altogether 12 per cent of our apparition subjects report feelings of this kind. For example, one percipient describes herself as 'absolutely spell-bound' during her experience. The following case also illustrates the type of reaction in question:

> I was working in a large girls' boarding school in Kent. I was 29 years old and in excellent health, good eye-sight, and of a normal and non-excitable disposition.
>
> One night I was going down-stairs, carrying an Aladdin Lamp, turned fairly low, there being no other form of lighting in the house, and as I reached the top of a long straight staircase I saw what appeared to be the figure of an elderly man walking down the staircase in front of me. He was five or six steps down when I saw him. His back was turned to me, his hair was grey, and one hand was on the bannister rail.
>
> I stood still and watched him go down until on reaching the bottom of the staircase with his hand on the newel post, he disappeared. There was no sound of footsteps although the staircase was not carpeted. He seemed to be wearing a long dark garment.
>
> I knew at once that he was 'a ghost' but was only conscious of extreme interest. The house was very old, reputedly haunted, and there were of course a great many people living in it although I suppose most of them were asleep at that time.
>
> Although I lived there for four years this was my only experience of the kind in that house, and although other people occasionally saw 'ghosts' these were not the same as the figure of the old man.

Sometimes the curiosity or fascination seems to be combined with a lack of fear which would apparently not be a characteristic reaction for the subject in a normal state. In fact, the lack of fear sometimes experienced by apparition subjects seems to resemble a less extreme form of the detachment reported by ecsomatic subjects, who often do not appear affected in the ecsomatic state by matters that would normally cause them concern, such as the fate of their own physical body.

The following is a case in which the subject reports feeling no fear but 'a strange fascination'.

> I attended a college situated in a small Wiltshire village and at the time was lodging with an elderly lady in a small pre-war terraced house.

I occupied a small bedroom at the back of the house and had been in the lodgings for about five weeks. One night I got back earlier than usual from the college and spent the whole evening working in my room. Being February, heating was necessary, and for the entire evening the one-bar radiator was on. Normally I had always found this form of heating quite adequate for such a small room, but on this particular evening I was aware of how cold the room was considering how long the radiator had been on. However I did not think too much about it and round about 11.30 I went to bed.

In bed, I rolled over and faced the wall but suddenly (literally in a matter of minutes) I had this extraordinary sense that I was being watched. I even felt a certain tingling at the back of my neck. Slowly I turned over, and standing about two feet from my head was a figure. It was a bright full moon that night, a shaft of its light penetrated the room between the slightly parted curtains, and it was in, or rather against, this light that the figure was silhouetted.

Naturally I was unsure, at first, of what I was seeing so I sat up in bed and pinched myself to make sure I was awake but after a few moments staring at this figure I knew I was not imagining things. I was actually seeing the silhouetted form of a small person, presumably a woman as it had long crinkly hair, as if it had been plaited when it was wet and then brushed out.

I can remember so well feeling no fear but a strange fascination. Perhaps it was this lack of fear that surprised me most. Anyway I simply lay down again feeling perplexed, nothing more, and the next I knew it was morning.

Although fascinated curiosity is mentioned by both apparitional and ecsomatic subjects, the emotional quality of this interest or fascination is not necessarily exactly the same in the two types of experience. Out-of-the-body subjects often mention that their fascinated interest in what is going on is combined with detachment, and use words such as 'academic', 'critical' or 'objective' to qualify it. Also, many out-of-the-body subjects refer to a kind of emotional detachment or complete disinterest in their normal affairs as a separate feature of their experience. This particular type of attitude is practically never mentioned by apparition subjects.

The following two, rather unusual, cases seem to be the closest apparition subjects come to the kind of complete emotional discontinuity with their normal concerns described by some ecsomatic subjects. The first percipient refers to being 'switched off . . . into another dimension', and the second to being only 'half in this world'. These expressions do not seem to refer to a particularly striking change of emotional outlook, and may

possibly be taken to refer to an awareness on the subject's part
that the experience was metachoric.

> My experience, one of several, is of my Mother who passed away
> 10 years ago. I came back from the shops. On coming into the house
> and on passing into the sitting room, I was suddenly switched off as
> it were from my surroundings and into another dimension and
> sitting in the arm-chair was my Mother. I looked hard at her. She
> appeared very happy, about 40 years old, and was smiling in a way
> she did when having done something clever. A voice in my head said,
> This is your Mother. She was wearing a jacket and skirt and hat,
> sitting on the edge of the chair as she often did. I wanted to talk with
> her, but all too soon I came back. She was a real person and not at all
> Ghost like. This is the third time I have seen her. The first time she
> was luminous.

> Some years ago (in the top flat where I reside) in November, one
> Saturday morning at about 9 a.m., as I came out of my bedroom,
> turned round a corner, to go down the stairs (in the flat—self
> contained) to the bathroom, I became rooted at the top of the stairs
> as, before me, was a woman—in a black cape and cowl—standing in
> the centre smiling at me. I must explain that, at that moment, I
> seemed (on looking back) to have been only 'half in this world'—I
> was not at all astonished, but stood at the top of the stairs smiling
> back at her—I was thinking—what lovely brown eyes she had, nice
> white teeth, and a particularly beautiful face. For how long I stood
> there, I have no idea, when suddenly she seemed to disintegrate, got
> very thin, and started floating up to the ceiling, when a huge white
> mist came up and she disappeared behind. The last thing I remem-
> bered then was that I was looking up at the ceiling and, when I 'came
> to' again, my head was down and I was watching the last wisps of
> mist disappearing—being absorbed, very rapidly, into the wall. My
> first thought was—'Fancy wood/paintwork etc., absorbing mist so
> rapidly!'
> Then I remembered all I had seen and my second thought was
> 'Goodness, I should be frightened' but I was not in the least, in
> fact, I felt completely uplifted and nearly floated down the stairs
> myself!

Another fairly common reaction among apparition subjects is
that of being 'puzzled', 'bewildered', 'disconcerted', 'mystified',
or 'bemused'. Altogether 8 per cent of our subjects report feelings
of this kind. Reactions of this kind are very rarely or never mentioned by out-of-the-body subjects.

Usually these feelings of puzzlement and bewilderment are
described as occurring after the apparition has ended. However,
in the following case the percipient was apparently bewildered

by the apparition while it was still visible. The subject of this case is 'Subject E':

> When I was 7 or 8 years old, while sleeping under the table one night (it was during the war), I awoke to see a black 'Scottie' dog, with red bow, sitting on the floor beside me (facing left). I couldn't believe my eyes! In bewilderment I turned over on my other side, presently taking a peep to see whether it had gone—but no, it was still placidly sitting there. I didn't dare take another peep, and tried to put it from my mind, and eventually fell asleep again. The image was utterly lifelike but unmoving, and as though self-illumined, not frightening in itself (rather the reverse)—but I just knew it shouldn't be there. The incident long puzzled me, for I felt sure I had been awake.

One or two apparition subjects made interesting remarks concerning their emotions which do not fall into any of the categories so far discussed. For example, one subject, who reported an auditory hallucination of footsteps passing her as she walked along a shingle-sand path, described her feelings afterwards as 'Slight amusement, and a feeling that I had done something clever.' And the subject who reports seeing a horse and two undergraduates in New College Lane (p. 1) says that afterwards she felt 'disconcerted', and says: 'I kept feeling everything I saw might not be real and normal. Avoided going down the road to New College for some weeks.'

*

Not all our apparition subjects report an emotion of some kind in connection with their experience. Eight per cent claim that they had no feelings at any stage, before, during, or after.

Nearly half of these are people who did not realise till after the apparition had ended that what they were perceiving was an apparition. Perhaps in some of these cases it is not surprising if they did not feel any particular emotion during the experience, since the apparition was of a familiar person or animal whom the subject was accustomed to seeing in everyday life.

However, a subject's emotions when perceiving an apparition are not always related in a very obvious way to the subject-matter of the apparition. For example, one subject reports seeing a black figure with a dog when, as a young girl, she was alone in a dark lane at night (see p. 158), something which one might expect would be a frightening experience. Yet she writes that the apparition did not frighten her, but rather that she regarded it as a 'guardian angel'. Another percipient reports that she twice saw a child-like creature floating in the air near her bed at night. The dress of the apparition was a pale and beautiful shade of brown, and it had golden hair and 'a wonderful smile' (see p. 162). At first this might sound a rather charming sight. However, it seems the subject was terrified by it and shouted 'Go away' on the first occasion, and screamed at her husband to get it out on the second.

It is possible that in a case such as this last, it is the mere fact that it is an apparition which frightens the percipient, rather than the nature of the apparition itself. Presumably this particular subject realised fairly quickly on seeing the creature that it was an apparition on account of the way it was floating in the air.

If we leave out of account those cases in which the subject is not aware at the time that he is perceiving an apparition, we still find that 4 per cent of our subjects report no feelings at all in connection with their experience.

In some cases the subject reports noticing afterwards that he did not feel the emotional response he might have expected. For example, one subject writes that she felt no emotions whatsoever, and adds: 'This is strange as I had never seen an apparition (ghost) before and thought if I ever did it would be in the dark and I should be terrified. I feel "she" [the apparition] knew this, consequently reassured me.'

The following is an account in which a subject comments on a somewhat similar absence of fear:

> My favourite Auntie had died and during the night before her funeral, after having slept for a few hours, I woke up. The room was quite dark and I saw, in a corner of the ceiling, a cameo-like picture of my Auntie's face. She looked radiant and was smiling happily down at me. She looked years younger than as I had known her (she was 64 when she died). She looked as she did in a tinted photo taken in her 20's. I closed and opened my eyes several times and also pinched my flesh to make sure that I was not dreaming, but she continued smiling at me for about 5 minutes and then disappeared. Afterwards, I was surprised that I had not felt any fear. I just felt happy in the knowledge that she was happy and free from pain.

The following is a case of the 'haunting' type, in which the subject reports having seen an apparition of a cat on a number of different occasions in a particular house. She stresses that she treated the apparition in a rather matter-of-fact way, and that it did not arouse any particular emotion in her.

> I have also had another experience, concerning a cat. This happened while I was a child of about six, seven and eight. I lived in a fairly old cottage with my grandparents and mother.
> It was just a grey barred cat that used to come down the stairs and along the hall and out through the back door. Once over the doorstep it disappeared. It frightened no-one and we used to shoo it out when we saw it. My grandmother disliked it, but I took it very matter of factly, even though I realized quite clearly that it 'didn't really exist'. The cat looked quite solid and ordinary, the only odd thing about it was that it wasn't a real one.
> . . . This cat would appear at intervals. We would see it perhaps 3 times a week for 3 or 4 weeks then not for another couple of months.
> I would like to emphasise that the above episodes appeared quite normal—I knew quite well that the cat wasn't real but it seemed a perfectly natural thing and about as ordinary as the postman calling.

This modification of what would normally be their expected emotional responses on the part of apparition subjects may be related to a similar phenomenon in the case of out-of-the-body experiences. As we have already remarked, many ecsomatic subjects seem to experience a kind of emotional detachment. However, in such cases the subject's emotional responses are often so distinctly different from normal—as when, for example, he views his injured body with emotions of cheerful interest and unconcern—that he frequently comments explicitly on his unusual state of mind. Apparition subjects may comment that they were surprised, for example, not to have been afraid, but do not usually relate this to having been in an extraordinary or remarkable state of mind. It appears that the modifications in the emotional responses of apparition subjects are less marked than in the case of out-of-the-body subjects.

On reading the accounts of apparitional experiences one sometimes notices that the subjects do not appear to have reacted in a completely normal way, even in cases in which they make no comment on this point themselves, and appear to have accepted their emotional reactions uncritically.

These indications that subjects may not always be in a completely normal state of mind are of relevance in considering their insight into the situation, that is, their realisation that what they are perceiving is an apparition and not a real person or object. As we have already remarked, subjects do not always realise this immediately, and sometimes seem abnormally slow in arriving at a normal assessment of the situation.

CHAPTER 8

Recurrent Apparitions

WHEN a subject perceives what he takes to be the same apparition on a number of different occasions these occasions may be spread over a length of time varying from minutes to years.

The number of separate occurrences in a recurrent case seems to vary considerably. There are cases in which the subject reports perceiving the same apparition only twice, and there are cases in which he reports perceiving it many times.

*

The majority of recurrent apparitions are perceived in the same place, or at least at different places in the same house, each time that they occur. The following is an example of a recurrent apparition which seemed to move in a variety of ways in a number of places within the same house. Incidentally, this case concerns an apparition of a cat, and recurrent apparitions of cats appear to form a distinct sub-group of their own. Recurrent apparitions of any other animal are much less common. The narrator of this case is an invalid.

> About two years ago during some alterations I was moved to another downstairs room in which are some large leather covered chairs and settee. I saw what appeared to be a large black cat jump down from the arm of these chairs and rush out of the door several times before I told my 19 year old daughter—who said she had seen it too. Several times after that we both saw it together at the same time. We would compare notes as to the route it had taken. Not always from the chairs, sometimes it came from a corner of the room, scuttled across the hearth and into the other corner where the door is —just disappearing there.
>
> We didn't tell anyone—for one reason we were afraid we should never get any more domestic help if they thought the house was haunted! However, one day the *daily* help said to me 'I think I must

be going daft I keep thinking I see your cat jump down out of that chair when I come in here.' (We have a large black cat.) Then later still a new *living-in help* said 'Have you got two cats ? Because I could have sworn one rushed past me in the passage but when I got to the kitchen he was lying asleep. (We have only the one cat!) I didn't tell her, it's hard enough to get them as it is!

Last night I told my husband of your broadcast and said I would write to you. I had never said anything to him of our 'ghost pussy' before this. When he suddenly said 'Oh *that* cat. I've often seen a black shadow like that in the conservatory, but I've never said anything because I wasn't sure enough of what it was and you would only be nervous anyway.'!!

. . . It seems very frightened of people and scuttles off just as cats do when they are startled.

In a later communication this subject adds the following note:

My daughter married and moved about 4 miles away about 7 years ago and some years later I said to her 'You know I've never seen the ghost cat since you moved.' To which she replied 'Oh I took it with me. I often see it.'

Curiously enough the observation by our correspondent's daughter, that the recurrent apparition of the cat appeared to have accompanied her to a new locality, is a feature that has also been reported to us in connection with another recurrent apparition of a cat. In neither of the cases was the apparitional cat that seemed to accompany a percipient to a new home a cat that the percipient identified as resembling any particular living cat he had known.

In yet another case concerning a cat, the apparition was also seen in two different places, but on only one occasion in each place.

In the beginning of the summer of 1884 we were sitting at dinner at home as usual, in the middle of the day. In the midst of the conversation I noticed my mother suddenly looking down at something beneath the table. I inquired whether she had dropped anything, and received the answer, 'No, but I wonder how that cat can have got into the room ?' Looking underneath the table, I was surprised to see a large white Angora cat beside my mother's chair. We both got up, and I opened the door to let the cat out. She marched round the table, went noiselessly out of the door, and when about half way down the passage turned round and faced us. For a short time she regularly stared at us with her green eyes, and then she dissolved away, like a mist, under our eyes.

Even apart from the mode of her disappearance, we felt convinced that the cat could not have been a real one, as we neither had one of our own, nor knew of any that would answer to the description in the place, and so this appearance made an unpleasant impression upon us.

This impression was, however, greatly enhanced by what happened in the following year, 1885, when we were staying in Leipzig with my married sister (the daughter of Mrs. Greiffenberg). We had come home one afternoon from a walk, when, on opening the door of the flat, we were met in the hall by the same white cat. It proceeded down the passage in front of us, and looked at us with the same melancholy gaze. When it got to the door of the cellar (which was locked), it again dissolved into nothing.

On this occasion also it was first seen by my mother, and we were both impressed by the uncanny and gruesome character of the appearance. In this case, also, the cat could not have been a real one, as there was no such cat in the neighbourhood. (*Census*, pp. 305–6)

An example of an apparition which is seen on a number of different occasions in exactly the same place and always performing the same more or less stereotyped actions is the following:

. . . I was living with my mother in a ground-floor flat in Sussex Gardens . . . This flat was shaped like a dog leg (or letter L) and there was a step in the long part of the corridor just before reaching the main bedroom. There were about seven rooms in this flat. I often saw an old lady with a stick pausing before she negotiated this step, presumably on her way back to the bedroom from the loo round the corner. I'm just saying what it looked like. I did not tell my mother about her, because I did not want to upset her, she slept in the main bedroom. One night, I can't think why, I spent the night in this room and had a terrible time scared stiff of something that appeared to resent my presence. I was too frightened to sleep. I can't think now why I was not in my own room round the corner—perhaps we had guests—but next day I told mother that I wouldn't sleep there again. She said 'I wonder if it was the old lady.' She had kept quiet about her for fear of worrying me.

The type of recurrent apparition which is least rigidly localised appears to be that in which the subject seems to become aware of the presence of some deceased person whom he knew well during life. This class includes, for example, cases like the following. The percipient's mother had recently died, and she had decided to redecorate her mother's old bedroom.

I went up in the evening to finish it off and was so tired I sat on the bed to criticise the result.

As I sat I realised I was not alone and there seemed to be a 'mouldy' smell in the room. Then came my mother's voice, plain and clear, saying 'Yes, I like that paper much better—I never cared for that yellowish one!'

I replied 'I didn't know that, why did you not say ?' My husband who was downstairs, hearing my voice, called me to come down out of that cold room!

With that I rose and went down, switching off the light. I had seen nothing, only heard the voice, but I realised I suddenly felt very cold. I felt no fear.

I heard her voice too on another occasion. We had to go to Thornton Heath as my son was looking for a lodging when his teaching job started.

I remembered how I had used to go with my mother to visit friends in that road and I had quite forgotten the number of the house.

'Why 69 of course!' came my mother's voice as though in answer to a query. So we went and found that number, and it was certainly the same house though I had not seen it since I was ten!

In this instance the two experiences apparently occurred in quite distinct physical locations, and the topics on which the percipient reports hearing her mother speak to her were quite different.

A contrasting example is the following, in which the subject sees a recurrent apparition of her deceased grandfather, but both experiences take place in the same room.

As a schoolgirl . . . I was in the habit of discussing my school problems with my grandfather, an old man with silky white hair and a little white goatee-beard, whom I adored. He was very well educated, and highly intelligent, and delighted in discussing with me the subjects I was studying in preparation for University entrance. When he died, I was about 18, and I was desolate.

About six months after his death, I had another big problem to resolve, and no-one to talk it over with. During that week once at about 3 a.m., my grandfather came through the outside wall of my bedroom, in a luminous circle of grey light, his head and shoulders clearly visible—and talked to me . . . Next day, I found I could understand my problem, and could proceed with my work. I told my mother about the happening, and she advised me to say nothing to anybody.

My 'grandfather' came again some months later when I again needed his help—but he has never come again since.

*

Subjects report recurrent apparitions involving most of the different senses. For example, different subjects have reported to us recurrent apparitions involving hearing, vision, touch and smell. Cases are also reported in which subjects have had recurrent experiences of a sense of presence, with no sensory accompaniment.

The following is an example of a recurrent hallucination of the sense of touch, and again forms part of the very distinctive group of cases concerning apparitional cats. It appears that this initially purely tactile experience came to incorporate an auditory element as time went by, since the subject writes that she used to hear the cat purr after a time.

> ... I was living in Sydney, and sleeping just underneath a window, which was always kept open. It was a ground floor flat. After I had been living there some time (and while I still had the light on and was reading in bed), a ghost cat visited me nightly. It was so vivid, I could feel it jumping on to the bed from the windowsill, and it would then walk up me towards my face. It seemed so real that I often involuntarily (while still reading, I became so used to it) put up my hand to stop it walking on my face. Sometimes it would walk across me and evidently jump on the floor, as it would return later on. Eventually we became so used to one another that I heard the little creature purr, though I never saw it. I told this story to many people at the time.
>
> I left the flat very suddenly, as I was offered a berth to come to London more or less at a moment's notice, and I've often wondered if the little thing visited the next tenant.

*

Before we leave recurrent apparitions, we should mention two striking cases we have received in which it is reported that the subject, over a period of time, repeatedly perceived an apparition at a particular place in his real environment, and took it for a real object until its disappearance led him to realise that it was not really there.

In the first case the subject reports seeing a stone effigy of a knight in a particular place in a church on the first three occasions on which she attended services there, only to find that nothing was to be seen in that spot on the fourth occasion she visited it.

> About six years ago my husband and I and four children moved to Tewkesbury in Gloucestershire. You may know already that Tewkesbury has the finest Norman Abbey in this country and being practising members of the C. of E. I made plans to attend services there.
>
> I took my three eldest children with me on my first visit, to 8 o'clock communion and through the entire service observed, admired, and

drew my children's attention to a figure of a knight in 13th century armour kneeling in prayer under a canopy of stone on top of a side chapel known as the founder's chantry chapel. The colouring was amazingly life-like and I thought it was a marvellous effigy.

The following Sunday and the one after that I again observed the knight, the entire service he was there whenever I looked. We were sitting on the right hand side in the choir stalls up near the altar. The knight was on the opposite side to us.

I here must tell you that there *is* an effigy in the abbey of a kneeling knight over a chapel on the *right* hand side, but it faces the altar and in fact can only be seen from the other side of the communion rail near the altar. It is quite unlike the one I saw and is very colourless.

On the third Sunday when I returned home I mentioned to my husband that I knew it sounded rather silly but I had that morning a very uneasy feeling as he was looking at me all the time. I felt that I was wrong to let my attention wander from the service so and I said that I had better sit elsewhere next visit.

My husband then on hearing where I had sat said that I could not possibly have seen the effigy already known to be in the abbey, as it was on the same side as I had sat and so could not be facing me. I was taken aback and annoyed with him and said he was quite mistaken over the position and after heated argument the matter was dropped.

The following Sunday I took my usual seat and the knight to my amazement was gone.

A friend of mine was the wife of the curate and I asked her if it had been taken down for cleaning. She looked amazed and said that there never had been an effigy in the place that I had seen what I thought to be one and I must have seen an apparition.

I was so shaken that I could not bring myself to enter the abbey for many weeks . . .

My husband is a graduate and is employed by the university, we are abolutely trustworthy people not given to any exaggeration or flights of fancy.

The following is the second case of this kind. The subject reports that she saw a bombed house in a London street at a spot where in reality there was an intact white house. It appears that the subject had seen the bombed house at the spot many times before she eventually discovered that the real house at the spot was intact.

Another strange incident happened in Queen Street, Mayfair round about 1950. I was a member of the English Speaking Union and was in the habit of going round there at lunch time. Going down Queen Street from Curzon Street, there was a bombed house on the left-hand side that I often noticed as I passed, as there was nothing left but one far wall and a small 'shelf' along it, level with the first floor I should say, obviously being all that was left of a room. This particular day, I suddenly saw a small boy in a red pullover and navy blue shorts run out on the ledge and along it (away from me). He was going quite fast and as he was only about seven or eight years old, I crossed the road to tell him to be careful. There was nobody there and nowhere he could have come from, or gone to. A little puzzling, and I can't understand it as I had hitherto seen this house quite often. I went back next day to look again and the house wasn't there. I tried the next street in case I had been mistaken, but it wasn't there either.

We asked this subject for various further particulars of this experience. She writes that prior to its disappearance, 'the "bombed" house was always just there—I did not doubt it'. She repeats her statement that she had 'often' passed it before. As regards the question of when the apparition of the bombed house was replaced by a perception of the intact house she adds the following:

> I went back down Queen Street next day and couldn't find the house—it had completely disappeared. It was still there when I crossed the road to tell the boy to be careful, and (as far as I know) when I continued on my way to the E.S.U. It had been about the —th house down on the left—between Curzon Street and Charles Street—if so, there was just a big white terraced house, more or less matching the rest, in its place.

Cases such as the last two we have quoted seem to be distinctly unusual. At any rate, these are the only two we have come across, either in our own collection or among published accounts.

Such cases are nevertheless of considerable theoretical interest, if we accept the percipients' accounts as being at least substantially accurate. They raise the question of how long a hallucinatory feature superimposed on the real world might go undetected. If a hallucination was collective, so that anyone passing a particular spot also hallucinated a similar non-existent object, might the hallucination remain undetected indefinitely?[1]

[1] This question is discussed further in Charles McCreery's book *Psychical Phenomena and the Physical World* (pp. 43–54).

CHAPTER 9

Apparitions Occurring just after Waking

ON analysing the apparition cases received by the Institute, one finds that in about a quarter of all the cases received the subject says that the experience occurred just after he had woken up, usually during the night.

The following is an example which will illustrate the type of case in question:

> One night, two years ago, I woke up, quite naturally, and saw a tall man standing close to my side of the bed. I was *not* still dreaming. I saw the large bay window, the street-lamp opposite, the furniture in the room, *and* the man. His face was long, melancholy, and slightly moustached. He wore a check overcoat, and a trilby hat. The overcoat had a wide belt at the waist. I think he seemed to me to be about fifty-ish, or perhaps less.
>
> Suddenly, I was afraid, and I screamed and screamed, waking my husband in a fright. As I was comforted, the man vanished. When I was somewhat pacified, I had an odd feeling that I had been wrong, precipitate in treating him as an enemy—that he had wanted to tell me something that concerned me, vitally. Of course, I got over the shock, but have always been certain he was no extended 'dream' figure. I have dreamed ever since I can remember, and no-one ever came so close to me with such clear, *breathing* reality. I have never forgotten exactly how the man looked at me.

Between a quarter and a fifth of all the subjects who report experiencing an apparition just after waking up say that they 'were woken' rather than that they merely 'woke up', as if they had been actively disturbed by some external cause. For example, the percipient may say that it was a 'radiance' in his room which roused him, or a feeling of cold, or a feeling that somebody was in his room, or he may say that he was awakened by someone calling his name, or touching him on the forehead. Alternatively, he may report that he was woken but say that he does not know what it was that woke him.

In the following example the subject reports that she was woken by her bedroom door opening. (This need not of course mean that the bedroom door actually opened; it may be that the subject hallucinated the sound of the door opening and possibly also the sight of it opening as well.)

> One night, about an hour after going to bed, I was awakened by the bedroom door being opened. Thinking it was my teenage daughter, who probably couldn't sleep etc., I raised myself up. Instead of my daughter, it was the full form of a very dear friend who had died a few weeks earlier. She was wearing a most beautiful green silk dressing-gown, which had a 'glow' about it. Her hand held the gown in place, and I noticed how white and thin the hand seemed to be. My eyes travelled up to her face, and I noticed that she looked so much younger than she was when she died.
>
> I was so surprised—and as I began to say, 'I thought it was Valerie coming in' (Valerie being my daughter), my friend faded away.
>
> She didn't speak to me, but her lovely brown eyes looked directly at me, with such love and understanding.

Subjects may also report that they woke 'for no reason at all'. Some remark explicitly that their waking in this way was most unusual. For example, one writes, 'I am a very sound sleeper but one night I suddenly awoke in the night for no reason at all.'

Again, subjects sometimes write that they woke 'suddenly', as if they were disturbed, although they do not say explicitly that they were. The following case, kindly sent to us by Mrs. Graham Greene, will illustrate this feature. The experience took place in a house in Holywell Street, Oxford.

> . . . I was sleeping in a back bedroom on the second floor and I woke extremely suddenly to see a hospital nurse sitting by my bed. The room was totally dark but the *figure* was coloured, and was entirely real, as if in daylight. She was perfectly 'friendly' and smiled, and I noticed she had a *gold filling* in a tooth on the side nearest to me. I was absolutely terrified—my heart seemed to stop and then thump: and I dived under the clothes. I remained there with my head bursting through lack of air, and finally after a long time, emerged for air—and *the figure was still there*! After that I remembered nothing—'blacked out' as they say.

In the great majority of nocturnal cases the subject wakes up and perceives the apparition immediately on waking, rather than after an interval of time. It appears, therefore, that the process of waking is an integral part of the experience of perceiving the apparition. It is as if the subconscious of the percipient is planning the production of the hallucination while the percipient is asleep, and then wakes him up at an appropriate moment.

Subjects sometimes remark that they felt fully awake when they perceived the apparition, even though they had only just woken up and it was the middle of the night. The subject of one such case, for example, writes that he 'woke one night feeling strangely alert under the circumstances . . .'

*

It is interesting to consider the time of night at which subjects report that they awake and have an apparitional experience. Cases are reported as occurring at all times of night, from very soon after the subject has fallen asleep to the time when he would be expected to wake anyway in the normal course of events. However, there seems to be a preponderance of cases occurring in the middle of the night—'in the early hours', as several subjects describe it, or two or three hours after falling asleep.

It would obviously be of the greatest interest to know at what stage in people's nightly sleep-cycle these nocturnal experiences occur. Most people's sleep is thought to follow a more or less definite rhythmical pattern, with periods of 'rapid eye-movement' (REM) sleep alternating with periods of orthodox sleep. Dreaming is thought to occur in the rapid eye-movement phase of sleep.

In addition, the successive phases of orthodox sleep are thought to become less deep as the night progresses, so that for most people the deepest sleep probably occurs within an hour or so of first falling asleep. So far as we can tell, it seems that people tend not to perceive apparitions during their period of deepest sleep at the start of the night.

It would obviously be of considerable interest to determine whether people tended to wake and experience apparitions following periods of REM-type sleep or following orthodox sleep. Of course, it might be that apparitions occurred following both kinds of sleep, in which case it would be interesting to discover whether there were any differences between the kinds of experience which occurred following REM sleep and those following orthodox sleep.

An interesting question is raised by collective cases in which two or more percipients report waking up simultaneously in the middle of the night and seeing (or hearing) an apparition. If some particular type of sleep is favourable for the occurrence of apparitions, we should like to know whether it is the case that both of them are at the favourable stage in their sleep cycle when they wake and perceive the apparition.

A small number of our subjects report that they had been dreaming just before they woke up and saw an apparition. The following is one of these cases:

> I have had a very clear vision of a man's head and shoulders on awakening from a nightmare.
> It was on the wall in front of me, and although the room was in darkness, the vision was brilliantly clear, in full colour. It was of an Indian man with a glistening white silk turban and smiling brown-skinned face.
> It happened about twenty years ago—but I can still remember the face and its expression. I had not seen this man before nor since.
> My anxiety (from the dream) passed away when I saw the man. It was reassuring.

Cases such as this, in which the apparitional experience is preceded by a dream or nightmare, clearly suggest that in at least some nocturnal experiences the subject wakes from an REM phase of sleep. However, cases of this kind are reported much less commonly than those in which the subject wakes and sees an apparition without remembering any mental events taking place just before he woke up.

*

Compared with the number of cases in which the subject woke during the night, we have received relatively few in which the subject said the experience occurred just after he had woken up at his normal time in the morning. The following is one of these cases:

> . . . I would like to relate an experience which occurred to me during the winter of 1965–6.
> At that time I was a Housemaster at —— School. I lived in a flat in an old part of the school building, with my wife and three daughters, who were then 9 years, 7 years and 4 years old. Unfortunately I cannot recall the exact month now, but remember that the mornings were dark until well after 7 a.m. On the morning in question I was due to rise at 6.45 a.m. to call the others in the school at 7.15 a.m. I normally awake by my alarm, which is not a loud ringing one, but which I normally get out of bed immediately it starts to ring and

switch it off. This particular morning when I awoke I saw my young daughter standing by me at the side of my bed. It was very dark in the room but I could clearly see her. I did not think that there was anything unusual about this. She had a bewildered look in her eyes, as if unsure of herself. To switch off the alarm I had to get out of bed and go to the mantleshelf above the old fireplace, at the foot of my bed, so on jumping out, I passed her at the same time, saying in a somewhat reassuring voice 'Hello darling'. I turned my back on her for barely a second, and turned around to discover that she was no longer there. I became immediately suspicious as the door in our room, which was a very large type of room door, creaked loudly when anyone opened it, or closed it, so I immediately felt for it and found that it was open by about 2–3 inches but certainly not sufficient to let her out or in.

My daughters at that time slept in the adjoining bedroom, so I immediately went in, switched on the light, and saw my youngest daughter lying asleep in her bed. I recall that she was partly un-covered, but it was fairly evident that, from the way she was lying, she was not out of her bed recently. I have a vague recollection of going to her bed and finding it warm where she lay, but cannot be quite certain now whether I did do this. I was certainly mystified by her sudden disappearance, and the fact that she was able to get out of the room without the door creaking. However, when I returned to my bedroom, I sat down and tried to recall exactly what I had seen— it was still fresh in my mind, in fact I still have the picture in my mind clear to-day as it was then. One point was; when I saw her, she was dressed in pyjamas which fitted her pefectly: this itself should have been odd, as at the time she had grown out of all her pyjamas. Secondly, the pyjamas appeared to be of a plain whitish colour. When I saw her in bed, the pyjamas she was wearing were ones which were ridiculously small for her, being too short in the arms and legs, and they were an odd set; the top being a yellow print and the bottom a red print.

A third point which then became apparent to me was, that it was so dark in the room that should she have been there in person I would not have seen her. I turned out my room light and tested this point by not being able to see my outstretched arm in front of me. The alarm clock, which has luminous numbers, I was able to see. The colour of the apparition I had seen was a grey misty colour, as one is often given to believe, but the only break in the colour was in the shaded areas, or where the shaded areas would normally be—such as creases, etc., in her clothing. Her whole figure was of the same colour. The thing that struck me most about what I had seen was the likeness of the apparition to that of the negative of a photograph. If you were to look at someone in the negative of a photograph, with a light behind the negative, you would see almost every detail of the indivi-dual down to the glint in their eyes—that is exactly how I saw my daughter.

CHAPTER 10

Informational Cases

SOMETIMES apparitions convey some kind of useful information to the subject. The information conveyed may be the solution to a problem with which the subject has been consciously occupied for some time, or it may be a spontaneous 'warning' of a danger which the subject has not previously thought about.

In both problem-solving and warning cases an element of extra-sensory perception may seem to be involved in the information conveyed to the subject, or it may seem clear that inferences from normal data would be sufficient to produce the correct solution or appropriate course of action.

Of course, there is an extremely large class of cases in which information of this kind is suddenly conveyed to the conscious mind of the subject, such as the various kinds of 'hunches' and 'premonitions', and sudden insights into problems. It is not particularly clear why the process should sometimes be associated with an apparition, or other type of hallucination. There seems to be no particular type of information-giving case which is always, or even usually, associated with an apparitional experience.

The following apparitional case is something of a borderline example between the 'problem-solving' and the 'warning' types of case. As a result of the apparition's advice, the subject took apparently appropriate action by discontinuing the taking of tablets which seemed to be harming her. But she had not been unaware of the possible danger in continuing to take them, as she says that the drug had seemed to be making her worse and she had wondered whether she should take any more. The subject's report is as follows:

> About 1951, when I was travelling to the City every day to work in an office, I was suddenly smitten with some virus. I never really

knew what it was, but I was prescribed a certain drug to be taken three times a day. I was of course in bed but as I was not seriously ill my doctor did not visit me every day and my late husband was able to look after me. However, the drug seemed to make me worse and worse and on the third day I felt so dreadful that I wondered whether I would take any more. My husband had to go out and I was lying in bed, knowing I was there quite comfortably, when I suddenly saw myself sitting on my bedside chair, dressed in a frock discarded quite a year before. I did not speak at all but myself in the chair told me that if I wished to recover I should stop taking the tablets at once or they might finish me off in so many words. At the time I had several troubles on my mind and was worried at being away from my job at a busy time and it passed through my mind why bother if they did finish me off. However, my chair self said that was a stupid thing to do and finally persuaded me to stop them immediately and tell the doctor, and then she disappeared. When my husband returned I simply told him I did not think the tablets agreed with me and I would stop taking them until I had seen the doctor and he agreed with me. I told the doctor I had stopped them as they seemed to make me worse and he said 'Good Heavens, quite right and I will give you something else!' This he did and I was back at the office in two weeks. I have never told anyone of this experience for fear of ridicule but the picture of myself sitting by my bed, in the old frock, and talking to me is as vivid as it was then. I should mention that there was no question whatever of delirium at any time.

It is not very clear why the solution of this particular problem in the subject's mind should be accompanied by an apparition of herself. People come to similar decisions without seeing apparitions, and similar apparitions are seen with no apparent connection with problem-solving. However, it is frequently suggested that apparitions seen in such circumstances are a method by which the subconscious mind is able to convey a certain piece of information to the conscious mind of the subject, in spite of the latter's emotional resistance. In this particular case, it is not possible to say whether the resistance of the subject to the idea presented was particularly profound. Did she, perhaps, have an emotional reluctance to accept the idea that a doctor might be fallible, and something prescribed by him might actually be bad for her?

The following case is similar to the last, in that the subject had been consciously preoccupied with a certain problem for some time, and was able to solve it after seeing an apparition of himself. In this case, the hallucination seems to provide the subject with actual information which he did not possess before, by showing

him the correct manipulations to repair a machine. (The subject
is a Dutchman writing in English.)

In the year 1944 I was asked by a milk condensation manufacturing
company named *CCF* in Leeuwarden to repair a very complicated
book-keeping machine (Burroughs) which I hardly knew how to work
with. I started with the repair and got the machine ready except
that she was not correct adding in the hundred figures. It was not so
easy to find out the defect, but . . .! During a night in the week I
was at work with the machine, I was awakened in my sleep and saw
(in colour) on the table of our bedroom that book-keeping machine,
while a brilliant electric lamp was lighting, and saw myself, fully
dressed, take out with the fingers of my left hand a little triangle
formed from the machine and give it with a pincher or pinner at one
end a pinch making it somewhat longer and placed that part back
in the machine.

At the day following on that nightly experiment I did the same
manipulation done in the preceding night and see, the machine was
working in the hundreds all correct. Mark please, the machine was
not in my workshop but I repaired her at the *CCF*.

The following case may be regarded as a 'warning' case, as
subsequent to seeing an apparition of her grandfather, and
possibly as a result of it, the subject went downstairs and discovered a dangerous escape of gas. This is distinct from a
problem-solving case, since the subject had no previous conscious
awareness of the possible danger.

I work in a mill, one night on returning home I had a feeling of
slight tummy upset and headache. I decided to have an early night in
bed. I put my husband's dinner in the gas oven on a low light to be
ready about ten o'clock when he came home. I went out to the coal
bunker and banked the fire up also. Then I retired to bed. I must
have slept for about three hours when I wakened up suddenly to see
my 'dead' Grandfather stood by my bedside. He had his back to me,
and was looking over his shoulder at me. I could see everything else
in the room. It did not appear to be a dream. I could see plainly his
snow-white hair just hanging over the top of his macintosh. I could
see the wrinkles on the cloth as he stood there. Just looking at me; he
looked so real I eventually stretched out my hand to touch him, and,
immediately the apparition slowly sort of broke up and melted away.
I was dumbfounded. Why, I asked myself, should I 'see' my Grandfather when he had been dead so long ago. My mother had died so
much more recently. Thoroughly awakened now by this unexplained
happening I decided to go down and take a look at the dinner in the
oven. As I went downstairs and opened the door at the bottom I
gasped. The house reeked of gas. I opened all the doors and turned
off the gas. I can only assume that when I went for the coal, on

shutting the back door the draught had blown the gas out. I have always thought since that somehow he came to *warn* me. It puzzled me so much as to why it should have been Grandfather I saw, when I had not seen him since I was a girl of fifteen. I was then forty seven. *He looked so really alive,* although he did not speak. I could not smell gas until I went downstairs.

'Warning' experiences of this kind, in which the subject seems to be alerted to some danger of which he had no previous knowledge, are often auditory. The following are two examples of the kind:

One of my regular jobs, on a certain farm in Western Australia, was to attend the wells and windmills during the summer, and see that the stock, sheep, cattle and horses, were not without water. Arriving at this particular well I found that I would have to go below to attend the pump. I sat down and had swung my legs over the edge of the well when a 'voice' said, 'There's death in the well.' I sat still for a moment, looked round, and said to myself, 'Rubbish, you're living alone too much.' At the bottom of the wells, and just above the 'high' water there is a platform on which to stand whilst working on the pump, which again is usually at eye level for comfortable working. I descended the well (perhaps 30 or 40 ft), stepped onto the platform, turned round to the pump, and there not more than a foot away was a snake coiled round the pump. I am not afraid of snakes, but I don't like to argue in the confined space of the bottom of a well. I don't remember getting out of the well. The next thing I knew I was lying 'on top' looking down into the dimness and thinking of that warning voice. I went back 'home', got a .410 shotgun, went back to the well, and blew that snake apart. I attended the pump the next day, and threw the two parts of the snake away.

Just before I sold my house near Enfield, I had a famous surgeon as a paying guest . . . My border collie 'Sally' . . . had had a puppy, and I put them to bed as usual on the settee, covering them up with an old soft woollen jacket. I went to my bed and slept for an hour, when a voice woke me up and told me 'to go downstairs and look at the dogs'—I refused saying the dogs were alright, again the voice said 'Go downstairs and look at the dogs', but I turned over to settle down to sleep again, but the voice repeated 'Go downstairs and look at the dogs'. So grumbling I got out of bed and opened my wardrobe, got out my dressing gown and went downstairs to speak to the dogs. It was as well I did so, for Sally had thrust her head and one paw right down the blue sleeve of the jacket and got stuck there, looking like a long blue sausage. I had to give a strong pull to get her out of the sleeve, and then I cut it up the seam so that she could not do the same again. Now whose voice was that which woke me up? I told the surgeon the next morning, he said he had heard me go downstairs and talk to the dogs and wondered why.

It is often suggested that such warnings are provided by the subject's subconscious for his protection, on the basis of information which it has obtained by inference or by extra-sensory perception. If this is so, however, the method of communication does not seem to be entirely perfect. The lady who owned the dogs at first refused to go downstairs and look at the dogs, as the voice told her to do, and went only reluctantly when the voice repeated the message. The subject who was going down the well took no notice of the voice which warned him of the danger in the well. It is not clear whether the warning was of any benefit to him at all, since presumably he would have noticed the presence of the snake in the well in any case. But it is possible that the warning voice had made him more alert than he might have been otherwise.

This, at any rate, is how the first case appears if we accept it at face value. If we do, the explanation which suggests itself for the subject's statement that he does not remember getting out of the well is that he climbed out in the normal way, but very hurriedly, and retained no memory of doing so on account of his state of panic.

However, the fact that the experience ends with a seeming discontinuity in the subject's physical position suggests the possibility that he may have hallucinated the descent into the well. We have already noticed that some apparitional experiences end with a discontinuity in the subject's physical position, and we shall later be discussing the possibility that sometimes, when a subject has an auditory hallucination, his visual environment may also temporarily be hallucinatory, although he may not necessarily realise this.

If the descent into the well were hallucinatory, it would seem that the information it gave him about the position and appearance of the snake tallied with observations he made later on. This is quite in accordance with reports of other spontaneous out-of-the-body experiences, in which information about the physical world obtained during the experience is seldom found to contain detectable inaccuracies afterwards. (Incidentally, in considering whether this case should be interpreted in this way, it is interesting to note that this subject has reported a number of ecsomatic experiences.)

CHAPTER 11

The Senses and Apparitions

WHEN subjects were asked which senses were affected in their apparitional experiences the proportions mentioning each sense were as follows:

	%
Sight	84
Hearing	37
Touch	15
Temperature	18
Smell	8
None of these .	4

These percentages add up to more than 100 because in some cases more than one sense is said to have been affected.

At first sight it might look as though visual hallucinations are more common among the population at large than hallucinations of any other sense.

However, we must bear in mind that our appeals for cases have usually included the word 'apparition' and to many people this may connote something specifically visual such as a human or animal figure.

There was also some indication that people tend to think visual hallucinations more worth describing in response to an appeal than auditory or other kinds.

Also, visual hallucinations may simply be better remembered than auditory and other kinds. The authors of the *Census of Hallucinations* thought they found some indications in their data that auditory and tactile hallucinations might be forgotten more quickly than visual ones. (*Census*, p. 66)

Finally, the data in the table above are based on questionnaire data, and there was some indication that people tended to be more willing to fill in questionnaires on visual experiences than on other kinds.

In view of all these factors it is difficult to conclude anything very definite concerning the relative frequency of different kinds of hallucination from the data given above. The authors of the *Census*, after attempting to make allowance for these and similar factors in their collection of data, concluded only that it was 'legitimate to infer that *impressive* hallucinations of the visual class are considerably more frequent than those of the auditory, and that auditory hallucinations in general are considerably more frequent than tactile'. (*Census*, p. 130)

*

The majority of cases reported to us involved only a single sense. However, experiences involving two, three or even more senses are also reported. The following table gives the relative frequency with which our subjects reported experiences involving a given number of senses.

	%
One sense	61
Two senses	25
Three senses	9
Four or more senses	5

It will be seen that the number of experiences falls off rapidly as the number of senses increases.

It seems that the more complicated types of hallucinatory experience may occur less frequently than the simple ones. A characteristic way in which apparitions may depart from complete realism is that some of the expected senses are missing. Thus we find subjects sometimes reporting apparitions which walk but make no sound with their feet, or apparitions which look quite solid, but do not feel solid to the touch.

It seems that virtually any combination of two or more senses may be hallucinated together. For example, in the following case the subject reports that his senses of hearing and temperature were involved. He heard a pleasant lady's voice saying 'Good morning' and at the same time felt a sensation of cold.

I neither believed, or disbelieved, in ghosts, or apparitions, until I stayed the night at G. Manor, near C— on the 11th of January this year.

G. Manor is an Adult Education Centre and on the night in question I attended a dinner there, given by a local organisation.

Due to snow and road conditions, I asked the Bursar at the Centre if I could stay overnight, to which he agreed except that he mentioned I would be the only person there as there was no course on and he and the staff slept out.

Just before the few remaining diners departed he mentioned that the Manor was haunted by a lady in a blue dress but that she was quite harmless, occasionally appearing in the early evening, or early dawn. He had met her and several others had seen her. In fact, he kept a record of her appearances. This did not worry me in the least.

I retired to bed and slept not very well being in a strange bed. In the early dawn, I was lying in bed *wide awake* when suddenly a woman's voice, gentle and pleasant, said 'Good morning' and then whispered it again as she appeared to pass through the room.

At the same time an icy wave swept through the room and bed clothes—my teeth chattered with cold, *not* fear. I sat up in bed, saw nothing. Turned on the light. The time was twenty to six. It was quite dark.

I reported the matter to the Bursar, Mr. P., when he came to his office at the Manor. He said that he was in no way surprised. I am afraid that I was!

*

As we have remarked, a typical form of unrealism in apparitional experiences is for too few senses to be involved in it, and the commonest sense to be missing is the sense of hearing, which results in the characteristic silent apparition. For example, subjects may remark that the apparition made no sound of footsteps as it walked, despite walking on a hard surface. Or they may be surprised at not having heard it breathing, although it seemed to be doing so very heavily.

In the following case the subject describes seeing an old man and apparently being surprised at not being able to hear the sound of his breathing:

As a nine and a half year old, one of my more pleasant household 'chores' was to take the baby up to bed at six p.m., and sing him to sleep . . . The baby having duly fallen asleep, I levered myself gingerly off the bed, so as not to waken him, and quietly opened the bedroom door, still watching the baby to make sure he didn't 'disturb'. As I turned my head, I was gazing directly at the window on top of the stairs, along the landing from me. Sitting on the landing window-sill was a very old man. I was startled into immobility ... He was very old, rheumy-eyed, grey-haired. He wore old, dirty looking dark trousers, a cream Welsh flannel shirt without a collar, unbuttoned at the neck, an extremely dirty looking old 'weskit' which were food and grease stained. He had a muffler tied round his neck ... On his head was an old bowler hat, black, and past its best by many a long day. The muffler, by the way, was black, red, and white, the old man was leaning on a walking stick, his two old hands folded one on the other on top of the stick. His mouth was open slightly, and slack, as some old men look, and I'm sure that if he had been a living man, I would have expected to hear his breathing quite clearly. As it was, I could only hear street noises from outside. The man's head was slightly inclined towards the window but he was not gazing out through the window. With hindsight, I realise now that he was *listening*, from his window seat. I suppose this apparition lasted about 10 seconds ... The apparition vanished as suddenly as a light goes out. I can't say I had been 'rooted to the spot', or felt incapable of movement, as though restrained by some other force, it was just that I had stood stock-still with surprise.

Curiously enough, on another occasion when she saw the same apparition this subject did hear the sound of breathing.

In another case the subject reports waking and seeing her late sister by a wardrobe. The apparition appeared to be laughing and talking to the percipient but nothing was audible. A similar case is one in which the subject reports seeing an apparition of himself and another man in his bedroom. They seemed to be arguing, but he could not hear any voices (see pp. 127–8).

It is interesting to note that on occasion subjects also report noticing a lack of sound during an out-of-the-body experience when they expected to hear something. For example, the subject may find himself apparently outside his body and observing some people engaged in conversation, and he may notice that he is unable to hear what they are saying, even though he seems to be close enough to do so were he really in the position he seems to be in. (Cf. Celia Green, *Out-of-the-Body Experiences*, pp. 67–8)

*

Subjects do not very often report sensations of pain in connection with apparitional experiences. However, in the following case the subject experienced a sensation of pain which seems to have been similar to what her husband must have been feeling at about the same time, even though there was no obvious physical reason why she should do so. The percipient and her husband lived near Lake Coniston.

> I woke up with a start, feeling I had had a hard blow on my mouth, and with a distinct sense that I had been cut, and was bleeding under my upper lip, and seized my pocket handkerchief, and held it (in a little pushed lump) to the part, as I sat up in bed, and after a few seconds, when I removed it, I was astonished not to see any blood, and only then realised that it was impossible anything could have struck me there as I lay fast asleep in bed, and so I thought it was only a dream!—but I looked at my watch, and saw it was seven, and finding Arthur (my husband) was not in the room, I concluded (rightly) that he must have gone out on the lake for an early sail, as it was so fine.
>
> I then fell asleep. At breakfast (half-past nine), Arthur came in rather late, and I noticed he rather purposely sat farther away from me than usual, and every now and then put his pocket-handkerchief furtively up to his lip, in the very way I had done. I said, 'Arthur, why are you doing that?' and added a little anxiously, 'I know you have hurt yourself! but I'll tell you why afterwards.' He said, 'Well, when I was sailing, a sudden squall came, throwing the tiller suddenly around, and it struck me a bad blow in the mouth, under the upper lip, and it has been bleeding a good deal and won't stop.' I then said, 'Have you any idea what o'clock it was when it happened?' and he answered, 'It must have been about seven.'
>
> I then told what had happened to me, much to his surprise, and all who were with us at breakfast. (Gurney, Vol. I, p. 188)

The percipient's husband wrote an independent account confirming that he had indeed got up early to go sailing on Lake Coniston and had had the accident his wife describes. He did not have a watch with him at the time of his accident, so could not be sure that it had happened at exactly the time his wife woke up with the sensation of pain, but, he writes, 'on comparing notes, it certainly looked as if it had been about the same time'.

CHAPTER 12

Purely Auditory Cases

IN this chapter we shall consider those cases, some 14 per cent of our collection, in which the subject reports that only his sense of hearing was involved.

The largest single item of subject-matter in these purely auditory cases is the sound of the human voice (36 per cent of all the purely auditory cases).

The following are two examples in which the subject beard a voice, in the first case recognised and in the second unrecognised:

> When I was ten, I was walking across country to the hamlet where my grandmother lived, in the quiet of a summer's afternoon. As I walked by a woodside, half a mile or so from the hamlet, I heard my grandmother distinctly say, 'I shalln't be long'. I looked all round, but nothing was to be seen, and arriving at the cottage, found it locked up, and no one about. I went down the lane towards the main road, and met my grandmother, who had just got off the carrier's cart. Over tea, I told her about hearing her say 'I shalln't be long', and she told me she had suddenly said this (but couldn't think why she did) when about a mile from home.

> It was in 1954[1] and the East Coast Flood Disaster had occurred a few days previously. I was sent to Immingham to help in repairing the damage to the sea wall, arriving at a time of confusion. I believe that it was my first day at Immingham and I was taken on an extensive tour of the sea wall terminating at nightfall. My guide suggested that after our evening meal we should drive to Grimsby and go to the cinema, to which I agreed. We proceeded as arranged and obtained seats in the circle which was well filled. The lights were dimmed and everyone stopped talking, settling back in their seats for the start of the performance. Then a voice said to me loudly and distinctly, 'You can't do it, you know.' It was so clear and resonant that I turned and looked at my companion who was gazing placidly

[1] The narrator presumably means 1953.

at the screen, then I looked at the people round about but nobody evinced the slightest interest in anything but the film being shown. I was amazed and somewhat relieved when it became apparent that I was the only person who had heard anything. Then I began to wonder if I really had heard the voice and this doubt persisted until the second occasion which I think was about two weeks later. It was just as I was dropping off to sleep in bed at about 11 p.m. when I heard the same voice utter exactly the same words and I was aware at once that had anyone been with me they would not have heard anything. At the same time I was confirmed in a belief which had grown since the first time I heard the voice, and that was that some subconscious part of myself was advising me that I could not do the job I had undertaken.

On considering the matter I can quite well understand how some people (I believe Joan of Arc was one) have claimed to have heard ghostly voices, because the voice is loud, clear and compelling—or I should say—it was in my experience.

In addition to cases in which the subject reports hearing articulate human speech there is a smaller proportion of cases (12 per cent of all the purely auditory ones) in which he reports hearing some inarticulate vocal sound such as a guffaw, sigh, whistle or scream. Also included in this category are a few cases in which the subject reports hearing the sound of breathing or panting, although strictly speaking these are not vocal sounds. A case of this kind will be quoted later in this chapter (p. 88).

After the various kinds of vocal sounds, articulate or inarticulate, which together account for just under half the auditory cases, the next most frequent category of sound to be reported is that of footsteps (28 per cent of all purely auditory cases). The following is an example of this type, in this case involving an animal:

> We had a very beloved old dog who, because of his age and stiffening joints, always went upstairs with the typical 'ker flop—ker flop' noise they make when they put both front paws on one step and then take the hind feet up on to the same step. The night after we had him put to sleep because he had by then gone quite blind, both my mother and I (who slept in separate rooms and always with our doors open) were wakened by 'something' at precisely the same moment and both heard old Snap come 'ker flop—ker flop' upstairs (I think on every step, although we did not, of course, count). There was complete silence after the regular rhythm stopped, and we neither of us ever again heard the sound. My mother was, incidentally, a most matter of fact and unimaginative woman. No successive dog has ever done this.

The remaining cases are made up of a wide variety of sounds which, if they were normally produced, would be considered as directly or indirectly due to human or animal agency; for example, the crunch of car wheels on gravel, the sound of threshing, the sound of drawers being opened, tapping, knocking, the scratch of a dog at a door, etc.

The following case will illustrate the type of account in question:

> I only heard noises once; that was when we lived in a very old house, the main part of which was used as a museum. In the room on the other side of my bedroom wall a row of ancient cannon-balls lay in the hearth. In the middle of the night there was a noise as of someone playing bowls or marbles, rolling the cannon-balls across the floor. This kept on for about an hour and was very disquieting.
>
> When I went into the museum in the morning, everything was in perfect order and showed no signs of disturbance.

*

It appears from subjects' accounts that many auditory hallucinations, if not the majority, sound as if they issue from a localised source, like real sounds. For example, one subject describes an old man's voice as having appeared to issue from a cupboard in her bedroom (see p. 132). Again, another writes that she heard her aunt calling her and the sound 'came from the window'.

Sometimes the sound even seems to move from one part of the subject's environment to another; for example, he may hear footsteps approaching or receding.

*

It is noticeable that in many purely auditory cases the apparent source of the sounds heard seems to have lain outside the subject's field of vision. This may have been because the sound appeared to originate outside the room in which the subject was situated, or because it seemed to come from behind him, or for some other reason.

The situation is particularly noticeable in relation to the cases in which the subject reports hearing footsteps. It is rare for the subject to report that he heard footsteps in the same room as himself and looked but was unable to see anything to account for them.

In the following case the subject reports hearing footsteps in a part of an L-shaped hospital ward that was not visible to her.

> . . . I was in another L-shaped surgical ward, and had sent for the Doctor as I was worried about a patient. I was in the part of the ward out of sight of the door, and heard a man's footsteps coming up the ward. Good, I said, he's got here quite quickly, collected the light and went to meet him and there was no one there!! I *definitely* heard clear footsteps—the ward was very quiet. I later heard *that* ward was 'haunted'! (What by I never asked!) What ward isn't said to be haunted!! It never bothered me—I'm not imaginative that way . . .

By contrast, in the following case the subject reports that she heard the panting of a dog 'right beside' her, but that she could see nothing. She seems to have found the experience rather alarming.

> When staying in the West of Ireland about eight years ago, near Bantry Bay, I was taking our dog for a short walk by the shore, through some trees. I had not gone very far before I heard the heavy panting breathing of an enormous dog, right beside me. My dog (a Cairn Terrier) was terrified and his hair stood on end. I could see nothing, and there was no cover near for a dog to be hiding in. In some alarm, I dashed back to the gate, and then, thinking I must have imagined it (although I couldn't think how as the presence of a large dog nearly touching me was hardly imaginary), I started again—and when I got to the exact same spot under a tree (no lower branches or any screen), the same thing occurred.
>
> A few days later a Bishop staying in our hotel who we had made friends with had the local vicar (now left) to dinner, and told him about it. He asked us to have coffee with them and brought up the subject. When I told him, he said I had undoubtedly heard and felt the presence of the Irish Wolf Hound, who was said to go for walks with people.

Why should there seem to be this tendency for people to hear hallucinatory sounds issuing from points outside their field of view, and seldom from within it?

Possibly in some instances the sounds in our purely auditory cases had a physical explanation, and if the subject had been able to see the point from which they originated, the physical cause of the sound would have been apparent to him. However, this explanation does not seem to be a possibility in a sufficiently large number of cases to account for the tendency.

It may be that the subconscious, when it presents an auditory hallucination to consciousness, sometimes does not wish to present a visual hallucination to accompany it. At the same time, it may wish to avoid the rather paradoxical situation in which the subject hears a normal kind of sound, such as a footstep, issuing from some place within his field of view where there is nothing to account for it.

It is interesting to compare certain purely auditory cases with certain experiences of the sense of presence, in which the subject similarly reports that he had a feeling that someone was present but in a spot that lay outside his field of vision (see pp. 121–2).

As we mentioned in the last chapter, there seems to be a general tendency to avoid hallucinations of more than one sense at a time.

*

In the case of visual apparitions we have seen that there are two possible ways in which the apparition may be related to the subject's normal environment. The subject's normal surroundings may be temporarily replaced by a hallucinatory alternative, or the apparition may appear to be superimposed on the subject's normal environment. In the case of auditory hallucinations we have also to ask whether the subject's normal train of auditory perceptions, arising from his surroundings, is temporarily suspended while he is having the auditory hallucination, or whether he experiences the two simultaneously.

In many cases of auditory hallucination it is difficult to obtain any impression from the subject's report whether his experience was one of these forms or the other. Many auditory hallucinations, such as the calling of a name, are very brief, and many take place indoors or in other quiet surroundings. In either of these circumstances the subject would probably not notice if there were a temporary intermission in his normal auditory perceptions, even if this actually took place.

There are, however, a few cases in which it seems likely that the subject might have noticed an intermission of this kind if it had happened. One of these is the case, quoted near the beginning of this chapter, of a man who heard a voice speaking to him while he was watching a film in a cinema. Another is the case of a woman who was walking along a shingle-sand path and heard hallucinatory footsteps walking past her. Presumably she might have been expected to notice if the sound of her own footsteps had stopped when she began to hear the hallucinatory ones, and started again when the hallucinatory ones could no longer be heard.

It does appear, therefore, that in at least some cases the auditory hallucination is superimposed on an uninterrupted sequence of auditory impressions arising from the environment, in the same way that the typical visual apparition seems to be superimposed on the subject's normal visual environment. However, in the case of visual apparitions we have observed that the experience may sometimes, and perhaps always, be entirely hallucinatory even when the subject's normal environment appears to remain constant, and only the apparitional figure to be added to it. This of course raises the question whether the same may not be true of some, or even of all, auditory hallucinations. Thus, in the case of the woman on the path, if she did hear her own footsteps and other surrounding noises continuing while she heard the apparitional footsteps, this may have been a hallucinatory reproduction of what she would have heard if she had still been perceiving her auditory environment in the normal way.

This interesting possibility requires further investigation.

CHAPTER 13

Other Auditory Experiences

In this chapter we shall consider experiences in which the sense of hearing seems to have been hallucinated more or less simultaneously with one or more other senses, most commonly the visual.

In some of the visual-auditory cases the sounds the subject hears contribute to the realism of the experience. For example, a visual apparition may make a rustling sound with its clothes as it walks, produce the sound of footsteps, speak, etc.

However, what the subject sees does not always seem to him to be the cause of what he hears. In some instances what is heard and what is seen seem to be quite unconnected with each other. For example, one of our subjects describes being woken by a 'buzzing sound' and then seeing a scene in his bedroom consisting of a column of men, led by a figure in a white robe carrying a red gothic cross. The scene appeared to be about a hundred yards from him although there was a wall about fifteen feet away in reality. The 'buzzing sound' did not persist during the visual part of the experience.

In this case the buzzing sound seems to have been quite unconnected with the subject-matter of the visual part of the experience.

There are a number of cases in which the auditory component of the experience seems to serve the function of drawing the percipient's attention towards a hallucinatory element in his visual field. For example, in the following case the subject reports first hearing the patter of footsteps and then seeing her dog, which had died.

It was one evening and my husband and I were listening to the wireless, and I decided to make some coffee. Whilst preparing for it,

> I hurried back to the door-way of the living room to listen to something funny on the radio. Whilst listening and laughing with my husband, I heard a patter of steps in the hall and thought a cat had got in. The next thing was I saw Wendy, our dog, who had been so loved, and mourned when she died after many years. She looked just as she did as when alive, although not quite as solid and heavy in build. She pushed her way past me and went straight across the room to where my husband was sitting. I then cried out to my husband, 'Wendy is here, she is quite near you'—and then Wendy disappeared.

The following example illustrates how the sense of hearing may be hallucinated at the same time as senses other than the visual. In this case the subject reports that an auditory hallucination of his late mother's voice was accompanied by a hallucination of touch.

> A second occasion occurred after her death (about two months). I was extremely worried about a certain matter and as I was living alone I decided to go for a walk to think it over. I had not been left the house for one minute when I felt a hand on my shoulder and I heard my mother's voice say 'Go home Ernie—everything will work out.' I returned home and thought no more about the problem. The 'voice' turned out to be correct.

*

In the last chapter we discussed whether the subject's normal auditory perceptions may be suppressed or replaced by a hallucinatory imitation while he is having an auditory hallucination. A similar question arises in connection with visual apparitions. That is to say, while the subject is seeing a hallucinatory figure, are his normal auditory perceptions suspended?

As in the case of auditory hallucinations, there are a certain number of visual hallucinations in which the subject would presumably not notice or not report on a temporary suspension of his normal auditory perceptions even if it had taken place, because his surroundings were quiet at the time in any case. But some visual apparitions do occur in circumstances in which a break in the normal auditory perceptions would be noticeable. For example, the subject who saw an apparition while he was walking round a cathedral (p. 35) might be expected to have noticed if the sound of his own footsteps on the cathedral floor and the other normal cathedral noises had stopped. Similarly, subjects who see visual apparitions while they are travelling by train or car would presumably notice a sudden silence.

Since subjects do not usually comment on any sudden silences of this kind, it seems to be clear that their normal auditory perceptions either continue, or are replaced by a hallucinatory imitation.

However, in a few cases such as the following, the subject does report that his surroundings seem to become abnormally silent:

> One evening about seven years ago I was on my way to work at office cleaning, the time was 8 p.m. It was winter and pouring with rain. As I reached the corner of the road I live in, suddenly everything faded away and became very silent. The building beside me, which incidentally is now a large shoe warehouse, suddenly appeared as a small old-fashioned house with pebble windows and sloping roof with a large lantern hanging over the door. I could see the roads were all cobble and I could hear the clip clop of horses' hooves. I felt a distinct presence of a woman in a full gown wearing a bonnet with ribbons. The feeling of elation and happiness was great for me. I know I tried to reach out and see more, when in a split second I was standing on familiar ground outside the shoe factory. Oh my disappointment in not being able to grasp it.
>
> Nothing has ever happened to me before or has since.

Similarly, while subjects are having an auditory hallucination their visual surroundings almost always appear to continue unchanged. But the possibility arises that the continuity is, in some cases, only apparent, and that what they are seeing is in fact a hallucinatory reproduction of their normal environment. The following case, which happened while the subject was suffering from Asian 'flu, provides an interesting illustration in which the whole sensory environment may have been temporarily hallucinatory.

> I was in bed with Asian Flu, and alone in the house as my landlady happened to be away. I do not know what my temperature was at the time of the experience I am about to relate, but it had been between 101° and 102° Fahrenheit some hours earlier.
>
> As I lay in bed I seemed to be listening to the ticking of a clock somewhere in the house. I lay listening to this for some time, and thought that it was ticking in a rather doleful way, as if re-echoing in the cavernous emptiness of the house.
>
> After a time I started to wonder where this clock might be that I was listening to, and it occurred to me that there was no clock in the house which I could be hearing in that way.
>
> As I thought this I 'came awake'. That is to say, there was a certain change in the quality of my awareness. It now seemed to me that I

was in a state in which I was aware of everything that I would normally be aware of, and that it was surprising I had not thought before of there being no clock in the house, so that before this I could not have been in a really normal state.

But what struck me very much was that my physical surroundings seemed to be completely continuous with before this scarcely perceptible discontinuity. I was still lying in the bed, in the same position, with my eyes open, looking at the room, as I had been doing while listening to the clock ticking. The only difference was that the ticking had stopped.[1]

[1] This case was not sent in to us as an example of an apparition or hallucination in response to an appeal, but was reported to us as an interesting experience by one of our lucid dreaming subjects.

CHAPTER 14

Speaking Apparitions

THERE seems to be a distinct tendency for visual apparitions not to speak. In our own collection only 14 per cent of all visual apparitions of human beings do so. Among this 14 per cent, few speak at length, and the speaking is not always realistic. It is an interesting question why this should be so.

However, speaking apparitions are reported, and in some cases they speak quite normally. Occasionally people even report holding quite long conversations with apparitions, as in the following case:

> The Transvaal war was at its height. One night, after reading for some time in the library of the club, I had gone to my rooms late. It must have been nearly one o'clock before I turned into bed. I had slept, perhaps, some three hours or so when I awoke with a start. The grey dawn was stealing in through the windows, and the light fell sharply and distinctly on the military chest of drawers which stood at the further end of the room, and which I had carried about with me everywhere during my service. Standing by my bed, between me and the chest of drawers, I saw a figure, which, in spite of the unwonted dress—unwonted, at least to me—and of a full black beard, I at once recognised as that of my older brother-officer. He had on the usual khaki coat, worn by officers on active service in eastern climates. A brown leather strap, which might have been the strap of his field service glass, crossed his breast. A brown leather girdle, with sword attached on the left side, and revolver case on the right, passed round his waist. On his head he wore the ordinary white pith helmet of service. I noted all these particulars in the moment that I started from sleep, and sat up in bed looking at him. His face was pale, but his bright black eyes shone as keenly as when, a year and a-half before, they had looked upon me as he stood with one foot on the hansom, bidding me adieu.
>
> Fully impressed for the brief moment that we were stationed together at C— in Ireland or somewhere, and thinking I was in my barrack-room, I said, 'Hallo! P., am I late for parade?' P. looked at me steadily, and replied, 'I'm shot.'

'Shot!' I exclaimed. 'Good God! how and where?'

'Through the lungs,' replied P., and as he spoke his right hand moved slowly up the breast, until the fingers rested over the right lung.

'What were you doing?' I asked.

'The General sent me forward,' he answered, and the right hand left the breast to move slowly to the front, pointing over my head to the window, and at the same moment the figure melted away. I rubbed my eyes, to make sure I was not dreaming, and sprang out of bed. It was then 4.10 a.m. by the clock on my mantelpiece. (*Proceedings of the S.P.R.*, Vol. V, 1888–9, pp. 413–14)

(It seems that the officer represented by this apparition had indeed been killed at about the time of the narrator's experience, and that he had been wearing the type of uniform the percipient saw and had died in the manner indicated, viz., by a bullet through the right lung.)

Cases of this kind are exceptional. Apparitions seem to have a certain reluctance to speak freely and realistically. It should not be supposed that all of the 14 per cent of cases in which visual apparitions speak correspond to cases in which the subject actually sees the apparition's lips move and hears the sound issuing from its mouth, as if it were a real person. In some cases the subject first hears someone speaking and then later sees what seems to be the author of the sound. In others he may see an apparition and at the same time hear a voice speaking, but the apparition's lips may not move, and it may seem as if the voice is coming from elsewhere and not from the apparition.

In a number of cases the apparition seems to show reluctance or inability to speak. For example, in the following case the apparition fails to speak, even though, had it been a real person, it would apparently have been appropriate for it to do so.

In 1942 I was working in a factory in High Wycombe. The commissionaire in the office there was a large and corpulent ex-serviceman nicknamed 'Major' due to the circumstance of his having been a sergeant-major during the First World War. I knew this man by sight and so was not surprised to meet him upon the landing of the office stairs about 11 a.m. one day. I wished him 'Good-Morning' as I passed him (at about eight feet distance), but he did not answer but looked at me in silence with the strained expression characteristic of a sufferer from stomach ulcers. I did not see him again, but upon remarking to my family that evening that 'The Major was in a pretty bad temper this morning', I was told that he had fallen upon a dwarf fence-post on the evening before and had been removed to High Wycombe Hospital, in which he had died at around the time at which I had seen him. I ought to point out that I had no prior knowledge of this event, nor did I know until after I had remarked upon his peculiar facial expression that he had actually died of peritonitis. I was about nineteen years old at this time.

When the percipient does not realise at first that what he is seeing is an apparition, its behaviour in not speaking to him may strike him as rude or peculiar. The following two cases will illustrate this feature. In the first the apparition was of a young man who (as we learn from the percipient's sister, a Lady M) had only met the percipient twice but had been 'greatly interested in her'. The percipient's account is as follows:

On the evening of Saturday, April 26th, 1890, I was engaged with my sister and other friends in giving an amateur performance of the *Antigone* at the Westminster Town Hall. A passage led down to several dressing-rooms used by ladies who were taking part in the representation, and nowhere else. None of the public had any business down this passage; although a friend came to the door of the dressing-room once to speak to some of us.

I was passing from one dressing-room to another, a few steps further along the passage, just before going on to the stage, when I saw in the passage, leaning against the door-post of the dressing-room which I left, a Mr. H., whom I had met only twice, but whom I knew well by sight, and as an acquaintance, though I had heard nothing of him for two years. I held out my hand to him, saying, 'Oh, Mr. H., I am so glad to see you.' In the excitement of the moment it did not occur to me as odd that he should have come thus to the door of the dressing-room—although this would have been an unlikely thing for a mere acquaintance to do. There was a brilliant light, and I did not feel the slightest doubt as to his identity. He was a tall, singular-looking man, and used to wear a frock-coat buttoned unusually high round the throat. I just observed this coat, but noticed nothing else about him specially except his face. He was looking at me with a sad expression. When I held out my hand he did not take it, but shook his head slowly, without a word, and walked away down the passage—back to the entrance. I did not stop to look at him, or to think over this strange conduct, being in a great hurry to finish dressing in time. Next day, as a number of us were talking over the performance, my sister called out to me, 'You will be sorry to hear that Mr. H. is dead.' 'Surely not,' I exclaimed, 'for I saw him last night at the *Antigone*.' It turned out that he had been dead two days when I saw the figure.

I have never experienced any other hallucination of the senses. (*Journal of the S.P.R.*, Vol. IV, 1889–90, p. 308)

Across the road from me, lived a brother and sister called Peggy and Bill Smith. They were very devoted to each other, having lived together for nearly fifty years, since the death of their parents. Both were in their seventies. (The sister is still alive, aged 86.) I was a great friend of both of them, as they were young in heart and spirit, no generation gap.

I had been away for several weeks at my home in Suffolk (my parents' home) and came back in the month of January. On coming back to Greenwich, I did not go out for three or four days, nor did I see any local friends, as I was busy clearing up the usual mess a family can make in a mother's absence! Then one day I decided to go to the library and had to pass the Smiths' house. It was bitterly cold and snowing, and to my surprise I saw—(?)— Bill Smith standing in the garden wearing a light coloured summer shirt. He looked very ill. I stopped to speak to him, telling him, gently, that he really ought not to be out in such cold weather without a warm coat etc. He never answered but looked straight through me, and after a short monologue on my part, I decided I'd better go. (Privately, I thought he'd gone a bit senile.) I looked back after some fifty yards, and he was still there, staring after me. When I got home, I remarked to my husband that I'd seen Bill, how ill he looked, and that he didn't seem to know I was there . . . .

Three days later I went to a female coffee morning—about ten people were there, including Peggy Smith, Bill's sister. The conversation turned to holidays, and someone mentioned a hotel in Scotland that catered specially for older people—and I remarked impulsively to Peggy 'Why, that sounds just the place for you and Bill! No stairs, etc.' There was a ghastly silence! I rambled on, wondering if I'd made some sort of faux pas . . . . then someone had the sense to say 'Bill died six weeks ago, suddenly, when you were away . . . .' I said 'But I was only talking to him three days ago . . .' Then to my embarrassment, Peggy Smith broke down in uncontrollable weeping, and I offered to take her home, which I did. I made feeble excuses to her—but—I *had* seen and spoken to her brother, several weeks after he was dead, although I had *no* previous knowledge of his death whatsoever. It was an incident none of my friends ever forgot!

Another indication that there is a tendency for apparitions not to speak normally is that in a few cases the subject reports having communicated with the apparition as if by telepathy, so that the use of speech has been avoided.

The following is one such case, in which the subject reports that an apparition conveyed a message of reassurance to her but 'did not actually SAY the words'.

A few years ago, one very sunny afternoon, my husband away and my siamese out, I was busy doing housework, dashing in and out of the kitchen, I saw at the door of our bedroom an apparition. At first I could not believe it. I went about my business. But on looking again, a white lady was standing there. She would seem elderly, but somehow ageless, in fact almost an exact copy of Princess Mary as she was in her youth. Her hair was short and very wavy. Her dress was early 1920's style . . . I just couldn't believe it, as I have always thought of 'ghosts' being only seen at night, and always the very thought of them gives me the creeps. But, I felt no fear at all. There must have been a questioning look on my face, because also a white-haired terrier appeared beside her . . . The lady had a pleasant face, and smiled and said 'It's alright.' She did not actually SAY the words, but they came to me. She seemed to give the impression that I was not to be afraid, and I wasn't. I then went about my business and have never seen her since.

Another subject reports twice having had a 'conversation' with an apparition of her late grandfather on the subject of her current work problems (see p. 66). She says the apparition spoke to her, 'but not in words—it communicated in thought. His lips could have moved slightly—but there were no spoken words—I am sure of that'.

How are we to account for this seeming reluctance of apparitions to engage in realistic speech?

It is possible that the subconscious of some subjects is reluctant to present to consciousness hallucinatory experiences that involve more than one sense. In general, as we have already mentioned, experiences involving more than one sense seem to be the exception rather than the rule among reported cases.

However, this does not seem to be a complete explanation of all cases of reticent apparitions, for in some cases an apparition does not speak but the subject nevertheless experiences an auditory hallucination accompanying his visual one.

For example, in one case of a recurrent apparition the chief percipient, Miss R. C. Morton, never heard the apparition speak. During one year, in particular, she tried to communicate with the figure—that of a tall lady dressed in black—'constantly speaking to it and asking it to make signs, if not able to speak, but with no result'. However, on one occasion the apparition 'gave a slight gasp'. She describes this incident as follows:

The first time I spoke to her was on the 29th January 1884. 'I opened the drawing-room door softly and went in, standing just by it. She came in past me and walked to the sofa and stood still there, so I went up to her and asked her if I could help her. She moved, and I thought she was going to speak, but she only gave a slight gasp and moved towards the door. Just by the door I spoke to her again, but she seemed as if she were quite unable to speak. She walked into the hall, then by the side door she seemed to disappear as before.' (*Proceedings of the S.P.R.*, Vol. VIII, 1892, p. 314)

In a case such as this it hardly seems possible to explain the apparition's apparent reluctance or inability to speak by supposing that the subconscious of the percipient experienced some difficulty or unwillingness to construct an auditory hallucination of any kind, since it seems that an auditory hallucination (of a gasp) was part of the experience. Of course, a gasp is not so complicated an auditory hallucination as speech, but there are other cases which show that complicated auditory-visual hallucinations can be produced. Also, we know that these sometimes occur in out-of-the-body experiences. So it does not appear likely that what is in question is merely the intrinsic difficulty of constructing a hallucination of this kind.

Possibly there is some subconscious tendency to avoid constructing apparitions which display too high a degree of realism, and possibly the sound of speech which actually seems to be issuing from the moving lips of a visual apparition is felt to violate this. We have seen in other contexts that the realism of most hallucinatory experiences seems to break down at certain points. For example, as we shall see in the next chapter, the subconscious of the percipient usually seems to draw the line at constructing a hallucination of touch to correlate with the visual one when the subject tries to touch an apparition. Instead of feeling his hand touch what seems to be a solid object he often sees his hand go through it or finds that the apparition disappears.

Whatever may be the cause of the psychological inhibition against visual apparitions which speak, it does not seem to be present in lucid dreams (dreams in which the subject is aware that he is dreaming), in which human figures usually speak quite normally. The lucid dreamer often engages in quite long conversations with the characters he meets in his dream, and he does not seem to notice any peculiarity in their manner of speaking, or any particular reluctance on their part to do so. It seems that both the sight of the person and the sound of his voice may be quite realistic, as in waking life, and these two hallucinatory components of the experience, the visual and the auditory, may be quite well integrated.

Of course, one difference between a lucid dream and an experience of perceiving an apparition is that in a lucid dream the subject has, by definition, insight into the nature of his experience—he realises that what he is perceiving is hallucinatory; the subject who sees an apparition on the other hand may not realise until afterwards that what he has seen was not a real person. Even if he realises that what he is seeing is not a real person, he does not necessarily think of it as hallucinatory.

The characteristic attitude of the lucid dreamer during a lucid dream is: 'Isn't it extraordinary what a splendid imitation of reality my subconscious can conjure up for me.' This is not a characteristic attitude for an apparition subject to adopt towards his experience, which he generally seems to regard, either at the time or subsequently, as the intrusion of something 'different' into the real world.

CHAPTER 15

Touch and Pressure

MOST of the hallucinations of touch reported to us were combined with hallucinations of other senses. For example, the subject might see an apparition and feel its clothing brushing him as it passes, or he might hear footsteps and feel someone sitting on his bed.

In the following example the subject sees an apparition of her husband, which then touches her under the chin. In this case a hallucination of temperature seems to have been involved as well, as the subject describes the touch as being icy cold.

> It happened about eleven years ago, one Sunday evening. I was alone, sitting knitting and listening to a talk on the radio. Suddenly I was aware of my husband standing at the side of my chair. He looked white and drawn and was gazing straight ahead. It seemed strange to me afterwards that I did not speak because at the time I really thought it was my husband come home, coming in so quietly that because of my concentration on my knitting and radio, I had not heard him. As I looked up at him, he raised his arm and his hand came to rest under my chin and it felt *icy cold*. I shrank back in my chair from the chill feeling of it and the arm then fell back to his side. When I straightened up again, again he raised his arm, but this time I shrank back before his hand touched me. Then as I still looked up at him, he disappeared. Only then, did I realize that my husband had never been physically in the room. I am not a widow, so even if I believed the spirit of loved ones could return (and I am not a Spiritualist) that could not be the explanation.

Hallucinations of touch alone seem to be reported rather rarely. However, it may be that they occur more frequently than the cases sent to us suggest. It is possible that they are less dramatic and memorable than visual or auditory cases, so that they are less likely to be reported. The following is an example of a case of touch alone:

While lying in bed one night wide awake, I distinctly felt a hand stroke my hand. It was a caress. I still was not frightened.

An example of a more elaborate and recurrent experience involving the sense of touch is the following. This, incidentally, is one of the very characteristic group of recurrent cat cases.

I live in a bungalow with my parents and a friend of the family. There is an upstairs room, this is occupied by my friend. For the past six or more years, she had mentioned that perhaps every few months she'd waken to feel a cat on her bed, either walking up it, or curled up against her. Each time she'd switch on the light, but could see nothing and had searched the room in case one of our three had got in without being noticed. As this usually happened during sleep, I assumed it to be imagination.

In September 1972 her room was being redecorated, and her bed moved down to my room. After we'd retired and put the light out we talked a little and suddenly I felt a cat jump on the bottom of my bed, walk up to my knees and curl up in the hollow of the back of my knees. The bedclothes were pressed hard against the back of my legs. I asked my friend to switch on the light as Jenny (our cat) was on my bed. I wanted to return her to her box. The light went on, the pressure instantly lifted, there was no cat, and Jenny was curled tightly asleep in her box. My friend said it looked as if I'd been visited by her ghost cat. I had no further experiences until late February last year, 1973. One night, in late February, I had gone to bed and switched out the light, at about 12.20, I felt a cat jump on the bed, so I switched on the light, no cat. I searched the room, still nothing . . . I returned to bed and switched out the light. A little while later, I felt it again, and later had a third visitation. And this has continued every night up to the present.

I feel the cat's paws as it walks over the bed, pressing down the covers, making 'puddings', the kneading motion a cat makes when it's pleased. Once as I tucked my chin in to the bedclothes I felt it push back, I pushed against it, it pushed back again, I did this several more times with the same result. We had a cat who died three years ago who would do this. I have heard, though faintly, purring and on one occasion it was quite loud.

Although I have looked very hard I never see anything. When it comes right up the bed and is standing on the clothes by my face I stare hard for it's odd not to be able to see a cat's face. I have switched on the light and even kept a torch in my hand to flash on the spot where I feel it. I have put my hand on the spot too but never feel anything that way. I just feel it walking about or lying down; it's the weight I feel.

*

Let us consider how the sense of touch enters into experiences of visual apparitions.

It is usually the apparition which touches the percipient, and not the percipient who touches the apparition. This is true both of our collection of cases, and of cases previously published. When a percipient does try to touch or catch hold of an apparition it often eludes him in some way. We shall proceed to illustrate some of the ways in which contact with an apparition may be avoided.

In the following case the apparition first recedes in front of the percipient, although the percipient pursues the apparition faster and faster. When eventually the percipient succeeds in catching up with the figure and tries to catch hold of it she seems to 'catch nothing':

> When I was a young girl, I resided with my father, mother, sister (named Ellen), and brother, at Clapham. My sister was in love with a man, but my father and mother disapproved of the attachment, and sent her to a friend in Brighton, to be out of the way. One evening during her absence, between 6 and 7 o'clock, my mother and brother were talking in the garden, at the back of the house. There was a wall at the bottom of the garden, and a gate, leading into a large enclosed space used for drilling, etc.; this enclosure was locked in the evening, and was certainly locked at the time in question. It was dusk, but not dark. My brother John (a very active boy, but who happened to have just sprained his ankle) looked over the wall, and suddenly exclaimed, 'Mother, there's Ellen!' My mother looked, saw, and recognised the figure of my sister, and said, 'John, go quick, and tell her to come in. Don't say anything to your father.' John replied, 'I can't because of my foot; call Mary.' Mother then called me, and whispered, 'There's Ellen; go and tell her to come in; her father shall not know anything about her coming back.' My mother's idea was to get her quietly into the house, and send her away again next day. I at once went through the garden-gate, and gave her the message. I particularly noticed her dress, a dark blue pelisse, buttoned, and the ribbon on her bonnet. A path led through the enclosure to the outside gate, and she kept receding from me along this path, while I followed more and more quickly, my mother and John watching us. There was a deep dip in the path, and here I overtook her and tried to catch hold of her, but seemed to catch nothing. She still receded, and at last stood by the watch-box, close to the gate; and here I repeated the message to her, but as she made no answer, I went back. My mother said, 'Why, where's Ellen?' I said, 'I left her by the gate.' My mother replied, 'But you caught hold of her.' 'Yes,' I said, 'but I did not seem to feel anything in my hand.'

My mother turned very pale, and went into the house and told my father, and both of them felt a conviction that some calamity had happened. The next day the news came that my sister had thrown herself into the sea and been drowned a little before 7 o'clock on the preceding evening. (Gurney II, pp. 615–16)

The following case is somewhat similar, in that the apparition seemed actively to avoid the percipient. A particularly interesting feature of this case is that the apparition always appeared to be walking slowly, even though the percipient was running in its pursuit. (The percipient and her sister had together seen a similar apparition on an earlier occasion at about the same spot— a road in the country near their home. The apparition was of a tall man dressed in a black coat, knee-breeches and a low-crowned hat, apparently in the manner of a clergyman of the eighteenth century.)

I have again seen the ghost, and under the following circumstances. On Sunday last, June 12th, at a few minutes before ten in the morning, having occasion to pass that way, I perceived far in front a dark figure, who at that distance was indistinguishable as to whether it were man or woman, but believing the person to be the latter, and one I was acquainted with and likely to meet at that hour, I determined to hurry on and overtake her. I had not gone far, however, when I soon discovered it to be none other than the apparition we had looked for and failed to see for so many months. I did not then feel at all afraid, and, hoping to get a nearer inspection, boldly followed, running in close pursuit; but here the strangest part of it all is that, though he was apparently walking slowly, I never could get any closer than within a few yards, for in but a moment he seemed to *float or skim away*. Presently he came to a standstill, and I began to feel very much afraid and stopped also. There he was!—the tall spectre dressed as I have described before. He turned round and gazed at me with a vacant expression, and the same ghastly, pallid features. I can liken him to no one I have ever seen. While I stood, he still looked intently at me for a few seconds, then resumed his former position. Moving on a few steps he again stood and looked back for the second time, finally *fading from view* at his usual spot by the hedge to the right.

There was no one else on the road but myself, and here I solemnly state that what I have written is not at all traded upon by imagination, as I was not thinking of the apparition at the time, he not having been seen for months previous to this visitation. (*Journal of the S.P.R.*, Vol. VI, 1893–4, pp. 149–50)

When a percipient does succeed in reaching an apparition and tries to touch or grasp it the results are variable. It may disappear, gradually or immediately, or his hands may go through it without his feeling any resistance. In only a few cases does he experience a more or less realistic sensation of solidity and texture.

In the following example the subject reports that she deliberately walked right through the apparition, and on turning round, found it was no longer visible.

It was while my friend was absent that I was going upstairs one night to bed, with candle in my hand, when standing in the open doorway in front of me (which led into the bedroom beside mine and immediately under the shut room) I saw distinctly a man standing looking at me. The only light was from my candle; the square was very badly lighted so that no light came through the window. He was a tall, dark man, dressed in a grey suit, with heavy dark beard and moustache; and at first I thought that he was some strange man who had been surreptitiously introduced by the servants, and my first expression was, I am afraid, not ladylike, for I exclaimed, 'Hulloa!' and walked straight up to him, intending to ask him who he was and what he was doing there. He never moved, and by some unaccountable impulse I *walked straight through him*, into the room. When I turned and looked, he was gone! and I found myself trembling from head to foot. I sat down on the bed to consider what had happened, and at first thought of calling the servants; but on consideration did not do so, as I thought they might laugh at me. I longed to go down for some brandy, but did not dare; and after a while I summoned up courage to creep into my room, which was next door. I then locked the door (contrary to my usual custom) and passed the night undisturbed, sleeping soundly. (*Journal of the S.P.R.*, Vol. III, 1887–8, p. 116)

In one case, which we will be quoting in full on pp. 153–4, a subject reports that he put his hand through an apparition and found that the part of his arm which was 'inside' the apparition was no longer visible, rather as if he had put his arm into some kind of opaque liquid. If we suppose that only the figure of the apparition in this experience was hallucinatory and the rest of the subject's environment was being perceived normally, this implies that in addition to the positive hallucination of the apparition the subject was experiencing a negative visual hallucination concerning part of his arm.

However, the picture is simplified somewhat if we suppose that this was a metachoric experience, in which the subject's whole visual field was hallucinatory, and not just the figure of the apparition.

*

In a few cases the percipient who succeeds in touching an apparition experiences a realistic feeling of solidity and texture. In the following case, for example, the subject, who was lying in bed, reached out and felt the apparition's coat. The sensation seems to have been reasonably realistic, because the subject continued for a little time afterwards to believe that the apparition was really her husband physically present in the room, and did not immediately conclude that she was only seeing an apparition.

We were living in a small house close upon the sea-shore, in a somewhat lonely situation, between Littlehampton and the village of Rustington. My husband and one of our sons, about sixteen, were to take the night boat from Littlehampton and cross to the French coast, returning in a few days. . . . With no cause for special anxiety, I felt a little lonely and depressed at the thought of [my husband's] leaving me, and of our being parted by the sea. I determined to go to bed before they started. . . .

I had slept for some hours when I was suddenly awakened by feeling some one bending over me. I was conscious of lying in the same position in which I had fallen asleep. My room was dark, yet I felt no doubt that it was my husband. I felt a strange thrill and a vague anxiety, but no fear. I did not doubt that it was himself in bodily presence, and yet I remember a strange momentary feeling that he could read my thoughts. I said, 'Oh, Willie, you have come back!' I put out my arms and felt his coat. He answered, 'Yes! I am come back.' I remember that the tone was very solemn and my fears were aroused. I asked, 'Has anything happened?' he replied in the same peculiar low, solemn tone, 'Yes! something has happened.' Then I thought of the boy and asked eagerly, 'Where is Eddy?' There was no answer, and after a moment's pause I felt that I was alone. I raised myself on my arm and endeavoured to penetrate the darkness. I looked towards the door; I was sure there was no one in the room, and equally sure that there had been no sound or stir of one leaving it. Then in an instant came the conviction that it was not in his ordinary bodily presence that he had been there, and at the same time the agonising realisation that it was himself to whom something had happened, although I reflected that he could not have been drowned, because his clothes had not been wet to my touch. I struck a light and went to look at my watch, for which purpose I had to get out of bed; it was five o'clock. (*Census*, pp. 295-6)

(It later transpired that neither the percipient's husband nor her son had been in any danger. However, during the voyage to France, at a moment when he had not been sure of his son's whereabouts on the ship, her husband had had a vivid imagination

of what it would be like if he had to announce to his wife that their
son had been lost overboard.)

In the following two cases the subjects describe shaking hands
with an apparition, and in both cases the percipient seems to have
experienced more or less normal sensations on doing so. Here is
the first case. (The subject, Baron B. von Driesen, was a
Russian.)

I must tell you that my father-in-law, M. N. J. Ponomareff, died
in the country. This did not happen at once, but after a long and
painful illness, whose sharp phases had obliged my wife and myself
to join him long before his death. I had not been on good terms with
M. Ponomareff. Different circumstances which are out of place in
this narrative had estranged us from each other, and these relations
did not change until after his death. He died very quietly, after
having given his blessing to all his family, including myself. A
liturgy for the rest of his soul was to be celebrated on the ninth day.
I remember very well how I went to bed between one and two o'clock
on the eve of that day and how I read the Gospel before falling asleep.
My wife was sleeping in the same room. It was perfectly quiet. I had
just put out the candle when footsteps were heard in the adjacent
room—a sound of slippers shuffling, I might say—which ceased
before the door of our bedroom. I called out, 'Who is there?' No
answer. I struck one match, then another, and when after the
stifling smell of the sulphur the fire had lighted up the room, I saw
M. Ponomareff standing before the closed door. Yes, it was he, in his
blue dressing-gown, lined with squirrel furs and only half-buttoned,
so that I could see his white waistcoat and his black trousers. It was
he undoubtedly. I was not frightened. They say that, as a rule, one
is *not* frightened when seeing a ghost, as ghosts possess the quality
of paralysing fear.

'What do you want?' I asked my father-in-law. M. Ponomareff
made two steps forward, stopped before my bed, and said, 'Basil
Feodorovitch, I have acted wrongly towards you. Forgive me!
Without this I do not feel at rest there.' He was pointing to the
ceiling with his left hand whilst holding out his right to me. I seized
this hand, which was long and cold, shook it and answered, 'Nicholas
Ivanovitch, God is my witness that I have never had anything
against you.'

[The ghost of] my father-in-law bowed [or bent down], moved
away and went through the opposite door into the billiard-room,
where he disappeared. I looked after him for a moment, crossed
myself, put out the candle, and fell asleep with the sense of joy which
a man who has done his duty must feel. (*Census*, p. 385)

In the second hand-shaking case the subject was again a

Russian; the original account is in French, and we have translated it into English.

> It was in Moscow, about 15th April, 1884 . . . Returning from my work at the local court at about 4 o'clock, I had dinner and sat down on a divan to read. It was then about 5 o'clock. It was sunny so the room was perfectly well-lit. From where I sat on the divan, I could see the door of my room. While still reading, I happened to cast a glance towards this door and noticed on it a little circle of light similar to what would be produced by the reflection of a mirror. But my room was on the 3rd floor, and I could see no-one at the windows of the house opposite. I got up and carefully examined these windows. Having resumed my place on the divan, I looked again towards the door. The luminous circle became larger and larger, until it finally embraced the whole door. Then something began to appear in the centre. A human figure formed more and more distinctly, then detached itself from the wall and began to advance slowly towards me. I remained motionless, as if petrified. I recognised in this figure my father, who had died in January 1880. He was in his dress-coat. His moustache was very grey, as in life, but in addition he had a short beard, completely white, which I did not recognise at all. The apparition approached the table which was in front of the divan, walked round it, and sat down next to me on the divan. I was unable to speak as my tongue was paralysed with fright. The apparition offered me his hand, and mechanically I offered him mine; his hand was not icy cold like that of a corpse; it was only cool. He began to speak: his voice was muffled, but it resembled that of my father.
>
> I cannot here quote his words, which related uniquely to myself and were of an intimate character. When he had finished speaking he suddenly disappeared.
>
> I was at that time in perfect health, had never suffered from hallucinations, and I am sure that at that moment I was fully awake, alert, and in command of myself.
>
> . . . The evening after this apparition, I visited my mother with the firm resolve to question her on the subject: I then learnt that my father had been buried in a black dress-coat; that up till his last illness he had never worn a beard, but that during his illness he had grown a small, perfectly white one, and that it was thus that he was buried. (*Census*, pp. 378–9)

*

When a subject does succeed in touching an apparition and experiences a realistic sensation, what is really happening? Does his hand really stop when it reaches the place where the apparition seems to be, or is the subject having a metachoric experience? If his hand really does stop, what causes it to do so; is it some subconscious motor impulse, or a psychokinetic force originating with the percipient but applied as if from outside his body?

Let us consider these questions in relation to the following case. The percipient did not succeed in actually touching the apparition, but she experienced an 'invisible barrier' some distance away from it which seemed to effectively prevent her hand getting to within a certain distance from the apparition.

This strange but fascinating experience happened during a holiday on the Greek island of Poros. My husband and I—much attracted by an old villa—were delighted to find ourselves staying there. Having travelled that day from Athens we retired early and were soon asleep. At about eleven o'clock I found myself wide awake and shivering with cold. It was a warm night with a bright moon, but I seemed to grow colder and colder—with an unexplained feeling of misery and sadness. At the same time I became aware of an elderly lady—quite ordinary looking with a dark complexion and white hair. She appeared to be in great distress and cried in a most heartrending way. I was compelled by some strange force to cry with her and this of course disturbed my husband. He looked quite astonished but was very good and understanding although he himself saw nothing. For the rest of our stay at the Villa P. this person appeared at different times duing the night. Sometimes she sat on my bed, always in great distress and sadness. One night I tried to touch her—to give some sort of comfort, but my hand met with a firm barrier . . .

The barrier seemed to be a kind of force, certainly invisible, and rather like holding one's hand out of a car window against the wind. There was no feeling of someone holding my arm back from behind. After the first time my attempts to touch the apparition were *not* spontaneous. I thought about it carefully and calmly. The distance between the figure and myself would be about one yard—perhaps less. My arms were not outstretched and met with the barrier in a bent position. I remember looking at them and pushing against the barrier.

There are a number of ways in which we might interpret this barrier.

It is possible that the subject's subconscious exercised some kind of control over her muscles so as to prevent her touching the apparition. We might compare this with the way the subconscious may exercise control over a subject's limbs in the hypnotic state. For example, the hypnotist may give a suggestion that the subject's arm will rise from the arm of the chair in which he is sitting, and the subject may find his arm rising into the air although he is not conscious of having tried to raise it. A hypnotist might well be able to reproduce the situation of our apparition subject with a suitably receptive subject. Thus he might tell the subject that there was a solid but invisible barrier two feet from his body in a given direction, and an observer might notice the hypnotised subject being unable to push his hand beyond a certain point in that direction although he was apparently making deliberate efforts to do so.

Another possibility that must be borne in mind is that psychokinesis was at work in this situation. Thus either the subject herself, or conceivably some other person in her environment, might have been using psychokinesis to prevent her arm from approaching the place at which she saw the apparition.

Another possibility is that our apparition subject was not really reaching out her hand at all, although she thought she was. It may have been a metachoric experience, in which she was hallucinating the entire situation: the sight of the apparition, the rest of her visual environment, including her own arm apparently approaching the apparition, the sensation of moving her arm in that direction, and the sensation of meeting with an invisible and irresistible force.

*

It is interesting to compare the situation when a percipient actively touches an apparition with the situation when a subject tries to touch his environment during an out-of-the-body experience.

Certain subjects who have found themselves apparently provided with a duplicate body in an ecsomatic experience have attempted to touch objects in their environment with this body and found themselves unable to do so. For example, one such subject attempted to turn on the light-switch in her bedroom but found that her parasomatic hand went right through the switch. The following is her account:

> I awoke during night while sleeping alone . . . . Suddenly I felt myself drawn gradually out of my body. There was a sound just like that of a sword leaving a metal sheath as I was drawn out through top of head. I stood beside bed, being a little nervous of dark, although room light enough from the moon coming through curtains.
> I travelled across room to far corner (it being a large room) to get to light switch. I travelled at the speed of thought, like lightning, till I

stood beside switch. I pressed switch down but my finger went right through the switch button. Tried this several times. My intelligence seemed sharper and I thought I would make a test. I put my flat hand not once but several times through the box, you know, where the wires are joined to electric switch. It travelled right through the box. Then I suddenly felt filled with the utmost joy and happiness. I felt such great freedom, like a bird just being let out of cage for first time in life, I flew, actually flew, round room, leastways it seemed like I was flying, though I didn't flap my arms . . . I glanced down at my body sleeping in bed. Then seconds later the thought suddenly came to my mind that it was time for me to return to my body. After that I seemed to black out, leastways I knew nothing more till I found I'd returned to my body.

If we assume that both the parasomatic body which this subject found herself occupying and the representation of her own bedroom she was looking at were hallucinatory then there seems no obvious reason why her subconscious might not have represented her hand interacting with the light-switch in the normal way and seeming to turn the bedroom light on.

Perhaps the explanation for both the out-of-the-body subject's hand seeming to go through the light-switch and some apparition subjects' hands going through an apparition may lie in the beliefs which subjects hold about them. In the case of an out-of-the-body experience, the majority of subjects to whom the ecsomatic state occurs spontaneously presumably believe that they are looking at their real, physical environment during the experience, since what they see looks identical with what they would be seeing if they were really in the position they appear to occupy. However they know that the duplicate or parasomatic body which they appear to possess cannot be their real, physical body, because they can see the latter lying on the bed, or wherever it may happen to be. They may thus think there is a fundamental difference in status between their parasomatic body and the rest of the environment they are perceiving.

Similarly, when a subject sees an apparition, the rest of his environment usually seems to remain unchanged, so that he believes he is still looking at this environment in the normal way. At the same time he is very often aware that the apparition cannot be a real physical person. So again, he may believe that there is a fundamental difference in status between the figure of the apparition and the rest of his perceptual environment.

In these circumstances it is perhaps not surprising that when he sees his own arm apparently interacting with an apparition, the interaction does not seem to follow normal physical laws.

Of course the apparitional subject may not be correct in thinking there is a fundamental difference in status between his arm and the apparition as he puts his hand through it. It may be that, at least in certain cases, the experience is metachoric, that is, his whole environment is hallucinatory as he views the apparition, and it is only a hallucinatory arm he sees.

It is interesting to note that when a lucid dreamer touches his perceptual environment in a lucid dream, which certainly is a metachoric experience, he does not find his hand passing through it, like the hand of an apparition subject passing through the body of an apparition. The lucid dreamer is by definition aware that he is dreaming and that both the body he seems to occupy and the rest of his perceptual environment are merely part of his dream. He thus believes their status to be equal, and it is interesting to note that when his dream-body interacts with its environment, it usually does so in realistic ways. For example, in the following case a lucid dreamer grasped the arm of another person during a lucid dream. The sensation she received was apparently quite normal, so much so, in fact, that the dreamer was quite shocked:

> Then I was standing at one end of the same room, again aware that I was dreaming. I spoke to a woman I did not know, and she told me she was a training college lecturer. (I am a teacher.) 'Oh no! You're a figment of my imagination,' I declared, and reached out to grasp her arm. At this I felt the most tremendous sense of shock, which was the most vivid moment of the dream. She was so real, solid, warm and fleshy. I remember thinking that it was exactly like holding a living arm, and yet I knew I was dreaming the contact.

CHAPTER 16

Sensations of Cold

THE subjects of apparitional experiences sometimes report feeling cold at some stage, but they practically never report feeling hot. An exception to this is the case, which we will be quoting on p. 136, in which the percipient first felt hot and then cold.

When there is a feeling of cold this may occur at any stage of the experience, not only during and after the apparitional experience, but sometimes before it. In the following example the subject reports first feeling cold and then opening her eyes and seeing the apparition, as if the cold sensation had alerted her to its presence. The percipient was sitting at home with her fiancé, Bill, after finishing work as a cinema usherette late one evening.

> I remember it was winter, and very cold when Bill and I came home . . . I put the kettle on, and poked at the now dwindling fire. I made two cups of cocoa, and we sat down. We turned the gas jet down and sat in the glow of the fire. We were getting warm and cosy, and I remember closing my eyes. I don't remember how long we sat like this, but suddenly I felt the room go icy cold and a chill came over me. I opened my eyes, and standing by the table was a woman in a long dress something like the Empire Line. It fell from the bust to her shoes. She had a large picture hat perched flat on her head. I clutched Bill's arm. He looked at me, saw I was staring toward the table. He then jumped up to turn the gas up. But as he did this, she raised her arm and pointed downwards as if trying to tell us something. Then she vanished, leaving in a swirly grey mist. I saw her very sad face. I'll never forget it. I was pretty shook up, and neither of us could speak for quite a while.

Sometimes the sensation of cold is felt when the percipient wakes in the middle of the night to see an apparition. In such cases the subject may wake up already feeling cold, before he starts to see the apparition, and he may assert that it was the cold that woke him.

The following is a case of this kind.

> I awoke in the early hours of the morning (a rare thing for me as I slept and still do sleep very heavily) feeling cold and shivery but the room I remember was warm. I turned over onto my left side to snuggle up to my husband and as I did I saw the figure of a man standing by his side of the bed looking down at my husband.
>
> He stood with his arms folded rocking backwards and forwards and was smiling.
>
> He was about 50–60 years of age and had a distinctly foreign appearance. Fat swarthy face, a large black moustache, crinkly dark hair and dark eyes but a kindly face. The clothes he was wearing were fairly modern. He was wearing a black dinner jacket and trousers, a white ruffled shirt and black bow tie.
>
> I distinctly remember seeing the wardrobe behind this chap (who was very solid looking) in the few seconds I was brave enough to keep my eyes open, though it seemed like an age at the time. I thought of waking my husband in case it was a burglar but I seemed to know it wasn't and so changed my mind, turned over away from it and tried to go back to sleep, which I did after the peculiar cold, shivery feeling had gone, but couldn't pluck up enough courage to turn back and see if he had gone.
>
> In the morning I told my husband what had happened and he laughed and said that I had dreamt it, but I was so firm in my belief that eventually I convinced him that what I had seen was there and I was very wide awake.

Percipients may describe either the environment or themselves as having been cold. Those who attribute it to the environment say, for example: 'I became aware of the sudden coldness of the room', or 'the kitchen went stone cold'. Some associate the cold with a wind or breeze, saying, for example: 'We . . . were hit by a very cold draught of air sweeping down the stairs', or 'An icy wave swept through the room and bedclothes.'

The sensation of cold does not seem to be connected in any very direct or obvious way with the emotions the subject is feeling at the time. In particular, it does not seem to be merely a side-effect of the subject feeling very frightened. Certainly some 'cold' subjects do report feeling afraid at some stage in their experience, but others do not seem to be particularly frightened. In the following case, for example, the subject seems to have had a rather detached and experimental attitude to the apparition, as he reports putting out his hand to her in the hope that she would come nearer. He was spending his first night in a hotel at the time.

I went to my bedroom and got into bed. I was just about to lie down when I heard a rustling sound. I thought it may be the cat which the owners had, getting into my bedroom. I am a cat lover and I called 'Puss Puss' a few times but couldn't see anything so I lay down. Directly on doing this I heard the local church clock strike 11.00 p.m. The strokes had hardly died away when the window was shaken as by a high wind, and I thought this could be the result of a sudden wind rising in a hilly country. Hardly having come to this conclusion when I became aware of a blue 'steam' which moved about itself and suddenly an apparition appeared. This was a girl. I would think about the age of 18 years. She wore what I take to be a gingham gown with a blue sash worn just below the bust. She was a beautiful looking girl and kept nodding her head and smiling at me. I did not recognise her, but I put out my hand to her hoping she would come nearer. I was sitting up in the bed and I then became aware of the sudden coldness of the room.

I thought to myself, 'Speak to her'—which I did, and she disappeared, becoming enveloped in the blue 'steam'.

Occasionally the sensations of cold are localised, and seem to affect only a particular part of the body, as in the following 'sense of presence' case in which the subject feels cold on the nape of her neck and head:

I took my son age just 11 yrs and daughter 6 yrs to Blackpool for a week and stayed in a boarding house where we had stayed two years previously.

. . . Friday night we went to bed fairly late and I was a long while getting off to sleep but was quite cosy. All at once I knew something had entered the room, and not through door or window, it just came and I knew exactly where it stood! in front of the wardrobe. I was rather frightened although I knew we couldn't be hurt I hoped nothing would frighten the boy although he slept. The thing paused a second or two and then slowly came down the room and stood by my head. I dare not open my eyes but just waited. Then the nape of my neck went icy cold, and up the back and over the top to my forehead as though a finger was drawn over and my hair stood on end, I could actually feel my hair rising as the icy cold passed over my head, a short pause and then it was repeated, another pause, repeated again and then I knew it had gone and the room was clear. I was now wide awake and about half an hour later exactly the same thing happened again. I was very glad we were going home the next day . . .

Not much is yet known about what causes the feeling of cold in apparitional cases, and it is of course possible that the feeling is not caused in the same way in all cases. However, we shall summarise the possible explanations.

In the first place, the environment may really get colder. This explanation might seem particularly likely in cases in which the subject refers to 'an icy wind' or something of the kind.

However, even in cases like this there are sometimes indications that the cold is not objective. For example, on one occasion three sisters and two maids were all standing at the doors of their bedrooms while footsteps were heard walking up and down the landing between them. As the footsteps passed they felt a sensation which they described as 'a cold wind'. However, the flames of the candles they were holding were not blown about, which seems to indicate that there was no real current of air which might have explained their sensations. (*Proceedings of the S.P.R.*, Vol. VIII, 1892, p. 320)

Sometimes, again, it appears that the coldness cannot be external to the subject, as it is not collective—that is to say, it is experienced by some, but not all of those present.

In other cases the subjects do not describe the coldness as originating in their environment, but explicitly comment on the fact that their environment was warm, despite their own feeling of cold. For example, the lady who was on holiday in Greece at the time of her experience writes that she 'seemed to grow colder and colder' before seeing an apparition, although it was a warm night (p. 110). Again, in the case quoted earlier in this chapter (p. 115) the percipient says, 'I awoke feeling cold and shivery but the room I remember was warm.'

When the subject's environment does not actually alter in temperature, we have to account for his sensation of cold by supposing that it is either hallucinatory or the result of his own physiological reactions.

It is not certain whether a physiological reaction could be rapid enough to account for the very intense and apparently quite sudden feelings of cold that are reported by some subjects. However, some observations do indirectly support the idea that a physiological reaction is involved. For example, in a number of cases, percipients report that someone commented on their facial pallor after their experience. Another indication is that certain subjects report fainting as a result of seeing an apparition, and of course fainting may be due to a sudden reduction in the flow of blood to the head.

CHAPTER 17

The Sense of Presence

SOMETIMES the subject feels someone is present, even though he cannot perceive anyone by any of the recognised senses. This type of experience was well known to William James at the turn of the century, who describes it thus: 'From the way in which this experience is spoken of by those who have had it, it would appear to be an extremely definite and positive state of mind, coupled with a belief in the reality of its object quite as strong as any direct sensation ever gives. And yet *no* sensation seems to be connected with it at all . . . The phenomenon would seem to be due to a pure *conception* becoming saturated with the sort of stinging urgency which ordinarily only sensations bring.' (*Principles of Psychology*, Vol. II, pp. 322–3 *n.*)

The following is an example of this type of experience:

> My husband died in June 1945, and 26 years afterwards when I was at Church, I felt him standing beside me during the singing of a hymn. I felt I would see him if I turned my head. The feeling was so strong I was reduced to tears. I had not been thinking of him before I felt his presence. I had not had this feeling before that day, neither has it happened since then.

This 'sense of presence' is reported in 8 per cent of the cases in our collection, either on its own or accompanied by a hallucination of one or more of the senses.

*

As with other sorts of apparitions, the majority of the sense of presence cases reported to us occurred indoors. However, it appears that the experience may occur out of doors as well. Our subjects included two people who referred to experiences of the sense of presence which they had had while mountaineering, and many similar cases are reported in books by mountaineers and by others who have survived dangerous situations in the open air. A celebrated published case is that described by the polar explorer Shackleton in his book *South* (p. 209); he claims that not only he but also his companions experienced an 'extra man' in the party when they were making their dangerous crossing of the mountains of Southern Georgia. The climber Frank Smythe, in his book *The Adventures of a Mountaineer* (p. 208), describes how, when alone on Everest, he offered a piece of food to an unseen 'companion' before realising the inappropriateness of his action.

One of our own mountain-climbing subjects reports behaving in a similar manner. He says that the feeling of presence is 'quite distinct so that you act as though there was someone there . . .'

*

It appears that experiences of a sense of presence, like other kinds of apparitions, may be experienced by more than one person at the same time. The following case is an example of this. However, other cases are reported in which, although one person had an intense sense of another person present, this was not noticed by anyone else who was there at the time.

> About nine years ago my wife and I went to view a house we thought of buying. We had no previous knowledge of the house, or indeed of the district, but just happened to see an advertisement and on impulse went to view.
>
> All the time I was in that house I had the most uncanny feeling that a third person was following us round and once or twice it was so strong that I actually turned to see whether the neighbour, who had given us the key, had come to see how we were getting along. On our way home my wife broached the subject though I had not mentioned it to her, of feeling that there was someone else there. Naturally, we didn't buy the house.

*

The sense of presence may, in some cases, precede or follow a sensory hallucination of some kind. Even when it occurs entirely on its own, with no hallucinatory accompaniment at all, the sense of presence sometimes seems to include quite specific impressions of the psychological, and even physical characteristics of the 'person' who is felt to be present. The presence is often described as located in a specific position, as in the following case, in which it is said to have been two feet above the floor.

On a day when I was free from care and occupied in my sitting-room reading a difficult scientific book, my mother (who had died 34 years before) came into the room. She had never done this before. I did not see or hear her, but suddenly knew—with a sense of shock—that she was there, in person, in front of the fireplace. I am not able to communicate verbally with unseen people, so could not ask her why she was there. By the time I had pulled myself together, she had gone. It only struck me afterwards as strange that she seemed to be about two feet off the ground!

In addition to the presence being associated with a specific position the subject sometimes reports being aware of it moving, as in the following example:

I suddenly developed violent asthmatic attacks in 1957 which got worse and worse as each year went by. My local Doctor could do nothing beyond injections so as I was beginning to feel I could no longer carry on with my school work, I made one last desperate appeal to Brompton Hospital. After a year's specialist treatment for allergies etc. I was told it was psychosomatic, but I could still receive treatment and pills to allay attacks.

One day in 1963 I was having a particularly bad attack when the vicar called to borrow my tape-recorder. Whilst he was trying to take my mind off the stressed condition I was in (by telling me some of his funny stories!) I was suddenly aware that someone else was in the room. I felt an enormous force coming towards me with all the serenity of the whole world in its presence. (The Vicar was still in the middle of his funny joke.) This force stood beside me, I felt if I put my hand out I would be able to *touch* it—it was so strong. The peace and serenity pervaded my whole body and away went the Asthma, as though I had had an injection. That was four years ago and I have *never* been bothered with Asthma ever again. The hospital specialist asked *me* to explain to him how I had got better, but I thought he'd think me completely mad if I told him about this. (The Vicar had looked very dubiously at me when I asked if he had been aware of anything in the room!)

The following case again illustrates the specific characteristics which 'presences' may seem to have. The subject felt she knew what the person present was wearing, although she was not actually looking in its direction.

In the year 1867 I was travelling to Switzerland with my husband, and we stopped at the Château de Prangins, near Nyon, which is now a collegiate school for boys.

Our bedroom was a large, oblong room, overlooking the Terrace and Lake Leman, with an old-fashioned black writing-table in the middle of it. There was nothing unusual about the room or the circumstances, and I went to bed and slept soundly. But in the middle of the night I suddenly awoke in a state of terror, not, apparently, from a dream, for I had no impression of having been dreaming, but with a sort of certainty that a tall, thin, old man, in a long flowered dressing-gown, was seated and writing at the table in the middle of the room. I cannot say what gave me this certainty, or this distinct picture, for I did not once turn my eyes to the place where I felt that the intruder was seated. It did not, in fact, occur to me at the time how odd it was that I thus knew of his appearance without seeing him. The room was flooded with brilliant moonlight; but I did not venture to turn my head. My cries awoke my husband, who naturally thought that I had had a nightmare, and could not understand my persistent assertion that an old man in a flowered dressing-gown was in the room. At last he persuaded me to look at the table where I had felt that the old man was sitting; and there was no one there.

Next morning my husband mentioned my extraordinary nocturnal terror; the account, to our great surprise, was received as a matter of course, the landlord's married daughter merely remarking, 'Ah, you have seen Voltaire.' It appeared on inquiry that Voltaire, in extreme old age, used often to visit this Château, then the property, I believe, of Lucien Bonaparte, and the room in which we slept was known to have been his sitting-room. Of this neither my husband nor myself knew anything. I had not been thinking about Voltaire, nor looking at any portrait of him, nor did it once occur to me that the figure could be his until I heard that morning from the landlord that the same figure was reported to have been seen in the same room, and that it was supposed to be Voltaire's.

I have never had any other hallucination of any kind. (*Proceedings of the S.P.R.*, Vol. VI, 1889–90, pp. 53–4)

The following are two cases in which the percipient felt the presence was behind him. (The percipient in the first case is a lady.)

I had a great friend who died. He was a convinced Christian and once I said to him that if he died first he'd have to come back and tell me if there was in reality an after life. I had a cat I was devoted to and had had for over 18 years. He had to be put to sleep and I was very upset and had no thought in my mind of X who had died over four years before. As the vet was in the act of giving the cat the injection I was so vividly aware that X was just behind me that I turned to look at him, all thought of the cat driven out of my mind by intense surprise. Of course there was nothing there.

Another time my wife and I were at a concert at the Royal Albert Hall and there were vacant seats to my left and immediately behind me. There were vacant seats throughout the concert. I could feel the presence of another person who seemed to be leaning from behind and enjoying the concert, yet each time I turned round to face him he disappeared.

In addition to cases in which the subject feels the presence to be behind him, there are several in which he could not or would not look at the place where he perceived the presence to be. For example, in two of our cases the presence was outside the door of the room in which the percipient was. It is relatively uncommon for the subject to feel that the presence is located in a place where he should be able to see it if it were a normal person.

This tendency to avoid too direct a conflict with the normal state of affairs is similar to that which we have already observed in purely auditory cases, in which the source of the sound also often seems to be in a position where the subject could not see a real person responsible for producing it, if there were one.

As well as occurring on its own, with no sensory accompaniments, the sense of presence may either precede or follow sensory hallucinations. One relatively common type of experience seems to be for the percipient to have a sense of presence first and then to see an apparition. The sense of presence appears to alert him to the existence of a visual apparition in his environment, as it were. For example, the subject may get a feeling of a presence and then deliberately look around for someone to account for it, or he may wake with the feeling that someone is in the room and then see the person.

The following is a case of this type:

> Last summer, whilst walking up the stairs of an old house in St. Thomas' Street, Newcastle upon Tyne, where I worked as a research secretary, I was suddenly aware of, firstly, an acute feeling of a presence near me; I looked behind me and then ahead up to another flight of stairs leading up to the attics; striding up this further flight, climbing at about three stairs at a time was a very tall man, wearing light-grey herringbone tweed clothing (he wore a cape in the same material), and a high grey hat. His face was extremely refined looking, thin, and his nose very sharp and pointed. He carried a black walking stick with a silver knob. I could not believe my eyes and stood at the bottom of the upper flight of stairs watching him striding up, as if in a great rush to get to his destination, and then he just simply disappeared. I later summoned my courage to go up to the attics and look around but there was absolutely no one about. The gentleman was so 'real' to me—the herringbone pattern of his clothing was so distinct and the purposeful way in which he strided up the stairs impressed me.

CHAPTER 18

The Occurrence of Apparitions

T HE majority of apparitional experiences (some 61 per cent of all our own cases) seem to occur in or near the subject's home. By 'near' we mean, for example, on the porch, in the garden or a short walk from the house.

Relatively few seem to occur while the percipient is at his or her regular place of work (only 4 per cent in our collection).

Another characteristic of apparitional experiences, at least as reported to us, is that most of them occur in familiar surroundings. For example, as well as at home or at work, they may occur at the home of relatives or friends, outdoors in some familiar place, in church, etc. Only 12 per cent of our cases occurred in some place which the percipient had never visited before. In the great majority (83 per cent) of cases reported to us, the subject was indoors rather than outdoors.

Visual apparitions are usually seen quite close to the percipient. The following table gives subjects' estimates of how far away from them the apparition was. In cases where the apparition moved, the table gives the nearest point of approach.

Estimated Distance of Percipient from Apparition	% of Cases
3 feet or less	41
3–6 feet	27
6–12 feet	16
12–30 feet	10
More than 10 yards	6

We asked all our subjects about their health at the time of their experience—whether it was better or worse than usual, or the same as usual. The majority (91 per cent) said it was the same as usual. Only 6 per cent said it was worse than usual, and 3 per cent said it was better than usual.

CHAPTER 19

The Posture and Muscle-Tone of the Subject

WE asked all our subjects to say what their physical posture was when they started to perceive the apparition. The results were as follows:

	% of cases
Lying down	38
Sitting	23
Standing still	19
Walking	18
Riding	1
Other	1

'Riding' includes such activities as riding a motor bicycle and riding a mule.

At first sight it might appear that lying down is the most favourable position for perceiving an apparition.

However, one possible interpretation of the data might be the following. The average person sleeps for about eight hours each night. He must therefore spend about a third of his life lying down. Let us suppose that the subconscious of the subject is responsible for timing the occurrence of the apparition, and that it is indifferent to what physical position he is in at the time of the occurrence and to whether he is awake or asleep. Then we might expect about a third of all cases, or $33\frac{1}{3}$ per cent, to occur when the subjects are lying down, on the purely statistical ground that the subject spends a third of his time in this position. In fact, we find that 38 per cent of our subjects report that they were lying down at the time of their experience.

On the whole it does not seem possible to conclude from our

data that any particular position or class of positions favours or inhibits the occurrence of apparitional experiences.

In our investigation of out-of-the-body experiences we found that approximately 70 per cent of the experiences reported to us were said to have occurred when the subject was lying down, which is approximately twice the comparable number for apparitional experiences. It therefore seems that physical posture may play a greater role in the occurrence of ecsomatic experiences than apparitional ones.

*

We also asked our apparition subjects whether they were more relaxed or more tense than usual at any stage in their experience, or whether they were just the same as usual throughout. About half (53 per cent) considered that they had been the same as usual throughout. Among those who thought they had noticed some change, there were nearly four times as many who thought they had noticed an increase in muscular tension as had noticed an increase in relaxation. However, many of the 'tense' subjects clearly regarded their muscular tension as a reaction to seeing the apparition rather than a condition that was present before the experience began. For example, one subject said he was 'rigidly tense through fear', another that he 'tensed for a moment then fled'.

On the whole the data do not seem to warrant a conclusion that either increased muscular tension or a state of muscular relaxation facilitate the occurrence of apparitional experiences.

In this respect experiences of seeing apparitions again seem to differ from experiences of seeming to leave one's body. In our study of out-of-the-body experiences we found some indication that subjects tended to consider the ecsomatic state was characterised by muscular relaxation more often than muscular tension. This may be because decreased muscle tone actually facilitates the occurrence of out-of-the-body experiences, or it may simply be that the ecsomatic state tends to be characterised by a decrease in muscle tone once it has been initiated.

We also found that among those subjects who were able to initiate the ecsomatic state more or less at will deliberate relaxation was a method sometimes employed to help bring about the state. A number of subjects also reported that their ecsomatic experience had come about as an unexpected by-product of their carrying out relaxation exercises, with or without some accompanying meditation practice. There is no parallel to this phenomenon in the case of apparitions. Subjects do not report methods for increasing the likelihood of these experiences, by means of relaxation or anything else.

CHAPTER 20

Paralysis and Aphasia

A SMALL proportion of apparition subjects (under 3 per cent in our collection) report feeling paralysed at some stage in their experience.

The following two cases will illustrate this feature. In the first the narrator is a schoolboy, who was away at boarding-school at the time of the experience.

> On Sunday night, March 20th, 1898, I had gone to bed as usual (about 9.30 or 10). I could not sleep and began thinking of home and especially of mother. My bed was so placed that I could see the staircase, and, after a bit, to my surprise, I heard someone coming up the stairs. It flashed into my mind that it was mother, and so it proved to be. She was dressed in a black dress that I had never seen before, and had on her pink shawl and gold chain, and as she came into the room her shoes creaked; in fact, they did so all the time. I did not feel at all frightened but tried to get out of bed to go to her, but something held me back. She went to the bed before mine, where my chum sleeps, and bent over him and looked at him. Then she came to me and kissed me; I tried to kiss her but could not. Then she disappeared and seemed to vanish in a mist; the face was the last thing I saw. I am quite sure that I was awake, and saw every object in the room when she was there. (*Journal of the S.P.R.*, Vol. VIII, 1897–8, p. 329)

> My wife and I were in bed; my eyes suddenly became aware of someone moving about the bedroom. I saw a person walking around the bedroom as though it was looking for something. I tried to shout and to jump out of bed, but no noise came from my voice and no response came from my legs or body. My eyes were still watching this person when suddenly it turned face towards me and I realized that I was face to face with my own double. It then walked towards me and climbed on to my physical body and quickly wormed itself into me.
>
> I immediately became aware that my voice and my body were again

active; I leaped out of bed, put on the electric light and had a good look around the room. I even examined my body expecting some minor puncture where my spiritual body had re-entered, but everything was normal.

My wife awoke and asked me what was I supposed to be messing about at, this time of night.

*

Paralysis may be reported at various stages in an experience of seeing an apparition—before, during or after. Usually the paralysis is noticed while the subject is perceiving the apparition. As an example of paralysis occurring before the apparitional experience, we may consider the case of the subject who reports that she found herself unable to move her arms and legs or shut her eyes, and then 'a little while later' heard a voice which seemed to come from the cupboard in her bedroom (p. 132). Another subject reports being unable to move only *after* pulling her sheet over herself and blotting out the sight of the apparition. Her account is as follows:

My experience took place in a bright sunny bedroom in (New York's) 90° heat . . .

I had just completed a sixteen hour shift, on-duty in a maternity unit. On returning to my apartment building, I was met by the superintendent who warned me that my apartment was to be included in a plumbing inspector's visit that a.m.

Utterly exhausted and desperate for sleep as I was due back on-duty at the hospital at 3:30 p.m., I advised the janitor not to call and disturb me till as late as possible.

Fearing that the water might be turned off, I had a shower and collapsed into bed. I willed myself to sleep and believe I dozed off. I woke, aware of a presence. On looking up, I saw a man bending over the bed.

I instinctively, ostrich like, closed my eyes and tugged the sheet over me. Inwardly furious at the man's impertinence (I assumed him to be the plumbing inspector) I thought him extremely objectionable as all apartments were similar and he couldn't mistake the bedroom for the bathroom.

Then, reason asserted itself. I kept the chain on the door and previously when someone had unlocked it, the crash of the chain had wakened me. I could never sleep through that. The janitor might have let the man in to save disturbing me, but his pass key wouldn't have solved the chain problem.

I recalled the man's appearance so vividly. He had snowy white hair, ruddy cheeks and wore a rough Harris tweed jacket. I didn't recognise him as I'd closed my eyes so quickly. I reasoned that I must have had a hallucination and tried to open my eyes. I soon discovered that I was unable to do so and my limbs and body felt leaden and I couldn't move. This unfamiliar sensation suddenly lifted. No one was there. I rose and checked that the chain was still in place.

In the following case it seems that the percipient was not paralysed in the early stages of the experience, as she describes moving her hand to stroke the apparition's forehead. Only when she realised that it was an apparition did she find herself temporarily unable to move. The percipient was fifteen at the time of her experience, and twenty-three at the time of writing to us. The apparition represented her grandmother who had died a few months previously.

> Then a few months later while my sister and I were in bed, a warm hand held mine. I thought it was my sister, but then I realised she was asleep the other side of me. I stroked the person's forehead who was lying next to me and I realised that it was my nan, then I noticed there was only half of her body, from her head to her waist. I suddenly panicked. I tried to move but my muscles wouldn't work, I tried to scream but no sound came. Eventually I pulled my hand free, although my nan seemed reluctant to let go. Then when I looked again she had gone. I decided not to wake my sister and tell her. The next morning my sister woke me up saying that my nan had been lying next to me. I was so tired after being awake half the night, I just said 'I know' and went back to sleep.

The percipient estimates that her experience occurred between midnight and two a.m. after she had been asleep for not more than an hour and a half and had just woken up. It is interesting to note that her sister seems to have had a somewhat similar experience on waking early the next morning. Her sister remembers the incident as follows:

> I am the sister of Mrs. ——, when at the time of the apparition I was asleep by her side, for at this time we slept together in a double bed. I was 11 years old at the time and was unaware of my sister's experience that night. However for some reason I awoke very early that same morning approximately between the hours of 6–6.30 a.m. I woke normally in a relaxed frame of mind and body, then I looked at my sister's face from side view, that is her profile as she lay on her back. I suddenly noticed how alike her nose was to our grandmother's and for some reason elevated myself up on my elbow to look at her face full on. To my absolute shock I realised it was not my sister's nose but that of my grandmother's which I had not realised or even expected. She appeared to be asleep or rather at rest herself,

her eyes being closed, she was lying on her back looking fresh and firm and in no way transparent, although her form appeared only to extend to her waist. As there was no impression of legs or feet beneath the blanket as there normally would be.

I remained motionless for a minute in a state of shock, I dare not speak or wake my sister for fear my grandmother would move or look at me. I cannot give an account of anything after this, whether she vanished or moved, for I slowly retreated beneath the blankets in fear. I must have gradually fallen asleep for when I awoke later she was gone and everything was as normal. I mentioned this to my sister that day unaware that she had already experienced this apparition, to which she replied she knew and had physical contact with her, which before I had mentioned this she was also unaware that I had experienced the same apparition.

Usually, when paralysis occurs, it lasts until the apparitional experience is over. However, in the following case the paralysis is described as passing off while the apparition was still there. The subject, a barrister, was staying overnight in a hotel when he woke up and thought he saw a fellow barrister in his bedroom. He reports that he was at first unable to move, but that after a few seconds the paralysis ended and he was able to spring out of bed and make two attempts to grasp the apparition with his hands before it disappeared. The following is his account:

In October, 1885, I was stopping for the night at the Swan Hotel at B., on circuit. My bedroom was No. 17. My friend K., a brother barrister, occupied No. 16. Between No. 17 (my room) and No. 18 there was a communicating door, and before retiring to rest I was under the impression that the door was between my room and my friend K.'s. I had told my friend K. so, when bidding him good-night, and he had jokingly remarked that he would come in and frighten me during the night. I discovered before going to bed that our rooms did *not* communicate. I must have been asleep some hours, when I woke up with a sensation that someone was close to my bed, and feeling about the other side of the chintz curtain at the head of the bed. I could hear the rustling and crackling of the curtain close to my face. I felt perfectly unable to move, or protect myself—not through any fear, but from a want of power of movement. After a few seconds this powerlessness went off, and I sprang out of bed, and saw the figure of my friend K. retreating towards the foot of the bed. He kept his face averted, his head bent a little, but I could see the wire and one of the glasses of his spectacles as he turned from me; he was dressed in his night-shirt. And what made me believe in the reality of the appearance was the 'solidity' of the white nightdress, and the light on the spectacles. The room was in dim light, owing to gas-lamps in street, and a fanlight over door admitting light from gas in passage. I grasped at my friend with both hands and supposed I had missed him as my hands met in the grasp. I attempted again to grasp him, when he disappeared as if through the floor under the washing-stand. I then realised, with some interest, that it was a hallucination, and I sat on the bed, wide awake, interested in thinking it over. I told K. of it next morning. (Gurney I, p. 513)

*

The majority of subjects who report paralysis are lying down, having just woken up, when they perceive the apparition, although there are exceptions to this. The following case is typical in that the subject was lying in bed when the paralysis occurred. In this case the subject had a 'sense of presence' of a tall dark figure but without actually seeing anything.

I was lying in bed one evening, gradually dropping off to sleep when I became aware of my bed moving—as if somebody was pushing the mattress up and down. Almost simultaneously, I felt there was a tall, dark figure standing in the doorway. I was unable to move, my muscles went completely rigid and I broke out in a cold sweat. As I was unable to turn, I could not confirm there was anything there but I would swear there was. There were no previous footsteps, no sound of breathing, no other noise at all except for passing traffic, and no member of my family came into my bedroom at that time.

*

There are a number of cases in our collection in which the subject associates his failure to move while perceiving an apparition with the emotions he experienced on perceiving it. The following case is one of these, in which the subject describes herself as 'too scared to move'. It seems probable that these cases are distinct from the type in which the subject is really paralysed, and that in cases such as the following he does not move because he feels disinclined to do so.

I am thirty three years of age and have never seen a ghost in my life. That is until a few months ago when I saw this apparition.

My husband was working nights. I was alone in bed and fast asleep. I woke up suddenly and looked towards the half open door. There was a child standing there. For a second I thought it was my little boy. I was just about to say, 'What are you doing out of bed,' when I realised it was no normal child. The only way I can describe it is by saying it was sort of transparent.

One hand was on the door and the face was turned towards me.

The hand was the clearest part. I could see the fingers plainly. I was too scared to move and as I watched it began to disappear, slowly from the outline towards the centre and was gone. It just seemed to fade away. I had the impression it was a little girl, though I don't know why.

I can assure you I was wide awake.

*

We have suggested at various points in this book that there may be a relationship between experiences of perceiving apparitions and out-of-the-body experiences, and also between some apparitional experiences and false awakenings. It is therefore interesting to note that paralysis is sometimes reported by the subjects of both out-of-the-body experiences and false awakenings. For example, in the following case the subject reports feeling paralysed, then hearing a voice apparently coming from a cupboard in her room, and seeming to leave her body and look at it lying on the bed.

> The second occurrence was at home. I was tired and went to bed late after my mother, my father being out on call. About half an hour after I was in bed, I found myself unable to move my legs, arms or shut my eyes (I was lying on my back). I started sweating and got very frightened. A little while later I heard a voice, like that of an old man reciting verses as in the Bible. I cannot remember what he said. I thought this noise was coming from a cupboard in my room and thought I would investigate, but I could not move anything. Within a very short time I had a strange feeling of leaving my feet, legs, body, etc., and being completely in my head. I could not feel my body. Then I literally squeezed upwards and found myself floating away with a light (blue white) joining me to my body which I could see lying on the bed. As soon as I realised my body was 'over there' I heard a door slam, just like our front door, and found myself in my bed shivering and lying in a pool of cold sweat, absolutely terrified. I got up and dashed downstairs thinking my father had returned. There was no one there and the front door was open. I had seen my mother shut it and check it before she went to bed, it was definitely shut properly then. I then went upstairs and looked in my mother's room, she was there sleeping.

*

Sometimes subjects who report paralysis also report that they were unable to speak or cry out while perceiving an apparition. An example is the case quoted at the beginning of this chapter, in which the subject reports seeing an apparition of himself in his bedroom. He says that he tried to shout out but that no sound resulted. The following case provides another example:

> The other thing is not so pleasant and I do have a dread of it. This happens in my bedroom. It started six years ago. One night I suddenly woke up. It was about 2 a.m., the room was very dark and there was a feeling of a horrible closeness so that I could hardly breathe. In the middle of the room there was a head, perfectly still. It was the most foul thing I have ever seen. It was looking at me and grinning. I was suddenly freezing cold. It was a round head with either black smooth hair or a beret on its head. It had small black eyes and a flat nose, and was creased and wrinkled. The colour was brown, the kind of brown sea-men go, like a nut colour, and shiny. It was an evil face.
>
> Since then I have seen it twice more, always the same way, I wake up, and there it is. After perhaps a minute it gets smoky all around it and it slowly goes into the smoke and then everything is clear again. I find this experience really shattering and I'm always worried in case it comes. Twice I've woken my husband to tell him, but I can't move or speak until it has gone, so although he doesn't say he doesn't believe me, he is very sceptical about the whole thing.

Only a minority of the subjects who report paralysis also mention that they were unable to speak. However, it is possible that some or all of the others did not try to speak, but would have found themselves unable to do so had they tried.

It seems that aphasia, or the inability to speak, may also occur on its own, without the subject being otherwise paralysed. For example, in the following case the subject says that she was 'struck dumb' and could not speak to the apparition as she wished; but she nevertheless seems to have retained the power of movement, since she describes sitting up with a start on seeing it:

> I had shut up all doors one afternoon and went with my dog Sally to sit in my lounge. I fell into a long doze and woke to see an elderly man dressed in a brown lounge-suit, with a brown trilby hat on his head, seated two yards away from me on the settee (I was in an armchair). The man looked about 80 yrs and very ill with a deep groove down his cheek, and sat looking at his hands. I sat up so suddenly Sally got up and went to the other side of the room. I wanted to ask the man 'Who are you and what are you doing here?' but I was struck dumb and could not speak. The spirit slowly sank through the floor, still with the brown trilby hat on his head, and disappeared through my blue carpet. I did not recognise him until about 5 minutes later— it was Mr. Crick![1] The brown suit and hat brought recognition to me too late.

[1] A former acquaintance of the subject's.

It is interesting to note that subjects who experience aphasia, like those who experience paralysis, sometimes state explicitly that they were not afraid during the experience, so what is in question is not merely a disinclination to speak arising from fear. The following case illustrates this point:

> During the month of August, 1908, whilst I was on a visit to my parents at Villa Finisterre, I saw what I believe to have been an apparition. Owing to the house being full, I shared a large bedroom with one of my brothers, which was in the top storey.
>
> One night I awoke suddenly, and, looking across the room, I saw the cloaked figure of a man bending over my brother's bed. I thought at first this might be a dream, and kept opening and shutting my eyes to make sure. My brother's bed was situated between the cross lights of two windows, and this enabled me to make out the outline of a figure fairly clearly. The time was between 2 and 3 a.m. I tried to call out to my brother, but was quite unable to do so. I did not feel in any way nervous, but merely curiously excited. My brother suddenly awoke, and said 'Who's that?' I tried to answer, but could not do so for at least ten seconds, and then I asked him what was the matter. Before my brother spoke the figure had quite disappeared. On discussing it with him, he said he thought he had been hit by some one on his side. We searched all round the room and found no sign of any one or anything. My brother did not see the figure.
>
> This is the only experience of the sort I have had at Villa Finisterre or elsewhere. (*Journal of the S.P.R.*, Vol. XIV, 1909–10, p. 380)

It is also interesting to note that aphasia is sometimes reported by the subjects of out-of-the-body experiences. For example, they may become alarmed while apparently viewing their body from outside and try to call out to someone in their vicinity to attract their attention, but find themselves unable to do so. The following account will illustrate this feature:

> The first occasion was ten years ago, on the 30th September, when I was 22 years old, and my first son was only one day old.
>
> I was sitting up in bed, holding my baby when suddenly I felt part of myself rise from the bed and float upwards, from where I could look down and see myself sitting with the baby in my arms. This was a terrifying experience, and I can clearly remember trying to call to my mother (who was downstairs) which I was unable to do, then desperately trying to return to my body. How long I was like this, I am unable to say, but when I did return, my whole body was shaken . . .

CHAPTER 21

The Initiation and Termination of Apparitional Experiences

IN this chapter we shall discuss how apparitional experiences begin and end.

Let us first consider the subject's state of mind at the start of the experience. When we asked our subjects whether they had any idea that they might perceive an apparition before they did, or whether it occurred without warning, 97 per cent said that it occurred completely unexpectedly. As we have already observed, apparitional experiences seem to occur most frequently in familiar, everyday surroundings, and only very rarely in unusual surroundings which might be thought likely to suggest thoughts of the supernatural.

When asked what emotions they were experiencing just before perceiving the apparition, hardly any subjects had anything definite to say. If there are states of mind which are more favourable than others as precursors of apparitional experiences, they seem to fall within the range of states which are commonly experienced in normal life.

Although some subjects have a number of apparitional experiences in the course of their life this does not seem to be something that people learn to induce, more or less at will, in the way that certain individuals train themselves to have frequent out-of-the-body experiences or lucid dreams.

When asked if they had noticed any kind of discontinuity in their experience at the beginning or end of their perception of the apparition, 92 per cent of our subjects replied that there was none. This does not rule out the possibility that some or even all of the experiences were metachoric, as we know that subjects can enter an out-of-the-body experience without any perceptible discontinuity.

Now let us consider how visual apparitions first present themselves. It seems to be more common for them to enter the subject's field of view as a complete figure rather than building up, solidifying or unfolding themselves before the subject's eyes.

The following case illustrates the gradual formation of an apparition while the subject watches. In this case the face of the percipient's late son seems to have 'unfolded' itself gradually like a piece of dress material:

> During the night, either in the late part of Nov., or early part Dec. 1917, I came over very hot indeed and turned down the eiderdown, etc. Some few moments later I became *extraordinarily* cold with a most unnatural coldness . . . I *doubled* the eiderdown over myself and tried to sleep and the feeling left me slightly, but came back again stronger than ever and far more intense. While I wondered what I could do a yellow-blue ray came right across the room and I at once blamed the housemaid (to myself) for not drawing the 'Raid' curtains together, thinking it was a light from the garage outside. I looked to make sure, but the curtains were well together, and as I looked the ray moved right across in front of where I lay. I watched, not at all nervously, and something like a crumpled filmy piece of chiffron unfolded, and the beautiful wavy top of Eldred's head appeared, a few seconds and his forehead and broad, beautiful brow appeared, still it waited and his lovely blue eyes came, but no mischievous twinkle, but a great intensity. It all shook and quivered, then his nose came. More waiting and quivering and then his tiny little moustache and mouth. At this point he turned his head very slightly and looked right into my face, and moistened his lips very slightly with his tongue. I kept quite quiet, but it quivered and shook so much and no chin came, and in my anxiety I put out my hands and said: '*Eldred*, I see you,' and it all flickered quite out, light and all. (*Journal of the S.P.R.*, Vol. XIX, 1919–20, pp. 45–6)

When, as is more common, the apparition is first seen as a complete figure, it is unusual for the subject to witness its 'arrival' out of thin air. More typically, the apparition enters the subject's field of view in some seemingly natural way. Thus the subject may look up and find the apparition standing beside him, or the apparition may seem to enter the room through a doorway. Many subjects report that they simply 'saw' or 'noticed' the apparition, as if it was already there, fully-formed, in their environment before they started to perceive it. Subjects quite frequently qualify such descriptions with the words 'suddenly', saying, for example, that they 'suddenly became aware' of the apparition in their environment.

Sometimes the subject may become aware of a presence, or feel a compulsion to turn round, whereupon he sees an apparition. Or he may suddenly feel cold, or apprehensive, or hear a sound, in a way which seems to draw his attention to an apparition in his environment.

Another characteristic way in which the experience may start is for the subject to wake up and perceive the apparition apparently already there in his environment, as if it had already been part of his environment before he woke (see pp.71–2).

*

The ways in which apparitional experiences come to an end seem to be more varied than the ways in which they begin. At the beginning of visual experiences there seems to be a tendency to avoid too abrupt an appearance of the apparition within the subject's field of view; the figures do not usually make their appearance out of thin air while the subject is looking at them. At the end of visual experiences this tendency is less; a far greater proportion come to an end while the subject is actually looking at them, and he may see them end in a great variety of ways. For example, in the following case the subject describes the apparition as vanishing 'like a bubble bursting'.

> One summer evening, when I was 20 yrs., I went for an evening drive in a car, with a friend. We lived in the town of Stroud, Glos. A short drive took us to a little road, which led out to X village. We stopped halfway, near J. Farm, where there were a few cottages. It was quite light. We sat quietly, just enjoying the evening. Looking up the road I saw an old lady walking slowly down, with a shawl round her shoulders, skirt to her feet. She was leaning heavily on a stick. I thought, she looks worn out, wondered why she had come so far, from the houses. She crossed right in front of the car, to the side. I turned my head, to look at her. She saw me, for the first time. A look of anger came on her face. She vanished like a bubble bursting. I looked round, said to my friend 'Where has the old lady gone?' He said 'What old lady?' I said, I have been watching an old lady, coming slowly down the road, she crossed in front of the car—vanished. He just said, Let's get out of here—we did. I was not frightened, but couldn't help wondering about the matter.

When an apparition fades away gradually while the percipient is looking at it, it may either do so by gradually becoming indistinct all over, or by first one part fading and then another until the whole apparition has disappeared. One subject describes

an apparition as disappearing slowly 'from the outline towards
the centre' (see pp. 131–2). The following percipient describes an
apparition which disappeared from the head downwards.

> I lived in an old Cotswold house in 1964. About six months before
> I moved away I saw one night while busy in the kitchen a tall grey
> haired woman dressed in a shabby dark dress, aquiline nose, pale
> face, pale grey or blue eyes. A heavy stiff long apron enveloped her.
> She stood in the hall facing the kitchen entrance. She moved her
> eyes and head and looked surprised at the kitchen unit and gas stove.
> When her eyes fell on me, she first disappeared from the head then
> slowly down until her very extremely thin legs and big men's shoes
> vanished also. I did not realise it was extraordinary until she started
> to disappear. In the grounds there was the remains of a laundry. She
> certainly looked dressed for the part, with the big waterproof apron.
> It appeared a stiff material. We lived 16 years in that particular
> house, *without* similar experience.

In other cases the apparition is said to fade from the bottom
upwards, until only the head is left. For example, in the following
case the face of the apparition seems to have been the last part to
disappear.

> My home was in Holland and I was 18 years old, on the point of
> leaving G. School, Tonbridge, Kent, where I had spent five terms to
> learn English. . .
> One night I was *compelled* to wake up in a state of absolute terror
> and saw a man in a trenchcoat sitting on my bed. Peering into my
> face. It was a bright moonlit night and I saw the girl who was sharing
> my room, Madeleine King, quite clearly, fast asleep. With a terrific
> effort I managed to raise myself into a sitting position and the man
> and I sat and stared at each other. I thought my heart was going to
> burst with fear. It was only when he slowly started to dissolve, his
> face disappearing last that I began to realise that he wasn't a live
> man at all.

The following case is a curious example of how different parts
of an apparition may disappear at different moments. The
subject reports that an apparition of a lady disappeared but that
the baby she was carrying persisted for a moment or two before
it also disappeared.

> August 1972. Approx. 3 a.m.
> I went to bed at 12.30 a.m. fell asleep around 1 a.m. I do not
> remember any dream. I awoke suddenly with slightly increased pulse
> rate, 'aware' of 'something' in the room. I opened my eyes but could
> not see anything as it was too dark.

Then to be more comfortable I turned over. Then I saw the apparition of a young woman of 20 years wearing a long white and blue sprigged muslin dress, small white lace edged shawl or large kerchief draped about her shoulders, light brown curly hair showing below a white lace edged mob cap.

She was holding a baby 8 months old and very healthy looking. They both had a fair skin and good complexion. The baby (boy) had sparse fairish hair.

She stood near the foot of the bed, looking towards the head, as if she was showing the baby to someone, in a bed about two feet to the right of our bed.

I sat up to get a better view. I contemplated waking my husband, but as he takes a long time to wake and does not usually register events immediately, I decided against it. I thought the disturbance might cause the apparition to disappear.

The apparition seemed to have a source of light of its own, not bright, but enough to show up clearly in the dark room. Then the woman suddenly disappeared, leaving the baby suspended in mid-air for a few seconds. Then the baby disappeared equally, if not more, quickly.

. . . Both [disappeared] suddenly, like pricking a balloon with a pin.

When an apparition vanishes while the subject is still looking at it, it sometimes seems to do so in response to some action on the observer's part. For example, if he is in a darkened room it may vanish when he puts on the light, or even when he merely reaches out to do so. Alternatively the apparition may come to an end when the subject tries to touch it, or makes some move towards it, or speaks to it.

An apparition may also disappear as if as a result of some inter-action with a real object. For example in the first case quoted in this book the subject reports seeing an apparition of a horse and two human figures disappear when a (real) bicyclist rode through the horse's hindquarters (p. 1). In the following case the subject reports that an apparition of a cyclist disappeared on running into the back of a cart:

One afternoon in the spring of 1896, as I was riding along the main road from Wheedon to Daventry, I became aware of the presence of a cyclist in grey who rode slowly ahead of me. The curious part of it was that a second before I had looked round, and the road, a very long and level one, had been absolutely void of life. For some distance we continued our course, until we came up to a large cart which was rattling along in the centre of the thoroughfare, the driver blissfully careless of any one else's welfare save his own.

To my horror my mysterious companion ran with great force right into the back of the cart and disappeared. Not a vestige of either him or his machine was to be seen, and I rode on wondering whether I had been dreaming. (*Journal of the S.P.R.*, Vol. IX, 1899–1900, p. 125)

Many apparitions are said to 'vanish', 'disappear', or simply 'stop being there', without any gradual process of dissolution, as in the following case, in which the subject remarks that while she looked at the apparition suddenly there was 'nothing'.

About 8 or 9 years ago I lived in a rather awful flat in the Hampstead area. It had two rooms, a long passage off which these opened and at the end a tiny kitchen with no door. I had hung a heavy curtain across the opening. One late afternoon I was in the kitchen, heard nothing, but felt a presence. I turned and saw a man, very solid, dressed in a longish mac, belted, and a felt hat—rather like the old Humphrey Bogart gangster character. I saw no face. He remained standing there for several seconds and then, suddenly, there was nothing. I did not see him disappear, I was not in the least alarmed and felt as if he had a protective feeling towards me . . . I never saw him again.

Not all apparitions disappear before the subject's very eyes, so to speak. Some leave the subject's visual field as if of their own accord, for example by walking out of the room. In other cases the percipient himself may, accidentally or intentionally, exclude the apparition from his visual field: he may close his eyes, look away from the apparition, faint, run away, or put his head under the bedclothes.

In the following case the apparition seemed to run out of the subject's visual field:

1957 it was Saturday afternoon 1.30 p.m. I was standing on a stool in the kitchen, fixing an electric door-bell. Suddenly my youngest son came charging past me and I nearly fell off the stool. I got off the stool and shouted after him to be more careful. I followed the direction he had gone but couldn't see him anywhere. I searched the backway of the house with no result. Then I realised the back door of the house hadn't opened so he couldn't have run into the street.

My wife was dusting things down in the front room. I shouted to her 'Where's that young 'un gone to, I'll give him a clip when I get hold of him.' She replied, 'Are you going daft or something, the lad's here.' I went into the front room and there he was with his head slumped on his chest in a deep sleep. I said to my wife 'How long has he been in here?' She replied about an hour.

I said 'There's something queer going on here, I swear to God that he ran by me and nearly knocked me off the stool.' My wife replied that I was going nuts. My son hadn't woken up a couple of hours later. I said to my wife, 'Why is the young 'un asleep all this time, he should be out playing.' My wife tried to waken him and she realized something was wrong. I rushed him to hospital and they found that he was suffering from acute pneumonia. Previous to this incident my wife said that my son had been playing in the street with other youngsters and had showed no sign of illness.

Sometimes apparitions leave the subject's visual field in ways that violate physical realism. For example, they may pass through windows, walls or closed doors, rise through the ceiling or sink through the floor.

In the following example the apparition disappears through a locked door. The percipient was living in a flat at the time.

It was Wimbledon time, and I am a tennis addict. That year I was emotionally involved with Christine Truman. On the day in question, before my daughter left for school, she prepared the laundry and, coming into the kitchen to say good bye, she said, 'Don't forget, in your involvement with Christine, that this is laundry day: I'll leave the bundle inside the front door so that all you will have to do when the laundry man rings is sprint down the stairs, hand the bundle to him and be back in time for the next "service"; good luck Christine.'

. . . It is relevant to mention here that, on the same floor and adjacent to our dining-room, there were two other rooms both locked, each door had two Yale locks.

. . . I was 'advising' Miss Truman on tactics when I thought I heard the door bell ring; it rang again but I waited for the end of the rally.

Then I sprang from my seat, took the two short flights of stairs in two bounds, thrust the bundle into the hand of an amazed man, shut the door and got up those stairs three at a time in the hope of seeing Christine serve. As I reached the landing outside the locked door, inches from the room I was making for, stood a man of some seventy years: he was dressed in a black heavy overcoat that reached to his ankles. His face was thin and swarthy, Mid-Eastern in appearance, but it was his eyes that riveted my attention: they were dark, very bright but infinitely sad.

I felt no fear whatever but I experienced a deep sense of sadness and sympathy for him to such an extent that tears welled up in my eyes. After what seemed to be a long time, I made to ask him if there was anything I could do to relieve his sadness.

As I started to speak, he turned and disappeared through the double-locked door only inches from where I would enter our room.

(The percipient later learnt that the figure she had seen resembled her landlady's late father, who had died 20 years before in the room the percipient was using as a dining-room.)

It is interesting to compare the beginnings and endings of apparitional experiences with those of out-of-the-body experiences.

Our subjects did not usually observe any discontinuity in their experience, either at the beginning or at the end of perceiving the apparition. But, as we have already pointed out, this does not rule out the possibility that the experience was a metachoric one.

Many out-of-the-body experiences start and end abruptly, without any apparent process of transition from the normal state. The subject may simply find himself without warning apparently viewing his body from outside. Then at the end of the experience he may abruptly find himself 'back inside his body'. We might compare such beginnings and endings of ecsomatic experiences with apparitional cases in which the apparition is suddenly seen as part of the environment without the subject observing any process of formation, or in which the apparition vanishes suddenly without seeming to undergo any gradual process of disintegration.

It is also interesting to note that when the subject of an out-of-the-body experience does describe a gradual process of transition to or from the ecsomatic state, this process may be described in highly idiosyncratic terms, paralleling the wide variety of ways in which apparitions may be seen to form or dissolve.

CHAPTER 22

Duration and Sense of Time

APPARITIONAL experiences seem to vary considerably in length. When our subjects were asked to estimate how long the apparition was perceptible to them, in minutes or seconds, about half estimated the experience as having lasted a minute or less. However, it is interesting to note that as many as 20 per cent considered it had lasted five minutes or more.

If we consider on their own the class of experiences estimated as having lasted a minute or less, we find that as many as 42 per cent of these are said to have lasted 15 seconds or less.

It seems that if the same subject has more than one apparitional experience their duration may vary considerably from one occasion to the next. For example, a subject might estimate one of his experiences in terms of seconds and another in minutes.

The following is an example of a relatively short-lived apparitional experience:

> The first time I saw 'Dorothy' (as we have named the figure which has appeared at different times to three of us) was in August—I forget the day of the month—1881. I was rather late for dinner and went hurriedly into my dressing-room to get ready when I was startled by seeing close to me, and close to my washing-stand a figure of a short woman. It looked to me, in the second that I saw it, like an old nurse. The dress was black, and a white apron covered her chest and the front of her dress. The face I could not see; all the head seemed enveloped in some light lavender-coloured gauze. It was gone so quickly I could hardly realise I had seen anything, and yet I know I did. She went so quickly; it reminds me now, when I think of it, of the sudden collapse of a bright-coloured soap bubble. The moment I got down to dinner I told my husband what I had seen. I have seen Dorothy three or four times since this, but never her face, and she invariably disappears, or goes out, so quickly that I have not time to be frightened. (*Journal of the S.P.R.*, Vol. V, 1891–2, p. 305)

The following are two examples of relatively prolonged experiences. In the first case, the percipient was a girl of fifteen and the apparition she saw was of a boy of seventeen with whom she had become friendly. The percipient knew that the boy, Bertie, was in delicate health, but says that she had not been told his life was in danger.

> There was a bright fire, and like many girls I delighted to sit by the fender, reading by firelight. Not knowing of my friend's danger I was not uneasy, only vexed that he could not come and spend the evening with me, so I felt lonely. I was reading quietly when the door opened, and Bertie (my friend) walked in. I jumped up to get him an arm-chair near the fire, as he looked cold, and he had no greatcoat on, and as it was snowing, I began to scold him for coming without his wraps. He did not speak but put up his hand to his chest and shook his head, which I mistook to mean his cold was on his chest, and that he had lost his voice, to which he was subject. So I reproached him again for his imprudence. While speaking, Mr. G. came in and asked me to whom I was speaking. I said, 'There's that tiresome boy without his coat, and such a bad cold he can't speak; lend him a coat and send him home.' I shall never forget the horror and amazement of the good doctor's face, as he knew (what I did not) that the poor boy had died half-an-hour ago, and he was coming to break the news to me. His first impression was that I had already heard it, and that I had lost my senses. I could not understand either why he made me leave the room, and spoke to me as if I were a small child. For a few moments we were at cross purposes . . .
>
> The apparition had been in the room about 5 minutes when Mr. G. came in. What to me has always been so strange is, that I *heard* the handle of the door turn and the door open; in fact, it was the noise of the lock turning which caused me to look up from my book. The figure walked across the room to the opposite side of the fireplace, and sat down while I lighted the candles. It was all so real and natural that I can hardly realise even now that it was not so. (Gurney I, p. 532)

In the second case, which follows, the subject reports playing with an apparitional dog for some ten minutes.

> Thirteen years ago, I was in the Army, stationed in Germany, and coming home on leave by ship, and train, usually meant arriving home somewhere during the early hours of the morning. My parents knew on which day I was arriving, and left the back door open. This meant going through a dark passage between the two houses to gain access.
>
> I was aged 19 at the time and had grown up from lonely childhood, and made good friends with the next door neighbour's dog 'Bobby', a large black mongrel. Before I went in the Army, we had grown very fond of each other, and an outsider would have thought he was my

dog—I would take him for walks every day without fail. I volunteered for the Army to be a Regular Soldier, but my attachment to the dog was so great, that I almost didn't 'join up'. Nevertheless, I did, but don't mind admitting I suffered quite a lot of emotional upset over the dog.

On the night in question, I arrived home at about 2 a.m., and sure enough, as soon as I opened the side gate, 'Bobby', who normally slept in a kennel outside the house, bounded up to me, and made a terrific fuss of me, nuzzling and licking my face. I stayed with him for some ten minutes or so, and then went indoors. There is no question in my mind, to this day, that I played with 'Bobby' for that short time. I knew and loved him so well, that there couldn't possibly be any mistake about his identity. As he left me, he disappeared out of sight into my neighbour's large Dahlia bed, and that was the last I saw of him.

The following morning after an enjoyable reunion with my family, I made my usual visit to my neighbour, the dog's owner, who was a very great friend of ours. I told him about meeting Bobby the previous night, and remarking quite casually that he was out of his kennel (he was normally kept chained in). My neighbour was thunderstruck, and said, 'Bobby died three months ago, and is buried in the middle of the Dahlias.'

My reaction to this was quite traumatic, and I was unable to speak to anyone, or eat for a couple of days.

. . . In conclusion, I should say that as long as the family lived in that house, I never used the back entrance after dark again, and insisted on having a spare key cut for the front door.

As we have already pointed out (p. 25), the possibility of the metachoric interpretation makes it easier to accept such accounts as this. For example, in the case just quoted, it is possible that the subject would have been seen by an external observer not to be going through the motions of playing with a dog, but standing with an abstracted air for some minutes.

Occasionally subjects report perceiving apparitions over a period of hours. However, it is to be presumed that in most such cases the subject is not perceiving the apparition continuously throughout that time. Thus the subject who describes seeing a lady in her bedroom while on holiday in Greece (p. 110) writes that her experience lasted 'approximately three hours'. However, it seems that the apparition was not continuously perceptible throughout this time. She writes:

I did not look at the apparition continuously. For part of the time I lay with my eyes closed, but aware of the figure sitting on my bed. From time to time the apparition vanished, leaving me with a dreadful feeling of sadness. There were times when I looked for the apparition but could not see it. I was in no way alarmed by this experience, and discussed with my husband all that was happening in the room.

★

When asked whether they had noticed any alteration in their sense of the passage of time at any stage in their experience, only 10 per cent of our subjects considered that they had done so. Among these subjects the most common remark was that the experience had seemed longer than it really was. For example, one subject commented: 'Although all over in a flash, time seemed endless whilst apparition in view.' Another wrote: 'What was probably only a minute seemed like hours.'

Even more commonly subjects suggested that time had actually seemed to 'stand still' while they were perceiving the apparition.

It seems that distortions of the time sense are less common in connection with experiences of perceiving apparitions than with out-of-the-body experiences. In our investigation of ecsomatic experiences we found that 17 per cent of those who had had a single out-of-the-body experience reported that their sense of time had seemed altered during it, and among those who had had more than one such experience the proportion who had noticed a change during at least one such experience was 37 per cent.

★

Sometimes a subject's perception of an apparition is interrupted rather than continuous. The subject may look away and continue with whatever activity he was engaged in before noticing the apparition, such as reading or doing housework, and on looking back a little while later he may see the apparition again. Alternatively, he may turn away in fright or hide his head under the bedclothes, as in the following case.

> I was in bed, having recovered from Quinsy, the doctor having said I must remain there for another week.
> It was half past ten in the morning. My mother and Auntie left me, asking if I would be alright, to do some shopping. I was all alone. Then as I looked towards the bedroom door, there, standing in the room, there was an Indian. He was dressed in a blue serge suit, and on his head a white turban. He had beautiful features, and smiled, but did not speak or move. I was terrified and put my head

under the bedclothes. I looked again. He was still there, and I cried out, 'Oh, please God send him away'. He slowly vanished.

When I told my mother, who was a lovely down to earth person, she just laughed, but I have never forgotten it.

Sometimes the subject opens and closes his eyes several times while looking at an apparition. In the following two cases, for example, the percipients report deliberately opening and closing their eyes, with a view to testing the reality of what they were seeing.

I thought that you might like to hear about an experience which I had earlier this year. On the morning of the 2nd January at about 5.30 a.m., I woke up and turned over in bed and standing by my fireplace (about ten feet away) was a figure of a woman in her late twenties. She was dressed in Victorian costume and was wearing the following—a long gathered camel coloured skirt, a tight fitting burgundy jacket and a high necked white lace blouse with a cameo brooch on the collar. I did not see her feet and she was standing about six inches above floor level. Her hair was scraped back into a bun and I was unable to see her facial features as she was in profile. Her figure was illuminated by her own light and she did not cast any shadow on the objects in the room, which is usually very dark at night with little or no light penetrating through the curtains. Her arms were outstretched and moving quickly in a rather jerky fashion (rather like a speeded up film) and it looked as though she was searching through some drawers. She was, in fact, standing in front of an armchair. She had a two-dimensioned quality and lacked solidity. When I saw her I could not believe my eyes and thought that I must be seeing things, so I shut my eyes and shook myself to clear my head, thinking that she would not be there when I looked again, only to find that she was and was still frantically looking for something. I looked for a few seconds and I then began to get frightened, although there was no need to as she did not appear to be unfriendly and she seemed unaware of my presence. However I could not stand it any longer so I switched on the light by my bed and the apparition (?) disappeared. I spent the rest of the night with the light on and I felt rather disturbed, as I did for the next few nights. I have not seen her again, however.

I saw what I believe must have been something of an apparition only a couple of months ago. I had wakened and, as is my custom, glanced towards the window—registered in my mind that it was early in the night or just after dawn. Then, sensing a movement the other side of the room, I saw a shadowy figure which I took to be my husband. He was wearing a dressing-gown and I assumed he had thought he heard me call (as he occasionally does think) and come here from his room to see if everything was all right.

I said, 'What is it, Jack' but the figure continued its walk round my bed till it stood, looking emaciated and shoulders drooping, on the mat the window side of my bed. Receiving no answer to my repeated 'What is it?' my mind registered the thought 'Good Lord—this is something ghostly'. But, being of an analytical bent, I had to find out really if I was dreaming, and closed my eyes tightly for a little longer. 'I must be dreaming' . . . When I opened them the second time, the figure seemed to have evaporated. But I was sufficiently interested to ask my husband—next morning—whether he had been 'thinking' of coming in during the night . . . or whether he had dreamed of doing so. The answer was 'no'.

It seems that when a subject closes and re-opens his eyes in this way while viewing an apparition, the apparition usually disappears, as if it was a real perception, while the subject's eyelids are closed, rather than remaining visible through closed eyelids.

The question might be raised whether the subject's eyes are really closed when he believes himself to be closing them during the experience of seeing an apparition, or whether the whole experience is metachoric. If the subject imagines that he is closing his eyes during the perception of an apparition and then looking at it again, he might be merely hallucinating the sensations of closing his eyelids. This question could of course be resolved if an independent observer, who was not hallucinating, happened to be watching the subject while he was perceiving the apparition, and seeing whether he really behaved as he thought he did during the intermission in his perception of the apparition.

In this connection it is interesting to note what happens when a subject closes his eyes in a different kind of metachoric experience, a lucid dream. A lucid dreamer may close his eyes in the course of the dream—that is, close the eyes of the hallucinatory body he finds himself occupying in the dream—and the scene he has been viewing previously may disappear, only to reappear when he opens his eyes again, just as if he had closed them and re-opened them in real life. Presumably in this situation the subject's subconscious is merely simulating reality by stopping all image-producing activity while the subject imagines his eyes are closed. In fact, of course, the whole experience is hallucinatory throughout, including the experience of blankness while the subject dreams that his eyes are closed.

We have observed that when a subject is seeing an apparition he may sometimes, if not always, be having a metachoric experience, that is, he may be seeing a completely hallucinatory environment. We have, therefore, to ask ourselves whether what happens when a subject looks away from an apparition and looks back to find it still there, is analogous to what happens when a lucid dreamer shuts out the dream-scenery before him by shutting his eyes and finds it still there when he opens them again. Does the subject's field of vision immediately cease to be hallucinatory once he looks away from the apparition, only to become hallucinatory again when he looks back at the apparition? Or does his field of vision remain hallucinatory throughout the period which intervenes between his two sightings of the apparition? For example, in the following case the subject reports looking away from an apparition to continue reading a book, and then looking back to see it still sitting opposite him. The question arises whether he was really seeing the book during the intervening period, or merely seeing a hallucinatory representation of the book.

> It also became apparent at this time that we had a gentleman resident who used to glide in and out of rooms, downstairs only, at any time of the day and night. At first my wife and I used just to say, 'Ooh,' as he glided through; but for a long time we never saw his face; in fact my wife never saw it. But one night, or rather early one morning, I was sat by the fire reading; now on this particular night, I did something I had never done before, I sat in the chair opposite to the one I normally occupied. While reading, I became aware of a person sitting opposite to me, and occupying my usual chair; I looked again at my book; and for the second time was compelled to look at this man sat opposite to me. There was no feeling of fear. Just the usual recognition of a normal person. He was sat there, normal, placid, and unsmiling. He was tall; near six feet; dark hair brushed back and parted to the side; it was a full head of hair. He had dark eyes, a pale, sallow complexion; he wore a navy blue serge suit, with a white shirt and dark tie. The third time I looked up he had gone. Now we believed, after, that this was the fellow who used to glide through the house at any old time, and he still did it until we left.

CHAPTER 23

Opacity and Transparency

THE majority of visual apparitions are opaque rather than transparent, the figure of the apparition seeming to blot out the part of the real environment behind it, as a real person would. Ninety-one per cent of our subjects who reported visual experiences said that the apparition they saw was completely opaque like a normal object so that nothing was visible through it, rather than at all transparent so that they could see what was behind it.

We shall first give some examples of the opaque type of apparition, and then discuss some problems they raise.

The following is a case in which the subject reports distinctly noticing that the apparition seemed to blot out part of the real environment which had been visible until the apparition suddenly appeared before him.

> At ——, Dublin, one evening, about 1878, in the twilight I was walking upstairs with a pair of shoes in my hand, when passing a landing on which there was a pedestal with a bust of Wm. Shakespeare on it, I saw a tall lady dressed in grey *suddenly* appear before me and stand in front of the pedestal, which became hidden—which would prove it was not a 'vapoury vision' I saw. I was so surprised and frightened at the extreme suddenness of the figure that I involuntarily threw my shoes at it, when the figure immediately vanished, my shoes striking the pedestal and seeming to pass *through* the impression. I was unnerved a good deal.
>
> I was in the best of health at the time. About 15 years [old].
> (*Journal of the S.P.R.*, Vol. VII, 1895–6, pp. 335–6)

Sometimes the opacity of the apparition is such that it appears to obscure the light of a candle or similar light-source as the apparition passes between the light-source and the percipient. The following is an interesting case in the present context. The percipient reports that the light from a candle which he was holding seems to be prevented from falling on a wall until the apparition disappeared, just as if it had been a solid figure.

> Last Easter Sunday, I was retiring to bed, just after 11 o'clock, and had stepped off the stairs on the landing that led to my room (my parents' bedroom being in front of me, about 10 or 12ft., and my door being about 2ft. to the right, so that I had to pass it to get to my room). I saw their bedroom door was open, and I was riveted to the spot by seeing standing in the room doorway in front of me, a figure of a female; although I could not distinguish the dress, I could plainly see the features, and especially the eyes. I must have stood there at least 20 seconds, for my mother, hearing me stop suddenly before reaching my room, at last opened the door (below) and asked what was the matter. I then came downstairs and stopped with them till we all retired together. The figure collapsed when my mother called upstairs, and the light I held in my hand shone through the doorway to the opposite wall, which had been obscured by the figure, as if it had had a tangible body. (Gurney II, pp. 59–60)

The percipient later identified this apparition as representing a former girl-friend, whom he had not seen for about six months, and who had died at about the time of his experience.

The fact that most visual apparitions are not transparent, but quite opaque, presents us with certain difficulties. If the subject is merely hallucinating the figure of the apparition and perceiving the rest of his field of vision normally, it seems that he must be having a negative hallucination to eliminate the part of his real environment which falls behind the apparition—otherwise, of course, he would see both the apparition and the normal environment behind it, so that we might expect the apparition to appear transparent.

The outlines of the hallucinatory figure and the negative hallucination which blocks out the real environment behind it would have to coincide very precisely. There is practically no indication that any kind of transparency or other peculiarity at the outline is a common feature of apparitions.

The difficulty seems to be compounded when we remember that many hallucinatory figures and objects (66 per cent) are seen to move in relation to the real environment. They may stand up, sit down, walk closer to or further from the percipient, etc. Throughout most of such movements the outline of the apparition presumably changes in shape, so that the negative hallucination of part of the real environment which would be necessary to prevent the apparition looking transparent would presumably have to change in shape as well.

The problem of the precise integration of a hallucinatory figure and a corresponding negative hallucination to block out the normal visual field behind it, does not arise if we suppose that the whole experience is metachoric. As we have pointed out in an earlier chapter, this interpretation seems preferable, in fact unavoidable, in cases in which the opacity of the figure leads to changes in the lighting of the scene which affect the whole field of view. The metachoric interpretation may also be correct in cases where there is no direct evidence to force it upon us.

If a hallucinatory experience is metachoric, there is no question of a negative hallucination having to blot out the area of the normal visual field covered by the figure of the apparition, since the representation of the real environment is hallucinatory as well as the figure of the apparition itself.

*

Although the great majority of visual apparitions seem to be opaque, blocking off from view the part of the environment that lies behind them, there are a minority which are transparent. In addition there are cases in which the apparition becomes transparent as it disappears. In such cases it looks normally solid and opaque at first but gradually lets the objects behind it become visible. We shall give some examples of these various types.

The following is a case in which the apparition is reported as looking transparent from the outset. The subject, a lady, describes rushing through her living-room drying her hands, and seeing a man with twinkling eyes sitting on her settee, and then realising that she could see the settee through him.

> On rushing through my living room, drying my hands, to dash upstairs, one sunny January morning, I stopped abruptly—went hot and cold.
> There on the settee, comfortably sitting in the sun, sat a short well bodied man—smiling—twinkling eyes—hands in lap—pure white curly hair—white ruffly cravate—knee length dark greeny-blue velvet coat—impression of gaiters—air of contentment and happiness and ease.
> All in a flash I realised that I could see the settee behind him. At the same moment I opened my mouth, 'What do you think

you're ——.' The words about to come out—he vanished—I sat, heart pounding!

I tried to re-act the scene, and have done since, all hours—in vain.

What is particularly interesting is that some apparitions are described as being quite solid-looking, despite the objects behind them being visible. The following case will illustrate this point:

> On Thursday evening, 14th November, 1867, I was sitting in the Birmingham Town Hall with my husband at a concert, when there came over me the icy chill which usually accompanies these occurrences. Almost immediately, I saw with perfect distinctness, between myself and the orchestra, my uncle, Mr. W., lying in bed with an appealing look on his face, like one dying. I had not heard anything of him for several months, and had no reason to think he was ill. The appearance was not transparent or filmy, but perfectly solid-looking; *and yet I could somehow see the orchestra, not through, but behind it.* I did not try turning my eyes to see whether the figure moved with them, but looked at it with a fascinated expression that made my husband ask if I was ill. I asked him not to speak to me for a minute or two; the vision gradually disappeared, and I told my husband, after the concert was over, what I had seen. A letter came shortly after telling of my uncle's death. He died at the time when I saw the vision. (Gurney II, p. 37)

The case already quoted on p. 115 appears to be another instance of this paradox. The subject describes the apparitional figure as 'very solid looking', yet she says, 'I distinctly remember seeing the wardrobe behind this chap'.

The following case will provide an example of how an apparition may first appear opaque and then gradually become transparent as it disappears:

> In the year 1863 . . . being about 26 years old, I was sleeping alone, without having indulged in any heavy supper. I woke up suddenly and with all my wits about me, but with a clear feeling that somebody was in the room. There was enough moonlight streaming in to cause lights and shadows. As I started up and raised myself on my elbow, I saw a tall lady in a rich black dress (silk, I think, with black beads and a train behind—I knew once, but I have forgotten), looking steadily at me with a most gentle, meditating gaze. About 40, I should say. I now saw that I [did] not at all recognise the face. There was a far-away look in her eyes, and I felt as if she had been reading me through. She rested the elbow of one hand in the palm of the other, and in the first hand there was a little duodecimo volume with rubric and, I think, 'black letter'. I was entirely calm, eagerly interested, but rather scientifically than imaginatively. I pinched myself to find out if I was really awake. I took my watch and held it

to my ear to hear whether it was ticking. I tried my pulse, which was normal. I then said aloud (in order to test my sobriety and calmness), 'This is an optical delusion. I shall now put my hand through this appearance.' I did so, and my hand went through as it would through water (only without the slightest sensation), the clothes kept their folds and position (as water keeps its level) making no break. My hand with the white night-shirt sleeve was wholly hid, and when I withdrew it, there was no hole left behind, any more than when one withdraws one's hand from water. After some 40 or 50 seconds I saw a straight white line crossing the figure. I could not make out what it was, till I perceived the apparition was slowly vanishing away in its place, and the white line was the top of my towel on the towel-horse behind. Bit by bit the white towel and other dimmer objects in the room came into sight, behind what was becoming a faint mist. In about 20 seconds it had completely vanished. (*Census*, pp. 117–18)

Sometimes an apparition looks quite normal and opaque from a certain distance, only to seem transparent when seen from closer to. The following is such a case from our own collection. The subject, who was staying in a guest-house at the time, says that though at first the apparition looked solid enough he then noticed that he could see the wall behind it.

My bedroom was on the first floor, the door of this was at the foot of the stairs leading to the next floor. The bathroom and toilet were on my floor at the end of a fairly long corridor amply lighted throughout the night. The time would be about 2.30 a.m. as I went *just as usual* to the toilet. Returning I saw what I was certain in my mind was a middle-aged or elderly female wearing a dressing gown partly over her head and shoulders, crossing the corridor toward the stairs outside my bedroom door. Quite sure that this was a flesh and blood person I wondered briefly why the gown was worn in that way. Visitors to Matlock Bath and to this and other houses near were very frequent, so I was not surprised to see a stranger, but assumed she was a guest.

I surmised that by the time she would be about three or four steps up the stairs we would just about draw level, and as we did so I turned my head towards her intending to say 'Hello, another Night Rake'. 'She' stood still, and turned 'her' head towards me. The words died in my throat and 'she' bent slightly forward as though to continue upwards. I saw with a dreadful shock, not a woman but the shadowy cadaverous face of a man wearing the hooded habit of a monk. I could see the wall through the phantom, yet 'she' had appeared solid enough from a few yards distant. The fact that the figure turned toward me convinces me that 'he' was fully aware of my presence. I was chilled with shock for a moment then dashed into my room, to lie awake wondering if the phantom would follow, I was badly scared.

Transparent apparitions do not at first sight present us with the same difficulties as opaque ones. What obviously suggests itself to the mind is that the subject is seeing a hallucinatory figure superimposed on the normal non-hallucinatory background. There are no problems about the need for the subject's subconscious to generate a negative hallucination to blot out the part of the normal environment behind the hallucinatory figure; it seems that the subject simply continues to see the normal environment through it.

However, we have already seen that in certain classes of apparitional case there are good reasons for supposing that the whole perceptual field is hallucinatory. In fact, the state of affairs is that we know for certain that some apparitional experiences are metachoric; and we do not know for certain that any are not. However, if we accept the simple view of transparent apparitions that they are transparent because the real environment, perceived in the normal way, is showing through a hallucination, we have to suppose that no case of a transparent apparition is of the metachoric variety.

It should be realised that it is in fact quite possible that some or all transparent apparitions are of the metachoric variety. If the subconscious can project a hallucinatory environment including an opaque figure, it can presumably project one which includes a transparent figure, and it may sometimes have some reason for wishing the apparition to look transparent, such as to convey to the conscious mind of the percipient that what he is seeing is not a normal figure.

CHAPTER 24

Colouring

BETWEEN a half and two thirds of the visual apparitions reported to us were coloured in some way. For example, they might represent someone wearing clothes of a certain colour, or having hair of a certain shade. The remainder appear to have been either black and white or monochrome.

Of the cases concerning apparitions incorporating some coloured feature (i.e. other than black and white or monochrome) the great majority are described as having normal colouring, just as it would have been if the apparition had been a real object. The following is an example:

> I have often attended summer holiday music courses at a girls boarding school: G. House. One year, about ten years ago, there were not so many of us on the course and a whole wing of dormitories were not in use. One morning, I decided to go along to the bathrooms in the unused wing so that I could have a bath in peace, so at 6.30 a.m. I went through the double fire doors into the corridor at the unused wing, and a few yards ahead of me and going in the same direction was a girl. She was of average height, short dark curly hair, slim, about sixteen years old, and was wearing a pale pink cotton ankle-length dressing gown. She had a towel draped over her left arm, and a plastic draw-string sponge bag swung from her right hand. She was so real I suspected nothing until she was level with a dormitory door half-way down the corridor—then she suddenly disappeared. She did not turn to go into the dormitory, just vanished! I looked into the dormitory in question but I knew I would find nothing and was right, as the dormitory was deserted—all the beds were stripped bare to the mattress. The next morning I had forgotten all about it and was only half awake as I went through the fire doors. It was exactly 6.30 a.m. again. It was an exact repeat performance of the morning before. But it did not happen on any other morning. I asked a teacher of the school who was helping in the course, and she told me that the girl had been worried about her exams and killed herself, but she did not tell me how or when.

Cases such as the following, in which the chariot and horses were evidently not coloured as a normal chariot and horses would be, seem to be relatively rare:

> One fine morning in early summer in either 1926 or 1927 my younger brother and I both saw something in the sky which I can only explain as being praeternatural. I remember seeing a chariot and horses moving through the sky. The driver was wielding a whip.
>
> I am not talking of a cloud formation. The figures were golden or fiery though not dazzling. The movement was distinct, the horses proceeding at a gallop and turning once they had reached one 'end' of the horizon.
>
> My brother and I have never had another similar experience.[1]

Among the group of apparitions that are described as being coloured only in black and white or monochrome, the great majority still probably do not depart in any detectable way from the colouring to be expected of a real object in the same circumstances. A number of these apparitions are seen at night, or in poor lighting conditions, or appear to be wearing black, white or grey garments. In a few of this class of cases, however, the figures are monochrome in a way which is clearly not compatible with the colouring of a real object.

The following is an example of the white kind of apparition:

> As a child of about 10 years old, I went out to play with my friends in the village. I had to pass a large house where there was a dog I was terrified of. He always barked at me, when I had occasion to fetch milk from this house. It was a moonlight night and as I was going near this house the man and this dog came out of the green door and went to some out-buildings. Being afraid of this dog I waited until they came back. This man was dressed in a top hat and long coat and a walking stick. But they were *all* white. When I went home I told my father what I had seen. He said I couldn't have seen him (*Mr. Bentall*) as he was dead and if I looked in the churchyard I would see his grave being dug. On my way to school I did and sure enough a grave was being dug. I asked the man whose grave it was. He said Mr. Bentall's.

The following are two examples of black apparitions, the first an interesting case of an apparition which was apparently seen more than once by the same subject:

[1] This case happens to have been a collective one, in which a chariot and horses were perceived simultaneously by two percipients. We have also received a description of his experience from the second percipient.

When I was a child, I lived in a village, with no street lamps.

Sometimes, after dark, my Mother would send me to the shop.

Part of the way, the road was between two high banks, on top of which were hedges, so you may imagine, it was very dark.

On my way home, when I came to this very lonely part, a man and a dog, I could see, blacker than night, walking about 3 yards in front of me.

When they came to the gulley (that was a pathway leading to the garden, through which I had to pass to get to my home), they would stop, and allow me to pass by.

I never saw them on my way to the shop, and I never felt frightened, but looked upon them as a guardian angel.

I share a bedroom with my brother and for some reason in the middle of this particular night I woke up. I had no idea of the time and the first thing I saw when I had woken up was a figure by the side of my bed.

I was extremely frightened and I tried to say 'Who is it?' but I couldn't speak. My mouth seemed to move but no sound came out. The figure was not anyone in the family but someone in a sort of cloak and hood rather like a monk's habit or that's how it seemed. I couldn't see the face and the whole of the figure seemed to be a three-dimensional shadow, all black and just a distinct shape.

The figure approached me and touched me and then disappeared and I can't truly remember if I fell asleep or stayed awake. Anyway I was extremely afraid. I think the fact that I could not speak worried me more than anything. It was as if my whole body had been paralysed except my eyes.

Apparitions may also appear in other uniform tones besides black and white. Thus in a number of our cases the apparition is described as grey. The following is one of these:

When as a child of six, I woke up in the middle of the night, I saw a little man. He had no decided clothing on but to me he looked grey all over. He had no age in his appearance, but looked more like a gnome. He had in his hands a great big ball of knitting wool, which seemed to unravel as he backed away across the bedroom and down the stairs. I never saw him again.

*

So far in this chapter we have only discussed cases in which the colouring of the apparition was normal or represented a simplification of the colouring that might be expected in the corresponding real object. However, in rare cases the colours of apparitions seem to be actually heightened, or abnormally intense in comparison with their real counterparts. For example, in one case the subject reports that while lying in bed she saw an apparition of her living daughter, then aged 11, floating across her bedroom between herself and the ceiling and out of the half-open door. She writes that the experience began with a 'glorious soft glow' developing in the corner of the bedroom, and that the ensuing picture of her daughter was 'all in colours too lovely to believe . . .'.

In the following somewhat similar case the subject was a child of seven or eight at the time of her experience; she described it as follows:

> My parents were in India, and I was living with an Aunt and Uncle and their five children in a Georgian Vicarage on the outskirts of H. Being the only girl child in the family I slept with the nurse and youngest child in a night nursery leading off the day nursery. Until the nurse came to bed the door between the two rooms was usually left ajar. On this particular night the light in the day nursery had been left on, and made a pathway of light through the half open door into the night nursery. My bed faced the door, and I had turned on to my right side, away from the light. After a short time I turned on to my left side, and there, vignetted between the pathway of light and the rest of the room, was this darling fair curly-haired blue eyed child. Only the head and shoulders were intensely colourful and clear, the rest faded into the light. It was completely unsubstantial and rainbow-like. I was startled and just stared, and the child smiled. Being very highly strung I *ought* to have been frightened! But the reverse happened, and a feeling of great peace and comfort enveloped me. It was somehow all GOOD. As I stared the colours faded gradually and disappeared, just as a rainbow might.

It is interesting to note that the characteristic of heightened coloration is also displayed by the environment seen in some out-of-the-body experiences. One of the Institute's subjects, for example, reported that the colours seen in the ecsomatic state seemed 'living and indescribable'. (Cf. Celia Green, *Out-of-the-Body Experiences*, p. 72.) However, heightening of colour seems to be more characteristic of ecsomatic experiences than apparitional ones.

CHAPTER 25

Incomplete Apparitions

NOT all visual apparitions of human beings are of complete human figures. Sometimes people report seeing apparitions of part of the human body only, such as the face, head, or head and shoulders. The following case will illustrate this type:

> About three years ago I went to stay with my niece for a short period in the summer and became ill with a septic throat. I had got over the worst but had not been out of doors. I was alone in the house on a beautiful afternoon, the rest of the family had gone out in the car. I was resting on my bed fully clothed with my eyes closed. Altogether I was there about 20 minutes. I thought I would get up to make a cup of tea but I got a shock because suspended between the ceiling and the foot of the bed in a lovely pale grey cloud and clearly visible was the head and shoulders of my mother. I sat on the bed and looked at her for a few seconds. She was not looking at me, she was looking out of the window and was profile to me.
>
> I spoke to her and told her to go away—she disappeared in a flash. I have often thought about this and wondered if I should have told her to go away. The strange part is my mother passed away 30 years ago and the house to which she came was not built.

Sometimes, as in the last case, the incomplete figure is surrounded by some kind of frame, such as a cloud. However, often no such frame is described, as in the following experience, in which the apparition seems to have consisted of nothing but a human mouth, resembling that of the percipient's late mother. The experience took place on the day of her mother's funeral.

> I could not go to the funeral on the Monday because of certain circumstances, so I carried on as usual that day, washing in the morning and ironing in the afternoon. As I ironed I felt pretty bad about not attending the funeral. I said aloud, 'I'm sorry, mother. I'm just carrying on as usual.' Then I looked up and saw in front of me my mother's smile, very distinctive, her lips not parted but lifted at the corners in a rather grim little smile she had.

The commonest type of incomplete apparition seems to be one of a head or face. However, apparitions of other parts of the body are sometimes reported, particularly hands, as in the following experience:

> I 'woke' in the early hours of the morning of Friday 6th January 1968, to 'see' two gaunt hands holding a ledger moving towards me, a yard distant from me and four feet from the floor. I wrote 'woke', because I believe that I was in a semiconscious state. I screamed three times, reported to me by my landlady, as I am only aware of one scream. Three days later I was informed by my superior at my place of employment, The V. Record Office, that my probationary period of work had been examined and that 'regrettably', I was not up to the required standard. And I was dismissed. I believe that this apparition was a product of my subconscious and projected by me, forewarning myself that my account of work was to my detriment.

In the following case the percipient reports seeing the lower half of a human figure only:

> This is an account of the only hallucination or apparition I have had. I am married (happily), in good health and 66 years old.
>
> A month ago my husband was undergoing a major eye operation and I was worried about him. It was a second operation. The first in September '61 proved unsuccessful. I felt in danger of losing my faith (I am a devout Christian). A man friend of my husband, an elderly gentleman, a devoted Christian, phoned me up when he heard the news and said he would pray for us both.
>
> In the train going to visit my husband, I was alone in the compartment. I fell asleep and on waking my eyes travelled to a gentleman's feet opposite. Then I saw the figure of a man. I could describe his clothes, up to his waist—then the figure disappeared (or half figure—I never saw its top half). This was no dream and I believe it was my elderly friend. I saw he was wearing the same clothes as I saw him wearing last. He had a deep concern for us both. This was not an alarming experience. It seemed quite natural; and I feel I was not asleep.
>
> P.S. The train was moving and between two stations—no-one could have got in or out.

CHAPTER 26

Apparitions Seen in the Air

THE great majority of visual apparitions of human beings appear on the ground, walking, standing, or sitting, just like real people. However, in a few cases they appear off the ground, or 'floating', as the following subject puts it:

> On two separate occasion I have woken up out of sleep, sat up and seen the same apparition quite clearly.
> My bedroom is half lighted from street lighting which is on all night.
> The vision was as follows: It was a creature—I think a child but her or his dress was (as far as earthly descriptions can describe) made of a gossamer thread and the colour was a pale and beautiful shade of brown.
> The child appeared to be floating above me slightly to the right of my bed. She or he was face downwards. The hair was showing like a fringe and was golden. He or she was smiling—such a wonderful smile!
> I was terrified and shouted 'Go away.' The same thing happened again a few weeks later. I woke up, recognised the apparition, screamed at my husband to get it out.

Sometimes the fact that the apparition is in the air seems to have a symbolic significance. For example, the subject may take it to indicate that the person the apparition represents is either dead or dying. In the following case the subject takes an apparition seen in the air to be an angel:

> Another time—I woke up early, and in the grey dawn, and saw the suspended figure of a young man in mid-air in a short tunic, at the end of my bed. I sat up to be quite sure I was not dreaming, and he gradually 'went up', and disappeared. Being a believing Christian I was quite sure I had seen an angel, and had the impression of this visitation strongly on me—all day.

When an apparition is seen to move in the air the movement is usually described as a floating one. In the following case, for example, the subject reports seeing an apparition floating across a field about one and a half feet above the ground:

> Some years ago, a friend and I were returning from an outlying village. It was a mild clear night with half-moon. Coming through an avenue of trees, we approached a large open field with houses on the opposite side of the road. Appearing to float across that field, just above ground level, was the figure of a woman with arms slightly outstretched. She was completely colourless, with the exception of her long fair hair which streamed behind her. We both stopped dead and watched. To our utter bewilderment, she disappeared straight through the wall of the convent school opposite. A man cycling towards us dismounted and enquired 'Did you see that?' We replied we certainly had. He left us saying 'That's the third time—I don't like it, I don't like it!'
> ... 'She' was gliding roughly $1\frac{1}{2}$ feet above ground level.

It is rare for an apparition to be described as making walking movements, as if on an invisible surface some way above the ground, particularly if it appears at some height above the ground. However, there are exceptions to this, such as the following case in which a tabby kitten was seen dancing along the top of a wall, but not quite touching it. The kitten had been born in the spring of the year in which the experience took place and the percipient had given it to her tenants who lived in a nearby row of houses. Before the experience took place the percipient had already rescued the kitten twice from a tree-trunk when visiting a shop next to her tenants' house.

> In July we sat at tea one day when there was a cloudburst of rain flooding the front. My husband suddenly said to me, 'I'm afraid the kitten is missing, and has been for two or three days.' This of course set me wondering where to look for him. After tea and the rain had stopped I was setting off from the back door to get out bottom of lawn past six more lawns to a side road leading to my destination. Before I could leave the doorway I suddenly saw the kitten dancing happily along the wall but NOT *touching* the wall, full of radiant happiness and its markings standing out so vivid, I shouted 'Tiggles' and flew down the path but it had gone ...

The percipient was told next day that her tenants had found the kitten dead in their shed and that it had obviously been dead two or three days, so it seems it was already dead at the time of the percipient's experience.

*

Subjects sometimes report that they saw an apparition outside a window which was too far off the ground for a real person to have been at that point, unless of course they had had the help of some mechanical contrivance such as a ladder. In one such case a number of army officers were having dinner in their mess, when the following incident occurred, described here by one of the percipients:

> At about 8.45 p.m. Atkinson suddenly glared at the window to his right, thereby attracting the notice of Russell, who, seizing his arm, said, 'Good gracious, Doctor, what's the matter with you?' This caused me to look in the direction in which I saw Atkinson looking, viz., at the window opposite, and I there saw (for the curtains were looped up, although the room was lighted by a powerful central gas light in the roof and by candles on the table) a young woman, in what appeared a soiled or somewhat worn bridal dress, walk or glide slowly past the window from east to west. She was about at the centre of the window when I observed her, and outside the window. No person could have actually been in the position where she appeared, as the window in question is about 30 feet above the ground. (Gurney II, p. 208)

In the following case the percipient reports seeing an apparition of a priest looking over a chalet roof in such a way that she assumed it was a real person standing on some kind of balcony on the other side, but when she looked at the chalet from behind she saw that there was no such balcony there. The percipient was walking towards a small village in the mountains of Savoy.

> I said before there was a turn which led to the village. To the right is a road leading up to the parish church, which is hidden by a large rock; to the left, a house with a barn, and next to it a sort of chalet with a painted roof. As I looked up, attracted by its old queer build, I saw behind the top of the roof, and seemingly resting his hands on the other side, a Curate in Roman Catholic clothing and with a strange sort of cap on his head, like those worn by Curates in church, but with what seemed stripes of white and black. The priest had a pale face with regular features and seemed to look at me *intently*, not even turning off his eyes when I stared back, wishing him to understand that I thought his manners strange. In this way I had a very good sight of him, and, if an artist, I could easily recall his features on paper. A stone, over which I stumbled, made me look down instinctively. When I turned my eyes again, the apparition was gone, and I went onwards thinking to myself how the manners of those village priests wanted improvement.
>
> A few steps further I arrived at a sort of little square, where the village fountain and the letter-box are, and after putting in a letter,

I sat on a stone staircase under it, and had a good look at the chalet, where I had seen the priest. It was uninhabited; its shutters were shut, and the whole place had an air of desolation. I could not see what was on the other side of the roof, where there must be a balcony, on which the Curate must have stood, so I moved on to the other side of the little square, from where I would have a view of the back. To my intense astonishment there was no balcony, nor anything but a roof as pointed as to the front, nor any means of getting to it in any way. Then the Curate must have been an apparition, and this thought sent an unpleasant sort of cold shiver through me, and I turned back home at once. (*Journal of the S.P.R.*, Vol. XVI, 1913–14, p. 152)

The percipient later learnt that the chalet was reputed to be haunted by the curate who had once inhabited it, and whose will could not be found when he died. Later still a member of the curate's family told the percipient that when he had been put in his coffin the women around him passed a white ribbon between the cloth stripes of his cap.

CHAPTER 27

Abnormalities of Movement

PERCIPIENTS quite often describe apparitions as walking from one place to another in the real environment and in such cases they usually say that the apparition's movements were normal, like those of a real person. However, in a few cases they seem to be unrealistic; for example, they may seem abnormally smooth. One of our subjects writes of the apparition she saw: 'It appeared to move past kitchen door with more of a panther-like glide rather than normal walk.'

In one case we have already quoted (pp. 50–1) a lady and her husband out for a walk saw the same apparition in two separate places within such a short space of time that it would not have been possible for the apparition to have got from one place to the other had it been a real person. The two spots were about a hundred and fifty yards apart; the wife remarks: 'Had he been shot out of a gun, he could not have gone faster.'

The following is an interesting case in the present connection. The subject describes an apparition as moving from one place to another but without traversing the intervening space:

> One night during [my husband's] absence the child woke me about midnight; having hushed him off to sleep, I said, 'Now sir, I hope you will let me rest!' I lay down, and instantly became conscious of two figures standing at the door of my room. One, M.N. [these are not the real initials], whom I recognised at once, was that of a former lover, whose misconduct and neglect had compelled me to renounce him. Of this I am sure, that if ever I saw him in my life, it was then. I was not in the least frightened; but said to myself, as it were, 'You never used to wear that kind of waistcoat.' The door close to where he stood was in a deep recess close to the fireplace, for there was no grate; we burnt logs only. In that recess stood a man in a tweed suit. I saw the whole figure distinctly, but not the face, and for this reason: on the edge of the mantelshelf always stood a morocco leather

medicine chest, which concealed the face from me . . . I had an impression that this other was a cousin of M.N.'s, who had been the means of leading him astray while in the North of England. I never saw him in my life; he died in India.

M.N. was in deep mourning; he had a look of unutterable sorrow upon his face, and was deadly pale. He never opened his lips, but I read his heart as if it were an open book, and it said, 'My father is dead, and I have come into his property.' I answered, 'How much you have grown like your father!' Then in a moment, *without appearing to walk,* he stood at the foot of the child's cot, and I saw *distinctly* the blueness of his eyes as he gazed on my boy, and then raised them to Heaven as if in prayer.

All vanished. (Gurney I, p. 425)

The percipient later discovered that M.N.'s father had died on the same day as her experience.

CHAPTER 28

'Hyperacuity' and 'Clairvoyance'

SOMETIMES people report that their hallucinatory perceptions were more clear and detailed than their ordinary perceptions would have been under the same circumstances. For example, they may see the figure of an apparition more clearly in a darkened room than they would have been able to if it had been a real person, even if the figure of the apparition is not luminous.

In one case a subject reported seeing an apparition of her father on a white horse out hunting, in a field where he did not actually go all day. He seemed to wave to her and her two companions with his hat, as if to sign them to follow him. She writes: 'As my father waved his hat I clearly saw the Lincoln and Bennet mark inside, though from the distance we were apart it ought to have been utterly impossible for me to have seen it.' (*Journal of the S.P.R.*, Vol. VI, 1893–4, p. 129)

The following is an interesting case, in which the percipient, a Miss Jessie Walker, reports a tactile hallucination which may have been more distinct than was strictly realistic:

About three years ago, I and a lady friend engaged apartments in the house of a widow lady with whom we resided about eight months, when the following incident occurred. One evening, we had been sitting up reading rather later than usual, and did not rise to retire until within a few minutes to 12 o'clock. We went upstairs together, I being perhaps a couple of steps behind my friend, when, on reaching the topmost step, I felt something suddenly slip behind me from an unoccupied room to the left of the stairs. Thinking it must be imagination, no one being in the house except the widow and servant, who occupied rooms on another landing, I did not speak to my friend, who turned off to a room on the right, but walked quickly into my own room which faced the staircase, still feeling as though a tall figure were behind and bending over me. I turned on the gas, struck a light and was in the act of applying it, when I felt a heavy grasp on my arm of a hand minus the middle finger. Upon this I uttered a loud cry, which brought my friend, the widow lady, and the servant girl into the room, to inquire the cause of my alarm. The two latter turned very pale on hearing the story. The house was thoroughly searched, but nothing was discovered.

Some weeks passed and I had ceased to be alarmed at the occurrence, when I chanced to mention it whilst out spending the afternoon with some friends. A gentleman present inquired if I had ever heard a description or seen a 'carte' of the lady's late husband. On receiving a reply in the negative, he said that singularly enough he was tall, had a slight stoop, and had lost the middle finger of his right hand. (*Proceedings of the S.P.R.*, Vol. V, 1888–9, p. 464)

As F. W. H. Myers remarks in introducing this case, 'It would not, under ordinary circumstances, be easy to be certain that a hand suddenly grasping one's arm lacked the middle finger.' It is possible that we have here an example of a hallucinatory perception having greater clarity or distinctness than its real counterpart.

Sometimes subjects with poor sight or hearing report that they could see or hear an apparition better than they would have been able to if it had been a real person. For example, one of our subjects reports seeing a visual apparition of an old lady in a long white night-dress in his home, and hearing the rustle of her dress, although he was 'totally deaf'.

It is interesting to compare such cases with an analogous phenomenon in out-of-the-body experiences. Sometimes ecsomatic subjects report that, while seeming to be outside their physical bodies, they could see or hear perfectly well although in the normal state their sight or hearing is impaired. The following case will illustrate this point:

One very interesting experience occurred when, in this 'floating' state, I decided to project my conscious self some distance away from my body, and 'willed' myself to travel some two hundred miles, to visit a theatre in my home town, where I knew there was a production in which I was very much interested.

Immediately the desire occurred, I was 'there', in the foyer of the theatre, and drifted towards the corridor which I knew led to the auditorium. To my surprise, everything appeared to be 'wrong way round': The stalls corridor was on the wrong side of the foyer, and the stage the wrong end of the auditorium, as I remember it.

I drifted some feet above the heads of the audience, in an upright position (and obviously invisible) and was able quite clearly to see and hear the play which was proceeding on the stage. A significant point is that I am rather deaf and could never, in the body, have heard stage dialogue without my hearing-aid; nor could I have seen so perfectly without my glasses. Despite the absence of both these artificial aids, I found no difficulty whatever in seeing and hearing perfectly . . .

I was greatly enjoying the play and delighting in my unique method of seeing it (not without a slight feeling of rather smug satisfaction at my own 'cleverness'!!) when something on the stage amused me, and I began to laugh. Immediately I was back in my physical body, and found it, to my disappointment, impossible to return.

*

Subjects sometimes seem to know more about an apparition than they can consciously justify. For example, the following subject reports that she somehow knew that the apparition was sitting in an apparitional rocking-chair, even though she could not see the lower half of the chair:

I am a very sound sleeper but one night about 3 months ago I suddenly awoke in the night for no reason at all and looked straight over to my husband's side of the bed. There I saw an old lady with her head bent sitting in a rocking chair. How it was a rocking chair I do not know as I only saw the top half as the rest was hidden by the bed. It had a high slatted back. Also I had the impression that she wore long skirts, but there was no fear at all. I only saw this for a second or two. I must also mention I had not been dreaming.

Andrew MacKenzie quotes an interesting case in which a subject 'knew' that an apparition's nails were dirty even though its hands were hidden in the sleeves of its monk's habit. (*Apparitions and Ghosts*, pp. 100–1)

Cases of this kind are similar to experiences of 'presences', in which the subject is convinced that someone is in his environment, even though he is not aware of any sensory impressions which could have given him this idea. As we have already seen, the subject may have a very detailed idea of the characteristics of the person whose 'presence' he senses, although he sees nothing (pp. 119–121).

CHAPTER 29

Apparitions Seen in Reflecting Surfaces

SOMETIMES subjects report seeing apparitions in reflecting surfaces, such as mirrors, highly polished furniture, and so forth. For example, in the following case the subject reports seeing a representation of her late mother's face above her own as she looked at her own reflection in the glass panel at the front of a bus. An unusual feature of this case is that the subject reports a vivid mental or 'internal' image following closely on the 'externalised' hallucination.

> Another strange thing. Last November, the anniversary of my mother's death (she died 17 years ago), I had completely forgotten about it. Though over the years, on the anniversary of her death, I have always got the feeling that somehow she came to me. But as I said, this last time I was very busy, and never gave it a thought. I had to go to town, and got on the bus sitting directly behind the driver. As you will know, your own reflection can be seen through the glass in the driver's back. Imagine then my surprise to see my face and above it the face of my mother's, looking at me reproachfully, because I had forgotten her anniversary I suppose. Then after I got over my surprise I caught myself saying 'Oh Mum, sorry I forgot.' She was *that much* real to me that I had to apologise. Then as her face faded the green and mauvy texture of a tweed coat she used to wear came vividly—really vividly—to my mind. This green and mauve coat was not a very bright coat, but seeing it then 17 years later, after I had forgotten about it anyway, it took on the most brilliant colours of green and mauve as to be almost jewel-like.

The following is a similar case. In this instance the reflecting surface was some protective glass through which the subject had to look while watching an arc-burning process at his place of work. It is interesting to note that the subject states explicitly that the figure of the apparition was not visible when he looked in the place where it should have been according to the optical laws of reflection if it had been a real person, but was only visible in the reflecting surface.

> . . . the time when my younger brother was killed at sea. This happened while I was at work. Part of my trade at that time was to watch a process of arc burning; to do this I had to look through a dark red glass; and in the reflection of this glass, I could see my desk and chair. I had done this same operation thousands of times, and always saw the same reflection. But this time, I saw a sailor sat in my chair. I turned and looked; the chair was empty. Three times I looked into the glass, and three times I saw a sailor sat there. Three times I turned and looked, and three times I turned and saw an empty chair. I knew then my brother was dead. I just knew. I can't, and couldn't then, say why, but I knew. He was an ordinary seaman in the Royal Navy; he and all his shipmates were lost.

It fairly frequently happens that an apparition seen in a reflecting surface is of only part of a human figure, as in the following two cases:

> During the 1950's my husband and I lived in a perfectly ordinary house at Mitcham, erected in the 30's and we had in our bedroom a suite of utility mahogany furniture, which included a wardrobe; this had a fairly good gloss on it, and it is only fair to mention this. I woke up one morning, a grey, late winter day, and not having been awoken by the alarm, peered over my husband's shoulder at the clock; the time was only 6.30 a.m. and I began to return to the warmth of the blankets, but as I did so my attention was riveted to the wardrobe. There, clearly on one of the panels, was the head and shoulders of a boy of about 10. It was in effect like a snapshot, except the size was about 24ins × 18ins. He was dark-haired, had a perfectly ordinary jacket—it looked like a blazer, but difficult to tell without colour, and a striped school tie. The picture was perfectly still, again like a snapshot, and even today, if I saw a photograph of this boy I would recognise it. It lasted about 30 seconds and then vanished. My family quite rightly state that a gloss can produce many illusions, but this was too clear and too definite to be one. We made enquiries about previous owners, but no-one seemed to know much about the original occupants. Nothing like that has happened again, and there did not seem any reason for it happening then.
>
> There was one other curious factor. In spite of the fact that the incident was rather odd, I never once had a feeling of fear, fright, terror or discomfort, either before, during or after.

> On the 5th April, 1873, my wife's father, Captain Towns, died at his residence, Cranbrook, Rose Bay, near Sydney, N.S.Wales. About 6 weeks after his death, my wife had occasion, one evening about 9 o'clock, to go to one of the bedrooms in the house. She was

accompanied by a young lady, Miss Berthon, and as they entered the room—the gas was burning all the time—they were amazed to see, reflected as it were on the polished surface of the wardrobe, the image of Captain Towns. It was barely half figure, the head, shoulders, and part of the arms only showing—in fact, it was like an ordinary medallion portrait, but life-size. The face appeared wan and pale, as it did before his death; and he wore a kind of grey flannel jacket, in which he had been accustomed to sleep. Surprised and half alarmed at what they saw, their first idea was that a portrait had been hung in the room, and that what they saw was its reflection—but there was no picture of the kind.

Whilst they were looking and wondering, my wife's sister, Miss Towns, came into the room, and before either of the others had time to speak she exclaimed, 'Good gracious! Do you see papa?' One of the housemaids happened to be passing down stairs at the moment, and she was called in, and asked if she saw anything, and her reply was, 'Oh, miss! the master.' Graham—Captain Towns' old body servant—was then sent for, and he also immediately exclaimed, 'Oh, Lord save us! Mrs. Lett, it's the Captain!' The butler was called, and then Mrs. Crane, my wife's nurse, and they both said what they saw. Finally, Mrs. Towns was sent for, and, seeing the apparition, she advanced towards it with her arm extended as if to touch it, and as she passed her hand over the panel of the wardrobe the figure gradually faded away, and never again appeared, though the room was regularly occupied for a long time after. (Gurney II, pp. 213–14)

(This account was signed by two of the percipients, the wife of the narrator and her sister, Miss Towns.)

There are a number of cases in which a percipient first sees an apparition in a mirror and then sees it directly or *vice versa*. However, it is seldom that a percipient reports seeing an apparition close enough to a mirror for him to have been able simultaneously to see both the figure and its reflection if it had been a real person. In the few cases in which the percipient has been suitably situated the results are inconsistent. Sometimes he sees the apparition reflected in the mirror and sometimes he does not.

In the following case the percipient reports seeing an apparition close in front of a mirror but being unable to see a reflection:

I had been sitting reading after the others had retired for the night, and it would be between twelve and one when I started to go up to bed. When I got to the top of the stairs I saw the door of my father's room was open, the gas full up, and standing before the dressing-table, resting her hands on it and gazing into the mirror, was the apparition. I stood still for a second, then moved to try to see past the figure into the mirror in order to get a view of her face. The first part of this was very easy, as the dressing-table was in the corner diagonally to the door, so that by moving a little to one side I could see very well into the glass, when what was my surprise to see there was no reflection. Just as I made this discovery she turned partly round, but not enough to enable me to see her face, and moved across the room beyond my vision. I rushed in, but there was nothing to be found . . . (*Journal of the S.P.R.*, Vol. X, 1901–2, pp. 309–10)

Subject E has deliberately experimented with a similar situation in lucid dreams, and describes one such experiment as follows:

When full lucidity dawned, I was still sitting at the table but the environment had changed—to a hall of some kind, occupied by people sitting at tables. It suddenly occurred to me that this was a good opportunity to try looking in a mirror in a lucid dream. I therefore approached the fireplace, above which (as hoped) hung a mirror, a large rectangular one. My image looked remarkably well and youthful, with *radiant* eyes, hair parted in the middle (I have never worn it thus) and rather long. I moved my hand across in front of the mirror and the reflected image followed this in a quite natural-looking manner. Turning my attention then to the other people and to the room in general, I could find no discrepancy in the reflection: in particular, a person clad in yellow, second from the counter/stage at the far end, was faithfully reflected.

It is interesting to note that two of our ecsomatic subjects deliberately approached the mirrors in their bedrooms during out-of-the-body experiences to see what they could see in them. The first appears to have seen a normal image of herself. She says 'I was certainly still "me" '. The second subject's experience was more paradoxical; she reports 'touching' the mirror, which seems to imply she felt as if she was located in some sort of 'body', but she could not see any reflection of 'herself', although she could see reflected in the mirror the rest of the room, including her own physical body lying on the bed. (See *Out-of-the-Body Experiences*, pp. 73–4)

CHAPTER 30

The Content of Apparitions

APPARITIONS may concern human beings, animals, and abstract or inanimate objects. Over 80 per cent of our cases are of human beings. However, we must bear in mind that such cases may be more memorable, or more likely to be reported in response to appeals for cases.

The following is an example of an auditory case concerning an animal.

> For some fifteen years I owned a working Sheep Dog, which I had destroyed because he was suffering, due to old age. Two hours after his death I was sitting in the lounge after lunch when I heard distinctly the pad of his feet and his characteristic snuffling at the bottom of the door, sounds which I had heard hundreds of times before when he wanted to come into the room. I half rose from the chair to go and open the door, realised I was imagining things and sat down again.

Our third category of apparitional subject-matter (abstract and inanimate objects) includes such things as geometrical figures, and pillars or rays of light, in addition to more recognisable everyday objects such as gravestones, inscriptions, buildings, machinery, and so forth.

The following case, which concerned an inscription on a building, will serve to illustrate the 'abstract or inanimate' category:

> I can report one [apparitional experience]—a stone date on the wall of a Quaker meeting-house, a date that may have been there when the building was erected but was not there when I 'saw' it.
>
> The meeting-house is at Marazion, Cornwall. I had seen a notice of a meeting advertised and I went there out of curiosity—I am not a Friend. There is a church-yard, with a path leading up to the door. When I reached the top of this path I paused and noticed the date, 1688, carved in stone over the door. I thought 'just 200 years before

I was born', and was meditating on this when one of the Friends came to me to say that the meeting was beginning and would I care to go in.

A few weeks later, after another meeting, I stood in front of the door, chatting with an Elder. I noticed that the wall over the door had been crudely repaired with a lighter-coloured cement or plaster. I remarked that it was a pity that the workmen had removed the date when they did the repairs. The Elder said that the repairs had been done years before, and neither he nor any other member knew anything about it. They said there was no record or picture of the original doorway, but the date was right and it was quite likely that it had been carved over the door.

I had no previous knowledge of the dates when Quakers flourished —my repertory of history dates is poor.

It is interesting to note that in this case at least part of the surroundings of the inscription appear to have been hallucinatory as well as the inscription itself, viz. the stone on which the inscription appeared, and which it seems was really not of the colour the percipient saw on the first occasion, but lighter.

Apparitions of plants on their own, unaccompanied by human beings or animals, are rarely reported. However, the following is an interesting example:

During 1962 I was cutting the grass round a fir tree with branches near ground level, when I saw a vivid colour underneath. On opening the branches I saw the most beautiful canterbury bells. On a long stem were two half hoops of huge bells. I immediately wondered if they were real, so I sat down, drew them out, smelt, and handled them. Deciding that they really were there, I thought it a pity to leave them, so went to prepare a bed for them in my small flower patch. On returning for them however, they were nowhere to be seen.

It is interesting to compare this experience with some reported by lucid dreamers. The subject handled and smelt the flowers, trying to decide if they were real and decided that they were. In a similar way, lucid dreamers sometimes examine the objects in their environment with care in an attempt to decide whether they are dreaming, and may conclude that they are not on account of their realistic texture.

*

It seems to be rare for an apparition to be of more than one person or animal at a time. Only 10 per cent of the visual apparitions of humans or animals in our collection involve more than one human being or animal, or a combination of a human and an animal.

The very first case quoted in this book, that of the two undergraduates and the horse seen in New College Lane, is an example of a relatively complex apparition, consisting as it does of two human figures and an animal.

Gurney, too, noticed that apparitions in which a second figure appeared are rare. Of course, most of the cases in *Phantasms of the Living* are 'crisis cases', in which the apparition represents a person at a distance who is undergoing some crisis, such as dying, or having an accident; and usually it is a single person known to the percipient who is undergoing this crisis. So it is perhaps not surprising that the apparition in such cases should usually be of a single person. However, Gurney also noticed the extreme rarity of more than one human figure in his cases with no obvious telepathic content. He writes: 'In my large collection of subjective hallucinations of vision . . . I find only seven cases, that is, less than 3 per cent, presenting more than one human figure . . .' (Gurney I, p. 546)

The Census authors also note: 'In the great majority of realistic cases, the apparition represents a single figure only, though there are exceptions.' (*Census*, p. 113)

CHAPTER 31

Apparitions of the Living

THE popular view of ghosts is that they are likely to be apparitions of the dead, and it is possible that this expectation may lead to a greater tendency to report cases concerning apparitions of deceased persons. However, subjects quite commonly report perceiving apparitions of people who are alive at the time of the experience. About a third of all the recognised apparitions of human beings reported to us are of this kind.

The apparitions reported represent a wide variety of living friends, acquaintances and relations of the percipient: parents, grandparents, children, husband or wife, in-laws, etc. If the apparition represents someone not related to the percipient by blood or marriage it may be a close friend, or merely an acquaintance, such as the subject's landlady or milkman. Occasionally, the apparition is identified as someone that the subject does not encounter until later. However, the majority of all apparitional cases reported to us (72 per cent) are unrecognised.

The following is an example of a case in which the subject reports seeing an apparition of a close relative, her mother.

> I would like to tell you of my experience of fifty years ago as a child of ten, and which has puzzled me ever since.
> It was my Sunday morning task to take mother her tea in bed before preparing for church and on this particular morning I was fastening my shoes and happened to turn my head to the left when I saw what I have always called since, 'mother's ghost'. At first I thought she had come downstairs because I said that I had not yet made the tea and on getting no answer I turned and looked again and there was this apparition. Mother used to wear a navy blue and white spotted dress but on this occasion the colours were reversed and I could see right through the 'ghost' to the sideboard behind. What did strike me, and I have thought of it since, that she looked so sad.
> Of course by that time I was scared and ran upstairs to tell mother who in her turn was somewhat perturbed.

I might add that I was not a very imaginative child, being the eldest of four brothers and sisters I was kept busy helping mother and so had little time for day-dreaming or otherwise.

I would also like to add that mother is still with me and has reached the age of 86 years.

There is little popular tradition relating to apparitions of the living, but what there is might lead one to expect that such apparitions would be associated with crisis situations in the life of the person perceived, or possibly with situations of emergency in the life of the percipient. In fact, although cases are reported in which circumstances of this kind obtain, in nearly two thirds of the cases in which the subject reports seeing an apparition of a living person his experience is not related in any very obvious way to events in the life of the person represented.

The following is one of these apparently inconsequential cases, in which the subject reports seeing an apparition of her husband, although he was lying asleep beside her.

My husband had a night out, with the 'boys', consequently was late home. I went to bed (we live in a bungalow) at midnight, and slept. At 2 a.m. I was aroused by the sound of my husband, trying to fit his key in the lock. Eventually I got up, and went and opened the door. He was rather cross, because, he said, there was something wrong with the lock, and I wasn't too happy at being wakened, as it takes a long time for me to get to sleep. He came to bed where I was lying wide awake, the room was filled with light from the moon, it being nearly full, and we always have the curtains drawn back at night and a window open. After a short space of time, I became aware of movement on his side of the bed, and thought to myself, 'Surely he is not getting up again, he's only been in bed five minutes.' I lifted my head, and saw him rising swiftly to nearly full height, but slightly bent at the waist, as if ready to run, which he was doing. I sat up startled, and put out a hand to stop him, thinking, by this time, that he was sleep-walking, then suddenly realised that I was leaning on him. He was still in bed, fast asleep, and breathing so quietly that I had to bend down to hear him. He didn't waken in spite of being leaned on. My husband is one of those people who say they never dream. The next morning I asked him if he had dreamt 'last night', and he said 'No'. It was very odd, because I could see his whole figure in the moonlight, looking solid and normal—in pyjamas.

The following is a rather similar case in which the subject reports seeing her husband apparently leaving his bed when in fact he was really still sleeping in it.

Two months ago, I woke suddenly at 1:30 a.m. and saw my husband walk from his bed to the window and stand looking out. I said 'Oh you are awake.' He did not answer. It was completely silent. I pulled the blanket on his bed and called his name three times. No answer. A car passed at that moment and the vision disappeared. My husband was sleeping very silently. After a little while I lay down and went to sleep.

The next case again concerns an apparition of the subject's mother, and illustrates the fact that these cases are not associated with crisis situations as often as tradition might suggest. In this case it occurs to the subject that her mother may have died, but in fact she finds her sleeping peacefully.

My mother lived with me, and at the time of which I write was aged about 83, so consequently went to bed a good deal earlier than I did. One night I was leaving the sitting room with my black cocker spaniel dog by my side, and on opening the door there was my mother standing just outside in the hall, perfectly solid and in her nightdress and with the little shawl around her shoulders that she always wore in bed. I thought she had just come to the door and spoke to her, when she immediately vanished. The dog's hackles rose slightly and I knew from his apparance that he had seen her too. My first thought was that she had died in her sleep, and that this was her ghost, so I went at once to her room, where she was lying peacefully asleep.
She lived for four years after this.

Again, in the following case concerning an apparition of the subject's son, no real crisis seems to have been involved although the percipient's son was in hospital at the time.

We were living in a gorgeous flat in Montreal at the time. My youngest son Donald was in hospital having one of many operations for osteomyelitis. My husband and I were in bed and asleep. I woke up with a start and looked towards the door which was wide open. I could see my son Don standing there in his white blouse and navy shorts on.
I thought, It can't be, he is in hospital, but he certainly seemed real enough. My husband woke up and said, 'What's the matter?' I replied that he wouldn't believe me. He said, 'Try me.' Then I told him what I saw, and he said, Yes he believed it. While we were talking Donald slowly disappeared backwards. Needless to say I didn't get to sleep again and worried until we phoned to see if he was alright. He is very much alive. He became an Englishman and also became a D— County councillor.

By contrast with the last case, in which the apparition was of the percipient's son, in the following case the subject apparently did not even know the person whose apparition he saw until that person later turned up in reality:

> A few years ago I was crossing the bridge over the River Idle here, 10 a.m. I saw at the end of a range of buildings fronting the river a young man, seated on a slab of cement. He was dressed in a grey suit, wore a grey cap, had on his knees a drawing board, and was obviously sketching. Seated on the grass behind him was a lady I knew, and with her, her small son. Passing the buildings, and going down the lane behind them, I came to the cement slab, but there wasn't the young man on it. Enquiry of the lady as to where he had gone, brought the reply, 'There hasn't been anyone here since we came, half an hour ago.' Rather puzzled, I didn't pursue the matter. At 4.30 p.m. I crossed the bridge, and there again was the young man. The afternoon was hot, and his coat was on the river bank. When I reached the spot, he was there in the flesh, so I asked him where he had disappeared to in the morning. He assured me he hadn't arrived in Retford until 1.30 p.m.

At first sight this might appear to be a case of precognition on the part of the percipient. However, we must bear in mind that the young man our percipient saw may have already formed the intention of sketching at that particular spot by the time our percipient saw the apparition of him there. The subconscious mind of our percipient may have acquired this information from the young man by extrasensory perception, and incorporated it in an apparition.

Sometimes a subject sees or hears an apparition of a person he knows shortly before that person really arrives at the same spot. Alternatively, he may see an apparition of someone he knows leaving the house, or seemingly returning to the house after they have really left it. The percipient nearly always takes the apparition to be the real person at first, and sometimes is only disabused when the real person turns up some time later.

In the following example the percipient was expecting her husband home at about the time she saw the apparition.

> My late husband had been to the hospital for a check-up, and on his way home he was to call at the local baker's for a plate pie. Around his time for return, and having the lunch just ready, I went to the front door, and saw him walking on the opposite side of the road, with the pie held in his outstretched hand. I went inside and was all prepared for his walking in the back door. Nothing happened. Half an hour elapsed before he came in with the pie, as I had seen it upon his hand. I asked him which side of the road he walked. The

same side I always do, and cross over at the Crescent, nearly opposite our house. Exactly the spot I had seen him.

In the following case, the subject saw an apparition of her sister leaving the house, and then discovered her sister was still upstairs.

> My sister and I were alone in the house, and I was washing up, when I heard the front door latch click. I went into the hall, and saw through the glass in the door my sister with her coat on walking away down the garden path, and tucking her hair into place with a habitual gesture. I have never understood why I didn't call to her. I returned to the sink, annoyed at being left to finish the dishes. Then I heard sounds of movements upstairs, which was frightening since I knew I was alone in the house. I looked up the stair well and saw my sister on the landing, still in her underwear, and without even the intention of going out.

The following experience, from the same subject, is similar. This time she saw an apparition of her father leaving the house and found he was still indoors.

> I experienced another example of this just two weeks ago. My young nephew was playing one of his new pop records. I was in the kitchen, and happening to glance out of the window saw my father out on the pavement, walking away from the house. (I described how I saw the back view of my sister going down the garden path, this time I could see my father side face on perfectly clearly. On both occasions the figure appeared clearly visible and perfectly normal.) He was not wearing a coat, but a light blue sweater which seemed strange on a cold day. I said to my mother 'Grandad didn't stand that record for long!' A minute or so later I went into the living room, and my father was sitting there with the rest of the family. He was dressed as I had seen him—I must add that I had not known previously what clothes he was actually wearing at that time.

The subject in the next case saw an apparition of her husband, apparently returning home after having left. Subsequently she found that he had not come back after leaving.

> One Saturday morning last autumn my husband went out shopping. Some ten minutes after he left I was in my kitchen, bending over a faulty vacuum cleaner. The outside door opened and my husband walked in again, dressed as usual, but looking rather pressed. He glanced at me without smiling, then turned away (out of my sight) along the corridor. A few minutes later I rose from my mending job on the floor and went to find him in the house. But no one had seen him anywhere, and he confirmed when he returned an hour later that

he had definitely *not* come back to the house after leaving. He had been in Hampstead and nothing abnormal had occurred.

So far as I know I have had no similar experience before or since.

In another case a Major Bigge saw his commanding officer in fishing gear, something he was evidently not expecting at the time and place in question. His account is as follows:

This afternoon, about 3 o'clock p.m., I was walking from my quarters towards the mess-room to put some letters into the letter-box, when I distinctly saw Lieut.-Colonel Reed, 70th Regiment, walking from the corner of the range of buildings occupied by the officers towards the mess-room door; and I saw him go into the passage. He was dressed in a brown shooting jacket, with grey summer regulation tweed trousers, and had a fishing rod and a landing net in his hand. Although at the time I saw him he was about 15 or 20 yards from me, and although anxious to speak to him at the moment, I did not do so, but followed him into the passage and turned into the ante-room on the left-hand side, where I expected to find him. On opening the door, to my great surprise, he was not there; the only person in the room was Quartermaster Nolan, 70th Regiment, and I immediately asked him if he had seen the colonel, and he replied he had not . . . I was very much surprised at not finding the colonel, and I walked back into the barrack-yard and joined Lieutenant Caulfield, 66th Regiment, who was walking there; and I told the story to him, and particularly described the dress in which I had seen the colonel. We walked up and down the barrack-yard talking about it for about 10 minutes, when, to my great surprise, never having kept my eye from the door leading to the mess-room (there is only one outlet from it), I saw the colonel walk into the barracks through the gate—which is in the opposite direction—accompanied by Ensign Willington, 70th Regiment, in precisely the same dress in which I had seen him, and with a fishing-rod and a land-net in his hand. Lieutenant Caulfield and I immediately walked to them, and we were joined by Lieut.-Colonel Goldie, 66th Regiment, and Captain Hartford, and I asked Colonel Reed if he had not gone into the mess-room about 10 minutes before. He replied that he certainly had not, for that he had been out fishing for more than two hours at some ponds about a mile from the barracks, and that he had not been near the mess-room at all since the morning.

At the time I saw Colonel Reed going into the mess-room, I was not aware that he had gone out fishing—a very unusual thing to do at this time of the year; neither had I seen him before in the dress I have described during that day. . . . (Gurney II, pp. 94–5)

CHAPTER 32

Autophany

SOMETIMES subjects report seeing apparitions of themselves. We have collected ten cases of this kind, two of them occurring to the same subject. The following is an example:

> . . . I was working as housekeeper, and was preparing the midday meal, which had to be ready by one o'clock. I wanted to see the time, and stepped to one side, from the cooker, to look into the next room where the clock was. The door of the room was open, as I only had to look across to the dresser where the clock stood, but standing looking at me was another me, dressed the same and looking very calm and spotless. I have never understood the meaning of it. It seems a wonderful thing to have happened.

We propose the term 'autophany' to denote the phenomenon of seeing an apparition of oneself, and the term 'autoscopy' to denote the phenomenon of apparently seeing one's own body from outside during an out-of-the-body experience. This usage was first suggested in *Out-of-the-Body Experiences* (p. 42), and appears more satisfactory than the usual one of using the term 'autoscopy' to denote the experience of seeing an apparition of oneself. In a case of autophany such as the one we have just quoted the percipient remains identified with his normal point of view throughout the experience, and an apparitional figure 'appears' to him. In an autoscopic out-of-the-body experience, on the other hand, the subject does not remain identified with his physical body but is the observer who views it—'himself'—from the outside.

A number of writers seem to have associated cases of autophany or 'seeing one's double' with illness on the part of the subject, taking them as a symptom of some underlying disorder. It may be true that experiences of autophany sometimes occur as a result of illness, and it may be mainly such cases that have come to the attention of earlier writers on the subject. However, it does not necessarily follow that all cases of autophany are of this kind. Among our own cases two are described as occurring when the subject was very ill, and a third when she was 'absolutely exhausted'. But in the remaining seven cases there is no indication that the subjects were ill or even sickening for an illness.

The following is the case in which the subject says she was exhausted at the time of the experience:

> I had a boarding house for a short period in Brisbane and as I fed and did the washing and ironing for fifteen young men as well as the house work by the end of the day I was absolutely exhausted.
>
> On the night on which the incident occurred I was sitting trying to relax in front of the television and must have dozed because I woke up with a start. Half asleep I looked around at the few young chaps that were also viewing the programme. For a few seconds I watched with interest the different expressions showing on their faces. Then I focused my eyes ahead on to the television screen. Imagine my surprise when I saw myself above myself. My other self was all white and transparent and lying in the same pose as I did myself: for a matter of moments I stared wonderingly and then suddenly it wasn't there. I looked around at my companions but they didn't seem to have noticed anything but were gazing intently at the television.

The following is a case of autophany that occurred to someone who says he was 'in excellent fettle' at the time of his experience:

> Through bereavement I have lived alone for over 10 yrs. Late in March, 1960 I retired at 12 midnight after a usual evening of writing, a light supper at 10.30 and my usual hour of light reading—nothing exciting at all to mind or digestion. . . . If I wake at all it is around 4–5 a.m., never in the first deep sleep.
>
> This night I awoke with a convulsive jerk all over, conscious of a nearby presence. There it was, within inches of my single bed and plain to see by the light of a half moon through my thin window curtains—the form of a human was covered by a pyjama-like covering like fine crumpled silk.
>
> As a precaution in these days of night-raiding I kept my bedroom door locked. It flashed across my mind that here was an intruder who had somehow got in and was trying to scare me prior to robbery.
>
> I jerked to a sitting position with my right hand drawn back. I let fly as hard as I could, but just before contacting I glanced up to the face and saw it was myself! Too late to stop, the fist went through the body which did not wait for a second, or a hundredth of a second—it was away!

It is interesting to note that at least one case of autophany on record was apparently collective. A Mrs. Hall saw an apparition of herself standing near a sideboard while she, her husband, and two relatives were having dinner one evening. We only have the account of Mrs. Hall in this case, but she maintains that the other three people present with her all saw the apparition too. The following is Mrs. Hall's narrative:

> As the weather became more wintry, a married cousin and her husband came on a visit. One night, when we were having supper, an apparition stood at the end of the sideboard. We four sat at the dining-table; and yet, with great inconsistency, I stood as this ghostly visitor again, in a spotted, light muslin summer dress, and without any terrible peculiarities of air or manner. We all four saw it, my husband having attracted our attention to it, saying 'It is Sarah,' in a tone of recognition, meaning me. It at once disappeared. None of us felt any fear, it seemed too natural and familiar.
>
> The apparition seemed utterly apart from myself and my feelings, as a picture or statue. (Gurney, II, pp. 217–18)

*

It would be interesting to know whether the subjects of autophany cases see themselves as others see them or as they normally see themselves in the mirror.

The image most people see of themselves in the mirror is of course somewhat different from the image of them seen by other people, because the two sides of the human face are usually not perfectly symmetrical and a mirror reverses these slight asymmetries.

Several of our ecsomatic subjects claimed that the image they saw of themselves while apparently looking at their own face from outside was not like the one they were accustomed to seeing in the mirror.

None of our subjects who report experiences of autophany mention that the face of the apparition they saw did not look quite like the face they are used to seeing in the mirror. However, this may simply be because we have received far fewer cases of autophany than cases of autoscopic out-of-the-body experiences. As already mentioned, we have received only ten cases of autophany, whereas we received some 300 cases of out-of-the-body experiences in which the subject reported looking at his own physical body from outside. Only a small proportion of these ecsomatic subjects remarked on the discrepancy between what they saw of their face during the out-of-the-body experience and what they were accustomed to seeing in the mirror. So it is possible that if 300 cases of autophany were studied, some cases might emerge in which a similar discrepancy was remarked upon.

Of course, it is also possible that when subjects see a representation of their own face in an ecsomatic experience, or in one of autophany, they are not actually seeing a precisely accurate reproduction of their features, either as normally seen by other people, or as normally seen by themselves in a mirror. When ecsomatic subjects comment that what they see looks a little unfamiliar, it may merely mean that the representation of their own face is not quite good enough to pass without attracting critical attention, and when they do not comment, it may only mean that the representation is good enough to be recognised as their own face without reservation.

*

The following is an example of what one might call auditory autophany, in which the subject seems to hear his own voice.

> About five years ago I was driving a car in the Isle of Wight along a road without a footpath. Two small children were walking steadily hand in hand along the left hand side of the road with their backs to me. I sounded my horn, but they did not turn their heads so I could not tell if they knew that I was there or not. However they were walking calmy and steadily along the side of the road, and I decided that it was safe for me to proceed. At that instant I heard the sound of my own voice as I explained to the Coroner how I had come to kill the children. It gave me such a shock that I stopped the car sharply about a yard short of the children, and at that instant, without any warning at all and without looking round, both children dashed straight across the road in front of me.

CHAPTER 33

Apparitions of the Dead

SUBJECTS sometimes report perceiving an apparition of someone
they know to be dead at the time. Such apparitions are even more
common than apparitions of the living in our collection. About
two thirds of all the recognised apparitions reported to us were
of people or animals whom the subject knew to be dead.

As with apparitions of the living, subjects report perceiving
apparitions of deceased people who were in a wide variety of
different relationships to themselves during life—relationships
by birth, marriage, friendship or acquaintance. It is perhaps
worth noting that the type of post-mortem apparition most commonly reported in our collection is one of the percipient's mother
or father.

The length of time that elapses between the death of the person
or animal represented and the apparitional experience varies
greatly from one case to the next. At one extreme there are cases
in which the apparitional experience occurs within a few days
of the death of the person concerned, and at the other extreme
there are cases in which the subject perceives an apparition of
someone who has died thirty or more years earlier. The cases
reported to us tend to occur most frequently within a week of the
death, and the number falls away as the length of time since the
death increases.

The following cases illustrate some of the variants that occur
in apparitions of the dead:

My mother died in December 1945, and my father in the following
January.

I saw my mother's ghost in the following May. I had done a day's
teaching, which had given me a rest from grief. I had come home, and
gone into a rather dark passage to leave my outdoor things. Suddenly
I saw my mother. She was about three feet away from me. The sun

never shone into the passage, but she was radiant as if in full sunlight. She looked quite solid and clear in outline. She looked very young, about twenty. I particularly noticed her rich, high colour. Her hair was arranged in two full puffs above her forehead. She was so clear that I could see the texture of her jacket and skirt. She was wearing a cinnamon brown woollen jacket of a twill weave and rather soft material, a skirt with a small black and white check, also woollen, and a dark blue and green shot silk blouse. The clothes were of the style of the 1890's.

I felt myself surrounded by her love and sympathy. It was not the sympathy she had given me in my adult sorrows, but the sympathy shown to my childish griefs.

I do not know how long I stood there. Suddenly she had gone. It then felt very cold. I do not know whether I saw her with my eyes or in my mind.

Later, I told my sister. She said, 'Yes, yes' but did not believe me. But when I described her clothes, she said, 'Yes, you've seen her, Mary. She had those clothes when she was in college.'

My mother was in college in the years 1895–97. As her college clothes were afterwards worn up by her three younger sisters, it is impossible for me to have seen them. (I was born in 1905.) There was no colour photography in my young days, so if I had seen a photograph I should not have known the colours.

About nine years ago my grandfather went into hospital for an operation from which he did not recover. My husband and I visited him in hospital and he said how sorry he was that he would not see his great grandchildren. Less than a year later our first child was born at home. The cot was in the room with me and at about one a.m. (eight hours after the birth) I suddenly woke to see a person at the foot of the cot. I knew it wasn't my husband as he was asleep next to me, and immediately struggled out of bed to see who it was and protect the baby. When the figure turned round I recognised my grandfather. I had the distinct impression that no harm was intended and he smiled and looked very happy. I climbed back into bed and he remained standing at the foot of the cot watching the baby. I went to sleep feeling quite secure overjoyed that he had seen the baby.

The time was March 1945, I gave our baby daughter her 10 a.m. feed a bit before the time, and towards the end of the routine, my Grandmother made a cup of tea. When Gran had finished her cuppa, she took the china into the kitchen. I finished my welcome drink, then turned the nappies airing at the side of the fireplace, after which I picked up the cup and saucer, turned around to go to the kitchen, and there on the brown velvet cushions of the settee was seated my Grandfather, who died on December 6th 1931. He wore a medium grey suit, white shirt, black tie, socks and shoes. Even the smoke was coming from his pipe. I stood rigid, clutching that cup and saucer, wanting to speak to him, but unable to utter a word. He smiled at me, and the expression in his grey eyes told me he was contented and happy. He vanished and I remember looking at the clock, it was nearly 10.10 a.m.

About 8 years ago I got up during the night to go to the toilet. Switching on the bathroom light, I saw a tall man in striped pyjamas standing in front of the lavatory. Thinking it was my 17 year old son, I said, 'Are you alright, Timothy?' At which the figure turned round. It was my father. I said, 'Dad, but you're dead.' He said rather sadly, 'Yes.' and I put my hand out to take his, but he disappeared. My father died 23 years ago. This house was built 21 years ago, so he had never been in it. I have never seen anything since then, nor do I ever dream about my father, though we were very close.

Our 8 year old daughter died in 1967 and about 2 weeks after she died, as I sat down after my lunch, I distinctly saw her in the chair opposite, just as we always sat at this time. I was conscious of my brain questioning what my eyes saw, and I was also conscious that there was no real solidity about what I saw, but that if I moved the vision would fade. I was, of course, in some state of shock or grief, but was overjoyed to see my daughter so clearly.

I'm sure I'd have always doubted my own eyes, but for the fact that Rosemary spoke so clearly. She said in a matter of fact way, 'My foot is better', and swung the foot towards me. This was something that had worried her during her long illness in hospital, but she had so much else to contend with that we never told the doctor about it. Although she was sitting facing me, I realized that it was the affected foot she swung. I had forgotten about it in the grief of her death.

I was sure somehow that although I 'heard' and 'saw' it was not in the same audible and visual way that one normally does.

My husband died in August 1970. The following Christmas, 1970, I spent with my married daughter (our only child), her husband and two teen-age children at their home in Bexley Heath, Kent. This was the first Christmas spent away from my home, my family having previously spent all the holidays with my husband and self at our home in Wimbledon. On Boxing Day Dec 27th between 11 o'clock and midnight we were all playing Monopoly and at that time I was not even thinking of my husband. I looked up from my game and my husband was sitting on the settee opposite. This I could not believe. I covered my eyes with my hands and looked again; he was still there. I then for some reason counted the people present and there were six of us not five. I must have looked very distressed, everyone looked up from the game and enquired what was wrong. I was a little incoherent and wept, and my husband got up from the settee, crossed the room, opened the door, and went out, turning at the last moment, putting his head back inside the door and smiling at me. He appeared, as in life (rather unusually dressed for a winter evening), wearing his charcoal coloured trousers and an open necked white shirt. I was overcome with grief and went to bed at once. At no time since have I heard or seen anything else of this nature.

Nearly 12 years ago my mother died. My son was then 11 years of age. A month after she died I went upstairs to fetch something. The landing light was on and my son's bedroom door was open and he was asleep. As I passed the door I saw my mother standing at the foot of the bed. She looked so normal that in that instant I forgot that she was dead and turned to laugh at her (we always said she spent more time looking at her grandson than talking to us when she came to stay). I suppose my amusement quickly turned to amazement, whereupon she put her finger to her lips and gently shook her head as much as to say, 'Don't make a sound. He would wake and be frightened.' As I watched she smiled a happy smile and disappeared. She had looked quite solid but as she went it was from the feet upwards. I have never to this day recalled what she wore but it looked quite normal to me.

I did not mention this to my husband for some weeks expecting he would think me fanciful. When I did he said, 'Oh yes, I saw her several times, but like you thought it was better kept to myself.'

I could tell you of one single and very simple experience of just hearing with the utmost clarity a single sentence spoken (or seeming to be spoken) by my father who had been dead for four years.

I was cleaning the grate out one morning, and thoughtlessly put the ashpan on the carpet, while it was still warm. I was of course kneeling facing the fireplace. I heard the voice of my father behind me say 'You pot-herb'. This is an old Lancashire saying, which I don't remember anyone else using but my father. I turned round fully expecting to see him, even having forgotten in that minute that he was in fact dead. There was nothing to be seen, but the absolute clarity of the voice still remains in my memory.

CHAPTER 34

Apparitions of Animals

MOST apparitions of animals are of cats and dogs. This is perhaps not surprising in view of the frequency with which these two kinds of animal are kept as domestic pets.

The first of the following two cases concerns a dog, while the second is an example involving a cat:

> I was cycling home alone from T. Hall, Norfolk, about 11.30 at night. I had been working late, because of a dinner party given by Lord and Lady B. It was a bright moonlight night, and I could see clearly right across the park and the fields. Between C. and what we local people call Bluebell Wood, the road was straight, and no high hedges either side. Then I became aware of an enormous dog running silently beside my cycle. I saw its tongue hanging out, and for some reason I didn't attempt to touch it, which was very unusual for me, as I am passionately fond of animals. I did wonder vaguely who it belonged to, as I'd never seen it around before, and I was afraid it would get too close to me, and throw me from my cycle, but I wasn't in the least disturbed otherwise. Then it suddenly vanished, as simple as that. I was living in a cottage belonging to Lord B., with my two daughters aged 12 and 16. I didn't say anything to anybody, mainly because I thought I wouldn't be believed. Exactly a month later, same time, same place and same conditions, I saw the dog again. This time I took a closer look and apart from it being an enormous dog, with its tongue hanging out, there was nothing odd about it. I still didn't attempt to touch it, and again it just vanished.
>
> . . . some months later I was waiting at the gate for my oldest daughter to come home. It was as bright as day at 11 o'clock, she had been working at the cinema at Fakenham, and as it was a lonely lane we lived in, I always watched for her. I saw her cycling along, and with this *same dog* immediately in *front* of her cycle. My first thought was that it would throw her from her cycle, but when she drew level with me the dog simply vanished. I asked her if the dog had frightened her, and she said she'd never seen a dog, and wondered what on earth I was talking about.
>
> I never saw it again.

The first [experience] was when I was upstairs in the bathroom and I saw a small brown cat walking across the floor. It was so real it never struck me that there was anything abnormal. Thinking that my little tabby cat Pussy Pockets had followed me from downstairs I bent down to pick her up. As I did so I noticed a curious thing, her right hindleg seemed to have faded rather from sight, although she still stood upright as if on four legs. By the time my hands had reached her level and I brought them together to gather her up I realised that I was only grasping thin air. There was no cat there at all.

The subject later identified this as the apparition of a cat she had known and which had died some ten years before, and attributed her not having recognised it immediately to the fact that the apparition looked in fine condition, whereas in reality the cat had always looked very thin and spindly.

We have already discussed the emotional state of the subject throughout an apparitional experience in an earlier chapter, but in passing we may note that the case just given possibly provides an example of a rather characteristic abnormality in the reactions of the percipient. The subject does not mention any particular shock or astonishment at finding that the cat's 'right hindleg seemed to have faded rather from sight'. As we have remarked, apparition subjects have a tendency at times to accept unusual features of their experience matter-of-factly, and not to call to mind facts which would make it clear to them that what they were seeing could not be real.

As we have already noted in Chapter 8 (p. 63), there seems to be a distinct class of case in which the subject reports seeing a recurrent apparition of a cat, often a black cat. The following are two further examples of the type. The first is from a Dutch lady writing in English.

First time, at broad day-light, 5 p.m. summertime, I think June (end of). It was sitting on the kitchen floor whilst I was cutting meat. It looked up at me. At first I did not pay attention to it, but at once I realised that it was a whole black cat, totally black, which in my opinion was impossible for my two cats have large white breasts and noses, so it had to be a strange cat. When I looked again it was gone.

We looked all over the place. The doors and windows were shut at the moment and our own cats were asleep. One in the living-room, one in the attic.

A strange cat in the house could not be possible for my cats would have attacked it immediately, they are very peculiar that way.

Second time I saw the cat, I was alone. I could not sleep and went down to the living-room. It was not dark in the room for there was a full moon. In the chair I saw three cats. My two ones, black and white, and a third one, black. I saw it very clearly, three heads and six eyes looking at me. I walked towards them and tried to touch the black cat, but it disappeared.

The third time, I went down at 11 p.m. because I wanted to fetch me a cup of cocoa. One cat was on the table, one in the chair, they were my own. The third cat, a black one was on the carpet, curled up. It looked at me with big green eyes. I went towards it and wanted to touch it, but all I felt was the rug.

When my husband and I were first married, in the autumn of 1964, we moved into the top flat in a newly converted house in Swinton, Manchester. The house had been split into two flats after the previous owner died.

On three occasions, separately, and once together, we saw a cat smallish and black, walk from the landing into the living room across to the window, and vanish. The windows in the flat were sash, and shut, and each time this happened we were decidedly incredulous, and shut all doors hastily in order to search each room thoroughly, at our leisure. On none of these occasions was there any trace of any animal.

This animal moved with us to another flat in London, where we saw it once, but after we brought two Siamese cats into our lives, the black one was not seen again.

Apparitions of dogs seem more often to occur in conjunction with apparitions of human beings than do apparitions of cats, which nearly always occur on their own. This may again reflect the relative frequency with which dogs and cats are seen in close connection with human beings in everyday life, cats usually being considered more aloof and independent than dogs.

Although the great majority of apparitions of animals represent dogs or cats, apparitions of quite a wide variety of other species have been reported to us; among them are horses, a deer, a tiger and a rabbit. The following is the case concerning a rabbit:

Some months after that, I had gone to bed and had slept for a couple of hours and had to get up to visit the bathroom. As I was about to leave the bedroom, the door of which opens inwards, I happened to see a fluffy white rabbit sitting at the foot of the door. I stood there for a couple of seconds to make sure of what I was seeing. I then bent down in attempt to touch the back of the rabbit and it disappeared. I even found myself turning the light on and running my hand over the carpet where the rabbit had been sitting.

A noticeable characteristic of the class of apparitions of animals, at least in our collection, is that hardly any of them represent *living* animals known to the percipient. They are nearly all either unrecognised or represent animals that have died. The following case is an exception to this, in which the subject reports seeing an apparition of a fox terrier outside her home at a time when the terrier in question was alive and well inside the house:

> We had a wire-haired fox terrier (all white but for a black-and-tan head) who was fanatically devoted to my mother and a great nuisance as he would do anything to be with her, jumping out of bedroom windows, digging under fences, and following the trail to shops, friends' houses, or even to the theatre.
>
> On this particular day my elder brother had had strict instructions to see that the dog was locked in the house before he left, no one else being at home. My mother and I returned about 4 o'clock. It was late spring and I was eight years old.
>
> Having lent her front-door key to my brother my mother had to go in by the back way. When she opened the side gate we had a clear view down a path bordered on one side by the house and a 6 foot fence on the other. At the end of the path our dog, Peter, suddenly appeared, stopped, bowed with waggling tail high in the air, as he always did, and then trotted up the path towards us.
>
> My mother said 'You naughty dog, what are you doing here?' and the poor creature, crestfallen, turned back and jumped into his kennel.
>
> My mother walked on, while I rushed to the kennel and thrust my head and shoulders inside to hug the dog. My arms only grasped straw. Unbelieving I unfastened the rear door of the kennel and looking into the sleeping compartment found that empty too. Astonished, I ran round the corner of the house to tell my mother. She unlocked the back door and the dog came from inside the house to welcome us.
>
> We were both convinced that in some way Peter had got out of the house and then in again, but went right through and found all doors and windows fastened, and my brother confirmed that he had certainly left the dog in the house.
>
> May I emphasize:
> (1) Visibility was perfect and the dog appeared at least 40 feet away, white against a dark path, and approached to about 10 feet.
> (2) We expected the dog to be locked in the house.
> (3) No conversation passed between my mother and I until after the incident was over.

A characteristic type of case concerning a dead animal which was well known to the percipient is that in which the footsteps and other sounds of the animal are heard, as they used to be heard in its habitual movements about the house. The following case concerning a cat was reported by a girl of 13, who was 10 when she had the experience:

About 3 years ago we had a siamese cat called Minky whom I loved a great deal. Unfortunately she was hit by a car and killed. It was a few weeks after this that she first visited me. When she was alive she would come up to my bedroom at about 10.00 at night. I could hear her paws on the floorboards, for about 5 seconds before she reached the carpet.

One night after her death I heard her paws 'walking' across the floorboards for about 5 seconds before she reached the carpet. I sat up in bed, but there was, of course, no-one there.

We had no other cats at that time so I cannot explain it other than that I was visited by Minky's ghost.

This happened at random intervals for some weeks but when I told my father of Minky's visits I never heard her again. I know for a fact that there are no pipes under my floor where Minky walked and since the floor had never creaked either before or after Minky visited me, I am convinced it was her ghost.

CHAPTER 35

Apparitions of Objects

THE following cases illustrate some of the variations that occur in apparitions of objects.

My father and I were living in a second floor flat in Gezira, Cairo, staying with us was a close friend, Mrs. B. One night in the early part of summer, some time after midnight, I was woken by Mrs. B. who asked me to come to her room; she could not tell me why. I went with her to the balcony of her room and looked out into the street; the street lamps were out, but the moon was near the full and it was bright enough to read by. On the opposite pavement I saw a drab coloured overcoat moving fairly slowly down the road, a few yards past our block it turned and came back along the pavement till it passed our block again, turned and repeated the movement. The range of movement was about thirty yards. No-one was wearing or carrying the coat which fell in folds as if it had been suspended by the neck lappet, from the way the folds fell it appeared to be of fairly thick material. The foot of the coat was about 18 in. clear of the ground, but nothing was visible between it and the pavement. Mrs. B. asked me if I saw anything and my description, she told me, agreed with what she saw. Mrs. B. had dragged the head of her bed on to the balcony for coolness, but could not sleep owing to the heat. She told me she had been aware of movement in the street and, as it had continued for some while, sat up to see what it was.

After watching this for some minutes, during which the coat continued to move back and forth, I went to call my father who came grumbling because I would not tell him why. After a few minutes I asked him to say what, if anything, he saw and his description tallied with mine and Mrs. B.'s.

The coat continued passing up and down the pavement; there was nothing in the least unusual about it—it was not shadowy or transparent and was clearly visible. Only the fact that it was an empty coat, moving without any visible means, rendered it uncanny.

We all watched this going on for some ten minutes and then my father and I returned to our rooms. The street was empty at the time and it was a still night.

My father, although he believed in the psychic experiences of others, was convinced that he, personally, was incapable of seeing a 'ghost'. On his first sight of the coat he said 'Good God' (or similar exclamation of surprise). However, he maintained firmly that he could *not* be a ghost—if only because he could see it. Although he would not accept it as an apparition he was unable to find any alternative explanation (I may say that this discussion took place while we were watching the apparition). After we had watched it for some while I suggested that my father and I (or myself alone) should go into the street and have a closer look at it. This my father vetoed because at that hour one could not enter or leave the building without disturbing the boab who dragged his bed across the main door. As my father pointed out—if the boab saw the apparition we would not only no longer have a boab, but doubtless all the servants in the block would leave in a body. I saw the force of this argument and we finally went back to our rooms, leaving the coat still going backwards and forwards on the opposite pavement.

We never saw the coat again, although I often looked for it late at night.

The following evening we were giving a fairly large party and among the guests who heard Mrs. B.'s account of what we saw was an Irish priest who lived in a ground floor in our block. Some weeks later the priest called on us and asked if we could tell him the date we had seen this apparition. On learning the date he told us that he had had news that an old friend, also a priest, had died then and left him, as a memento, an overcoat.

I have had an experience of seeing, quite clearly in detail, when passing through my old home town, a shop that I used long ago. As the whole of the town-centre has been re-developed, I was delighted to see it, and parked the car opposite. As I turned to cross the road it just wasn't there. I cannot exactly say that I saw it go, it just was not there, although I had seen it clearly.

I, together with my family, had gone on a short holiday to Daylesford [Australia] to drink the famous spa waters, and there we rented a cottage on the Hepburn road about a mile from the town.

Whilst there, I walked alone out of the house and decided to explore the gully sloping steeply down from the back of it. As I walked I became (about 150 yards) conscious of a thudding sound (as of machinery) and between the trees there came into view a collection of iron grey buildings and pipes and the sound of water gushing forth. In the foreground was a pool of stagnant, green water.

I stopped and gazed for a few moments (there was no sign of life) and then returned to the house where I told my father what I had seen. Some time later he remarked to me that he, also, had gone down into the gully but had seen nothing—just a dry, rocky gully.

Some four or five years later, a local resident informed my mother that there *had been* just such an installation as I described, back in the old mining days.

On Saturday morning (28 November 1931) I received a letter from my lawyer saying that he enclosed a cheque for £10.

As I was away from home, and too busy to have any opportunity either to reply to the lawyer or to send the cheque to my bank, I carried it about whilst I was talking to some friends, peering into the envelope occasionaly to see whether the cheque was safely there (as I had a good many papers with me and was anxious not to lose it). It was finally packed with special care, and I had pleasing memories throughout the day of seeing the marbled pale colours of the cheque and the look of the writing on it.

I got home late that evening, and next morning when I looked inside the envelope, to my extreme surprise there was no cheque. Completely puzzled I spent the morning looking through all my papers and into the lining of my trunk and into every imaginable crevice. Finally in despair I decided it must somehow have slipped out of the envelope and I sadly wrote a letter to the lawyer to confess my carelessness and to ask them to stop the cheque. My lawyer replied by return saying he had looked through their counterfoils but could find no record of the cheque, and that he must somehow have omitted to send it; he made good the oversight with apologies. (*Journal of the S.P.R.*, Vol. XXVII, 1931–2, p. 184)

Early in January I was staying with my sister. The day before I left I had a letter from my daughter R in which I read, 'Nanny is in bed with bronchitis.' I read it out to my sister.

I wrote to my daughter V to tell her.

When I got home next day my first question was 'How's Nanny?'

R. She's all right I suppose.

I. But you said she was in bed with bronchitis.

R. No. I never said such a thing.

Next morning I went to see how things were and found N just out of bed and very sadly indeed, having had bronchitis.

I. Miss R told me you had had bronchitis.

N. Miss R! but she didn't know; I wouldn't tell her to trouble her.

Getting home I looked again at the letter. I knew exactly the place on the page where I'd seen 'Nanny is in bed with bronchitis'; it wasn't there or anywhere else in the letter, nor was there room in it for a single extra line. Nanny had been greatly longing to see me to pour all out but wouldn't write as I was on a holiday. (*Journal of the S.P.R.*, Vol. XXXI, 1939–40, p. 53)

CHAPTER 36

Reassuring Apparitions

SUBJECTS sometimes report that they had a feeling of 'peace', 'calm', 'comfort', or 'tranquility', either while perceiving an apparition, or afterwards. Four per cent of our subjects report this type of reaction.

In particular, there seems to be a distinct class of experiences in which the apparition has the effect of reassuring the percipient at a time when he is undergoing some crisis or situation of stress. The following examples illustrate the range of variations. It will be seen that the apparition may be recognised or unrecognised, and the experience may be visual, auditory or tactile.

> I was expecting a baby in March of 1965 and a week or so before the birth I had gone to bed at my usual time. I am a sound sleeper and never wake up during the night, having to be called each morning. I had not suffered any uncomfortable nights throughout my pregnancy so I was a little surprized to find that I woke up during this particular night. I felt absolutely wide awake and then I saw what appeared to be an elderly lady stood by the bed looking at me and smiling. She seemed to have on a dark, long dress and had curly hair and what I call a mob cap on her head. She didn't move at all and I felt surprizingly calm and peaceful, and not afraid as I would have expected to feel upon seeing a 'ghost'. I watched her for what must have been several seconds but seemed much longer and then she gradually faded away, and I never saw her again. Immediately she disappeared I put the light on and looked round the bedroom to see if anything was lying about which could have caused a shadow or reflection but there was nothing. I then woke my husband and told him and I felt a little nervous afterwards . . .

> I had never seen an apparition before that time and I have never seen one since, but I am convinced I was not dreaming as I never dream that I know of and also I felt so calm and awake at the time . . .

> I woke up feeling that the lady I saw had wanted me to wake up

but without touching me or speaking to me. I didn't even ask myself why I had seen it at the time. I just remember that I had never felt so relaxed and at peace before in my life and I have not done so since that experience as I am a person who lives 'on my nerves'. The feeling I had was one I couldn't forget as long as I lived as it was something I have never been able to repeat—to relax so completely.

My mother died in June 1952. One Sunday morning early, we had a terrible thunderstorm. My husband was working away at the time, and as I have always been nery nervous of storms, I went downstairs, taking the baby with me, and my eldest daughter also came down with me. She could see how I was shaking with fright. Suddenly I felt a very slight pressure on my shoulders, and heard my Mother's voice say, 'Don't be afraid Winnie dear, nothing will harm you'. I immediately stopped shaking, and felt quite calm, and my daughter noticed the change in me, and said, 'What's happened, Mum, you don't look frightened any more.' This was early in August, my daughter was 17.

It was a time of great stress for me, and I had been unable to sleep for weeks it seemed to me. This particular night I felt at the end of my tether and as I laid down I thought to myself, if I don't get some sleep soon I shall go mad. Well, I shut my eyes and tried to sleep but something caused me to open them and there at the side of my bed stood a young monk. I saw his tonsured head and he wore a brown robe. I don't know why but I thought he was twenty-six years old. He had the kindest face I have ever seen, and he said to me, 'My child, I will give you a blessing.' Then he laid his hand on my head. Immediately, I felt the tired lines ease away from my face and I felt so peaceful. I saw him go through my bedside table and then through the wall. I went to sleep as sweetly as a child and in the morning I felt a different person. I have never forgotten it. I am not a religious person nor had I been reading anything about Monks. Why he came to me I do not know but it was the most wonderful thing to happen to me.

When I was 21 and expecting our first child, I often felt faint and shaky in the first three months. One Sunday morning in church I felt as though I would pass out. I was kneeling down. I prayed to God to help me because I did not want to pass out, and disturb everyone while they were in church and praying. My head was going round and round. Then I felt as though a cold and soothing hand had been put on my forehead. I could feel the fingers. This steadied me and I was alright for the rest of the service.

About 27 years ago my son had just started school and became quite ill for many months—continually under the doctor with little result. Eventually we sent him to Ealing Chest Clinic to have an x-ray. (These facts could be checked.) There the picture told a nasty story. A little spot on the lung. The doctor there drew a diagram and filled in the spot etc. with mother watching in dismay. My own mother had died of T.B. when I was five.

We were to go on holiday, which we were advised to do, so it was a couple of months before visiting the clinic again.

Meanwhile I had gone home and was taking it all very badly. My husband just demobbed and our son with T.B.—it wasn't what I had envisaged for the end of the war. Night after night I laid awake. I had him dead and buried. Oh it was a lovely funeral!! Of course I was in a state which may explain what happened.

One night my mother came to the side of the bed. I instantly recognised her although I had previously no remembrance of her as she was ill for a couple of years and I saw very little of her from the age of three onwards. She was to me at the time perfectly normal although I believe all in white. She spoke very clearly and told me not to worry; all was well. We had a pleasant little conversation about the illness. I wasn't a little bit amazed at her coming. It seemed perfectly natural. In the morning I could hardly believe it had happened. I told my husband who said not to be stupid, but I felt a different person. I honestly didn't worry again.

Eventually another picture was taken at the chest clinic. NO SPOT. The doctor looked at the diagram then at the picture backwards and forwards—NO SPOT. I was not surprised.

My mother's 'ghost' had definitely visited me. It was not eerie or supernatural, just a perfectly normal occurrence. In all fairness I don't think a 'miracle' had occurred. My own doctor on hearing and seeing he was better decided she should have diagnosed glandular fever and much earlier.

So much for the medical side, but my mother definitely came to me for my peace of mind. Of that I for one at least am certain.

I was going through a very bad time and was finding it very difficult to keep myself and my 2½ year old daughter following the break-up of my marriage.

We were living in rooms in a house which, I discovered later, had been occupied by spiritualists. Our beds were on opposite sides of a fairly large room and one morning, just as dawn was breaking, I woke up and, as usually happened, the worries of the day came crowding into my mind. As I opened my eyes I was aware of a presence in the room and, taking shape in the centre of the room, was the figure of a woman. She was tall and slender and dressed in Edwardian style with a long skirt, and high-necked blouse with long full sleeves. Her hair was piled up in the style common in those days and she was wearing a small straw hat.

I did not feel any fear because she was smiling at me in the most reassuring way. As the daylight increased she slowly faded away and at the same time it was as though she had told me not to worry and that things would be all right with me. I still had my problems but I felt as though I had been given strength to cope with them.

In 1924 my husband and I were travelling from Cuyabá the Capital of Matto Grosso in a northwesterly direction along the Telegraph line which runs from Cuyabá to Porto Velho on the River Madeira. Our object was to commence Christian work among a tribe of Red Skinned Indians known as the Nhambiquàras. Our journey took us three months on mule back to reach Barão-de-Melgaço, where we commenced missionary work.

We had been on our journey about 6 weeks when the following incident occurred. We had reached the foot of a hill, when to my horror there appeared at the top a group of Nhambiquàra Indians. My husband was not so disturbed as he had previously travelled in this region. The group consisted entirely of men, each one carrying a bow and several arrows. These were normally used for intertribal warfare and attacks on strangers. They were naked except for arm bands, beads, necklaces of monkeys teeth, nose ornaments and a piece of native string tied round their waists from which was suspended a bunch of vegetable fibre about 5 inches wide and 10 inches long. Their hair was dishevelled and long to their shoulders and their bodies were covered in an evil smelling red pigment. I was terrified and afraid to go any further, when, suddenly, over my right shoulder came the words in a man's clear voice 'Lo, I am with you alway.' I turned to see who the person could be but no one was there. I knew then it was a voice from Heaven and my fear went, faith and strength returned and I was able to meet them without fear.

After over 40 years I am still as conscious of that voice as I was in 1924.

CHAPTER 37

Apparitions and Psychokinesis

HALLUCINATORY figures of human beings often appear to be closely integrated with the subject's real environment, sitting in chairs, walking up and down stairs, resting their elbows on tables, and so forth. Sometimes the figure actually seems to be moving physical objects in the environment around in some way. This at once suggests the question, do these objects really move?

Of course, in most cases where the apparition appears to have some effect on the physical environment, it is impossible to tell whether the effect is real or hallucinatory. For example, the following case is one in which no independent observer was present to say whether they saw the table-cloth moving, even though they did not see the hallucinatory figure of the child. And a disturbance of the table-cloth of the kind described would leave no permanent trace afterwards, whether it were a genuine physical happening or not.

> I saw my eldest child Daisy run down the two lowest steps of the staircase into the drawing-room. I followed, calling her, but obtaining no answer. The figure ran under the table, and the cloth where she passed under shook. . . . At the time she was at the top of the house. (*Census*, pp. 191–2)

The following is a similar case. The subject reports blowing a puff of smoke at an apparition of a human figure. He saw the smoke divide and pass on either side of the apparition as if it had been a real person, but naturally such a happening would leave no permanent physical trace once the experience was over.

The original account is in French, and we have translated it into English.

> In the year 1883, at St. Petersburg, I witnessed the following apparition.
> I was then aged 19 and on the point of finishing my course of

studies in the first corps of cadets at St. Petersburg. In December of the same year (the exact date has escaped me) I was in my mother's lodgings in Petersburg. I was then convalescing after a throat illness, and as the doctor had found my state of health satisfactory, I was proposing to get up the following day. It was around midnight, and there was complete silence in the house. I had put out the candle, which was placed on a little table beside the bed. At the foot of the bed was a stool.

I was tired of turning in bed without being able to go to sleep and I had the idea of smoking. I stretched out my arm in the feeble light of a match to pick up my cigarettes. At that moment I distinctly perceived on the stool at the foot of the bed my late grandmother, Marie Alexeevna Volchoff (my mother's mother), who had been dead 5 years, that is to say, since 1878. She sat on the stool, leaning her elbows on the table, and stared at me fixedly. I was terrified, threw down the match, and fell back on the pillows. When I had calmed myself a little, I lit a candle, and saw the apparition again. It was still there, as before, with its elbows on the table.

Summoning up all my sang-froid, I took a cigarette and blew the smoke from it towards the apparition. Imagine my surprise when I *saw the smoke divide on either side of the apparition*, as if encountering an obstacle. Then the apparition got up; I distinctly heard the noise of the stool being pushed back, and I saw my grandmother standing on her crutches (her feet were paralysed some years before her death). She was wearing her usual black dress, and had a coffee-pot in her hand, from which she was hardly ever separated while she was alive. The apparition took a few paces backwards; then, still backing away, it went out into the corridor through the door of my room, which was open. It stopped to speak the following words to me: 'Do not forget me, Daniel, and visit my tomb,' then disappeared.

I sprang from my bed and rushed down the corridor to my mother's bedroom, where I woke her and my step-father, and told them of the occurrence. For a long time after this incident I was afraid of sleeping in a dark room. (*Census*, p. 192)

In certain cases the apparition does seem to effect some change in the environment that ought to be detectable after the experience is over if the change really took place and was not merely hallucinatory. For example, in the last case quoted the percipient heard the apparition push back a stool at the foot of the bed. If the stool had really moved, the percipient might presumably have noticed that it was in a different position after the experience than it had been before. In fact he does not mention any difference in its position.

This is typical, as subjects frequently do not comment spontaneously on whether things moved by the apparition were or were not found in a new position at the end of the experience. However, when asked they almost always say that the apparition left no permanent physical effects behind it.

Those few subjects who do perform some action at the time of the experience which has the effect of testing whether the physical effect really happened, usually find that it did not. In the following case, for example, the subject saw an apparition ostensibly open a door, but on trying to push the door shut he found it had not really opened at all.

> On the second occasion it was about the same hour in the morning and on the same day of the week. The bedroom door was shut all night on this occasion, and I was lying awake when I saw the door open and some one peep round. I thought it was one of our assistants come for a lark to pull me out of bed (as we do those kind of tricks sometimes); however, I lay still, and then the door seemed to open wide, so I leaned out of bed to give it a hard push and everything vanished, and I nearly fell out of bed, for the door was shut as when I went to bed. (*Proceedings of the S.P.R.*, Vol. XXXIII, 1922, p. 36)

The following is a similar case. In this instance the percipient saw a door open, an apparition walk out through it and the door close again after it. But on going to the door she found it locked.

> When my mother was ill, and I sat up during the night with her, I heard some one trying the lock of our door, which I had locked. I thought it was W. come home late, as usual, so I went up close to the door and whispered through, 'Do not come in; mother's asleep.' I went back to the fire, and I do not know what made me do it, but I gave a great jump, and on looking round found we were no longer alone—a short, stout, elderly man was midway between the bed and the door. He went and stood near the bed, but not close, and while I looked I seemed to know he could do no harm. He stood looking a long time. He clasped and unclasped his hands frequently. Upon the little finger of his left hand he wore a wedding ring, and he turned it round and round in his hand as he stood, and his lips moved, though I could not hear a sound. I tried to flap him away with a towel, as I had heard that a current of air will make these things go sometimes, but to no purpose. He took his own time to go. After seeming to speak to some person, whom I could not see, and pointing to the ceiling a good deal, he *moved*, I cannot say *walked*, to the door; it opened; he went out; it closed; and I went, too, to try the door. It was still *locked*. I never saw him again. (*Proceedings of the S.P.R.*, Vol. III, 1885, p. 144, *n.*)

Since cases of this kind clearly have to be regarded as among those in which at least part of the subject's environment as well as the apparition was hallucinatory, the question arises whether these are among the cases in which the subject's whole environment is actually hallucinatory while he is seeing the apparition.

There are only one or two anomalous reports in which a physical effect which seems to have been caused by an apparition persisted after the end of the experience. We shall quote two such cases. In both cases the change in the environment was of such a kind that it might have arisen naturally. In the following case the subject describes an apparition as releasing the blind in his bedroom so that it shot up with a crack, and he maintains that it was still up after the end of the experience.

> I slept alone in a back bedroom and woke up suddenly one bright, windy, moonlit night at about 10.30 p.m. with the feeling that there was someone in the room. By the window, and clearly visible in the moonlight, there was a woman in a white nightdress, and I can still recall a double frilled yoke over the shoulders and a frilled collar.
>
> She was holding the cream roller blind away from the curtains and the window, looking down into the yard of the house next door. After watching her for a while, I said 'Mother, what are you looking at ?' but there was no reply. The question was repeated and the figure at the window turned to look at me and I was surprised to realise that it was not my mother.
>
> At the same moment the figure gave the blind the sharp downard tug necessary to release it and it shot up to the roller with a crack like a shot.
>
> I screamed twice for my father and disappeared under the bedclothes and he and my mother, fully dressed of course, ran upstairs from the room where they had both been reading. The incident, of course, was treated as a dream or nightmare but I would never sleep in that room again.
>
> I found out months later that my 'dream' had caused quite a bit of interest amongst friends of the family, one of whom knew the owner of the house. We were told that he had married for the second time, a younger woman of whom he was very fond. She had died in that room of 'Spanish 'flu', as it was referred to then, about a year before, and my description of her face, hair style and height bore some resemblance to her. . . .
>
> There were white lace curtains in a squared pattern at the window, which was partly open. There was a stiff breeze and moonlight and perhaps the wind had caused the blind to flap and release itself but I was aware during the incident of complete silence and of no movement for quite a time until the figure turned and the blind shot up.
>
> . . . the blind which was always pulled down was up when my parents came into the room.

On the information given we cannot rule out the possibility

that the blind may have been unstable, and released itself in some natural way. Possibly the hallucination which the subject saw was constructed by his subconscious to fit in with the spontaneous release of the blind.

In the following case the two percipients both maintain that a night-light, which had been burning before their experience, was extinguished after it. One of them saw the figure of an apparition gesture towards the mantel-piece on which the night-light had been burning, and the other claims to have seen the apparition actually put its hand over the night-light and extinguish it. The first percipient is the Rev. D. W. G. Gwynne:

> During the night I became aware of a draped figure passing across the foot of the bed towards the fire-place. I had the impression that the arm was raised, pointing with the hand towards the mantel-piece, on which a night-light was burning. Mrs. Gwynne at this moment seized my arm, and the light was extinguished. Notwithstanding, I distinctly saw a figure returning towards the door, and being under the impression that one of our servants had found her way into our room, I leapt out of bed to intercept the intruder, but found, and saw, nothing. I rushed to the door, and endeavoured to follow the supposed intruder, and it was not until I found the door locked, as usual, that I was painfully impressed. I need hardly say that Mrs. Gwynne was in a very nervous state. She asked me what I had seen, and I told her. She had seen the same figure, but her impression was that the figure placed its hand over the night-light and extinguished it.
>
> The night-light in question was relit and placed in a toilette basin, and burned naturally. I tried to convince myself that it might have been a gust of wind down the chimney that put the light out; but that will not account for the spectral appearance, which remains a mystery.

Mrs. Gwynne's account is as follows:

> In addition to my husband's statement, which I read, I can only say that the account he has given you accords with my remembrance of the 'unearthly vision', but I distinctly saw the hand of the phantom placed over the night-light, which was at once extinguished. I tried to cling to Dr. Gwynne, but he leapt out of bed with a view, as he afterwards said, of intercepting some supposed intruder. The door was locked as usual, and was so when he tried it. He lit a candle at once, and looked under the bed, and into a closet, but saw nothing. The night-light was also relit, which was placed on the wash-stand, and together with the candle, remained burning all night. I must observe that I had never taken to use night-lights before we lived there, and only did so when I had been so often disturbed and

alarmed by sighs and heavy breathing close to my side of the bed. Dr. Gwynne, on the appearance of the phantom, in order to calm my agitated state, tried to reason with me, and to persuade me that it might have been the effects of the moonlight and clouds passing over the openings of the shutter, and possibly that a gust of wind might have extinguished the light, but I knew differently. When we had both been awakened at the same moment apparently, and together saw that unpleasant figure, tall and as it were draped like a nun, deliberately walk up to the mantel-piece and put out the light with the right-hand, there could be no mistake about it; and I distinctly heard the rustling sound of garments as the figure turned and left through the door, after my husband's attempts to stop it with his open arms. The moonlight was very clear and the white dimity curtains only partly closed. (Gurney II, pp. 202–3)

In this case a possible explanation is that the night-light went out on account of a draught or some other natural cause, and that the subconscious minds of the percipients arranged their apparitional experience to synchronise with this fact.

An alternative explanation might be that this was a metachoric experience in which the percipients' whole visual field was hallucinatory, so that the night-light may never have gone out at all. The presence or otherwise of the night-light flame would affect the level of illumination of the whole environment, so the period for which they were perceiving a hallucinatory representation of their entire environment would have to cover at least the time from the night-light's appearing to go out to the time at which they thought it was relighted.

A further possibility is that the night-light went out due to some physical cause, such as a gust of wind, while the two subjects were asleep before the experience. The subconscious of each percipient might have registered the fact that the night-light had gone out and judged the moment opportune to wake the subject and present to his consciousness a hallucinatory scene similar to that which the subjects describe in their accounts. On this view, everything the percipients saw from the moment they woke and opened their eyes may have been hallucinatory, up till the disappearance of the apparition. The night-light was already extinguished before they woke up, and the burning night-light they saw up till the moment when the apparition seemed to gesture in its direction was only a hallucinatory one.

It is of course possible that in both the cases last quoted the physical effects in question, i.e. the release of the blind and the extinguishing of the night-light, were caused by psychokinesis. There seems no reason why psychokinesis should not operate in such a way as to produce physical effects, suitably synchronised with the movements of hallucinatory figures, even if this only happens rarely.

Glossary

This glossary is in logical, not alphabetical, order, as some of the concepts depend on others which need to be explained previously.

A *lucid dream* is a dream in which the subject is aware that he is dreaming.

A *false awakening* is a dream in which the subject seems to wake up in bed, or elsewhere, in the normal way. It may then occur to him to doubt whether he is really awake, and he may proceed to examine his environment in the hope of obtaining clues. Sometimes he realises that what he is experiencing is only a dream in which case a lucid dream may follow.

The phenomenon of the false awakening may occur after both lucid and non-lucid dreams, but it seems to be particularly common among subjects who have frequent lucid dreams.

A *Type 2 false awakening* is one in which the subject appears to wake up normally and find himself in bed. His surroundings may at first appear normal, but he gradually becomes aware of something unusual or 'uncanny' in the atmosphere. Alternatively he may 'awake' immediately to a 'stressed' and 'stormy' atmosphere. In either case the subject tends to experience feelings of suspense, excitement or apprehension. He may experience 'hallucinatory' or 'apparitional' effects. If he attempts to move or get out of bed while in this state, he tends to find himself in an ecsomatic state. It is presumed that throughout a Type 2 false awakening the subject is actually lying with his eyes closed, and would appear asleep to an observer.

An *out-of-the-body* or *ecsomatic* experience is one in which the observer seems to himself to be observing the normal world from a point of view which is not coincident with his physical body.

A *parasomatic* experience is an out-of-the-body experience in which the percipient is associated with a seemingly spatial entity in place of his physical body. This seemingly spatial entity may or may not resemble a normal physical body, and is referred to as the subject's 'parasomatic body'. This usage is for convenience of reference only, and does not imply any theoretical assumptions concerning the status of the entity in question.

A *metachoric* experience is one in which the subject's normal environment is completely replaced by a hallucinatory one. The most obvious examples of such experiences are dreams and lucid dreams. It should be noticed that although the subject's environment is temporarily completely hallucinatory it may provide an exact, or nearly exact, replica of his real one, as in a false awakening or an out-of-the-body experience.

A *negative hallucination* is an experience in which the subject fails to perceive some element of his environment when there is no physical reason why he should not do so. For example, under hypnosis certain subjects can be told by the hypnotist that an object in their environment is not really there, and the subject may subsequently report that he was unable to see the object referred to.

An experience of *autophany* is one in which the observer sees an apparition of himself.

Autoscopy is the experience of seeming to see one's own physical body from outside during an out-of-the-body experience.

Aphasia is the inability to express oneself properly through speech.

The subconscious: the term 'subconscious' is used in this book to refer to whatever components of the percipient's mind may be responsible for constructing his conscious experience of the apparition. Such a usage does not, of course, rule out the possibility that factors external to the percipient's mind may play a part in initiating the apparitional experience.

Bibliography

SIR ERNEST BENNETT, *Apparitions and Haunted Houses*, Faber and Faber, London, 1939.

SIR FRANCIS GALTON, *Enquiries into Human Faculty and its Development*, J. M. Dent and Sons, London, 1883.

CELIA GREEN, *Lucid Dreams*, Hamish Hamilton, London, 1968.

CELIA GREEN, *Out-of-the-Body Experiences*, Hamish Hamilton, London, 1968.

E. GURNEY, F. W. H. MYERS and F. PODMORE, *Phantasms of the Living*, Vols. I and II, Trübner and Co., London, 1886.

WILLIAM JAMES, *Principles of Psychology*, Dover Publications, New York, 1950 (first published 1890).

CHARLES MCCREERY, *Psychical Phenomena and the Physical World*, Hamish Hamilton, London, 1973.

CHARLES MCCREERY, *Science, Philosophy and ESP*, Hamish Hamilton, London, 1972 (first published 1967).

ANDREW MACKENZIE, *Apparitions and Ghosts*, Arthur Barker, London, 1971.

SIR ERNEST SHACKLETON, *South*, William Heinemann, London, 1919.

ELEANOR SIDGWICK, ALICE JOHNSON, and others, *Report on the Census of Hallucinations*, Proceedings of the Society for Psychical Research, London, Vol. X, 1894.

F. S. SMYTHE, *The Adventures of a Mountaineer*, J. M. Dent and Sons, London, 1940.

G. N. M. TYRRELL, *Apparitions*, Gerald Duckworth, London, 1943.

Index

THE HUMAN EVASION
Celia Green

The Human Evasion is an attack on the way of thought of twentieth-century man, revealing the patterns of prejudice which underlie his most cherished and sacrosanct opinions. For all its seriousness, the book is written with sustained wit and intellectual audacity. Surveying the whole field of modern thought, the author reveals the same disease at work in modern Christianity as in theoretical physics. Trenchant and provocative, this book is profoundly controversial—and brilliantly funny.

The Human Evasion is a book for anyone who has ever wondered about the purpose of life, or felt dissatisfied with current 'solutions' to the fundamental problems of life, death and human destiny.

'Very witty'—*The Guardian*
'Refreshing . . . so much sparkle'—Philip Toynbee, *The Observer*

Hardback   £1·75
HAMISH HAMILTON

LUCID DREAMS

Celia Green

Have you ever realised you were dreaming in the middle of a nightmare, or just before waking up? Celia Green's book shows how people have learnt to realise they were dreaming during ordinary dreams, and without waking up, so that they could then control the dream and bring about whatever their heart desired—for example, they could fly, do 'miracles', conjure up visions of beautiful women. Celia Green also discusses how people have used lucid dreams as a means of preventing nightmares, and the question of telepathy or extra-sensory perception in lucid dreams.

'Fascinating'—J. B. Priestley

Hardback   £1·75

HAMISH HAMILTON

OUT-OF-THE-BODY EXPERIENCES
Celia Green

Where do you go while you're 'unconscious'?

As far back as ancient Egypt, man had recorded out-of-the-body experiences, episodes in which the 'soul' could wander while the body lay inert. The soul could experience pain, joy and knowledge, could see the body as if from a distance, while the physical body lay unresponsive to external stimuli.

This absorbing and documented study shows how it is possible for someone to continue functioning in an apparently normal way while his consciousness is concerned only in watching his movements from an external point. Learn what evidence for extra-sensory perception is provided by the information obtained by the subjects of out-of-the-body experiences, and how people have learnt to leave their bodies deliberately, 'travelling' at will in time and space.

'Extraordinarily interesting'—*Times Literary Supplement*

Hardback   £1·75

HAMISH HAMILTON

PSYCHICAL PHENOMENA AND THE PHYSICAL WORLD

Charles McCreery

A fascinating discussion, with numerous detailed examples, of ghosts and apparitions, 'materializations', out-of-the-body experiences, lucid dreams, extra-sensory perception, and psychokinesis. The author discusses such remarkable phenomena as the materialized 'hands' that appeared at the séances of Eusapia Palladino; an apparition of a man with a hook in place of an arm with whom the percipient shook hands; and a nineteenth-century Marquis who 'travelled' to the moon during an out-of-the-body experience.

'The real thing . . . a fascinating and well-written book'—
Kingston News

Hardback   £2·30

HAMISH HAMILTON

SCIENCE, PHILOSOPHY AND ESP
Charles McCreery

The phenomena of extra-sensory perception and psychokinesis (the direct influence of mind over matter) present a disturbing challenge to accepted ways of thought. Charles McCreery's book provides a fascinating introduction to the subject for the general reader. It assumes no previous knowledge of the subject, and numerous examples of both telepathic and psychokinetic phenomena are presented vividly, and discussed in detail. We read of an apparition of an airman which spoke to a friend just at the moment when the airman met his death in a plane crash; a remarkable nineteenth-century medium, Eusapia Palladino, who could move tables and chairs by will-power; and the card-guessing feats of Basil Shackleton, who became known as 'the man who was $2\frac{1}{2}$ seconds ahead of time'. Mr. McCreery also discusses the EEG or 'brain waves' of the ESP subject, and the relationship of meditation, Yoga and such drugs as mescalin and LSD to the ESP state.

'Most lively'—*Times Literary Supplement*

Hardback   £2·25

HAMISH HAMILTON

TO YOUNG PEOPLE IN SEARCH OF THEIR DESTINY

'Ein Licht ging mir auf: Gefährten brauche ich, und lebendige—nicht tote Gefährten und Leichname, die ich mit mir trage, wohin ich will.

'Sondern lebendige Gefährten brauche ich, die mir folgen, weil sie sich selber folgen wollen—und dorthin, wohin ich will.'

To be a genius has never been too easy, granted the tendency of the human race to like frustrating them. It is no easier in this century than any other time. In fact, it is rather more difficult, as in this century it is believed that an unrecognised genius is impossible.

However, I have in Oxford a place in which it is possible to carry on the struggle for survival, and I am looking for people to join me. There are at present too few of us, and this makes the struggle for survival even more difficult.

I cannot give a brief summary of my ideas; they are original, and that means they are difficult to communicate. However, I have written a book, *The Human Evasion*, which while containing rather a small fraction of what I think, does give an introductory impression of my outlook. If you find this too uncongenial, I think you should not bother to get in touch with me to find out any more.

If, on the other hand, having read the book, you do want to know anything more about what I think, and to see whether you would like to join us, there is no alternative to coming to Oxford for a time.

Please write to me, in the first instance, care of the publishers of this book.

CELIA GREEN